FEDERAL SUPPORT OF HIGHER EDUCATION

THE GROWING CHALLENGE TO INTELLECTUAL FREEDOM

D1528660

FEDERAL
SUPPORT
OF
HIGHER
EDUCATION

THE GROWING CHALLENGE
TO INTELLECTUAL
FREEDOM

Edited by

Roger E. Meiners
and
Ryan C. Amacher

A PWPA Book

PARAGON HOUSE
New York

Published in the United States by
Professors World Peace Academy
481 8th Avenue
New York, New York 10001
Distributed by Paragon House Publishers
90 Fifth Avenue
New York, New York 10011

A Professors World Peace Academy Book

The Professors World Peace Academy (PWPA) is an international association of professors, scholars and academics from diverse backgrounds,
devoted to issues concerning world peace. PWPA sustains a program of conferences and publications on topics in peace studies, area and cultural
studies, national and international development, education, economics
and international relations.

Library of Congress Cataloging-in-Publication Data

Federal support of higher education.

    Includes index.
    1. Federal aid to higher education—United States—Congresses. 2. Higher
education and state—United States—Congresses. I. Meiners, Roger E. II.
Amacher, Ryan C.
LB2342.4.U6F43   1989   379.1'214'0973   89–10189
ISBN 0–943852–76–5
ISBN 0–943852–78–1 (pbk.)

Table of Contents

TABLE OF CONTENTS

FOREWORD

THE ACADEMY AND THE STATE

Ryan C. Amacher and Roger E. Meiners

Higher education around the world is dominated by government. In all countries the government provides the bulk of the funding for higher education and most colleges (even private institutions in the US) are governmental institutions. Understanding of the impact of governmental domination of the academy by scholars is not very good. If one ignores the academic literature that seeks to justify ever expanded support for higher education and looks only for scholarly literature that examines higher education in a dispassionate manner—the kind of analysis scholars apply within their fields of specialization—one finds few academic studies of academic organizations.

This book presents papers given at a conference that was organized to bring together senior scholars from a variety of academic disciplines and allow them to consider some aspect of the consequences of government involvement in higher education.

Because colleges are government institutions, or rely heavily on government support even if they are private, they must respond to political pressures. The idea that the academy is a place of pristine scholarship, where a collection of selfless Mr. Chips dote on students and scholarship, is obviously a naive ideal that some outsiders (and even more curiously some insiders) have of academe.

In this book we only look at American higher education. We live in institutions that scramble for tuition dollars, donor support, and added state or federal dollars. The results are impressive in many respects—most other advanced nations have university systems that appear to produce inferior results. Americans certainly dominate in research if we look to Nobel prizes (and other such surrogates) as a measure of quality. Even more impressive, the Japanese, who supposedly excel in public education, look to the US for advanced university education.

Evidence about the apparent quality of American higher education must be tempered by two thoughts: the cost of the system and the possibility that we might be able to obtain better results for the same number of dollars. We can never know what could have been, but we can consider evidence about what has emerged as guidance in helping structure a more productive system of higher education.

The authors here were given free rein to examine some aspects of higher education important from their professional perspective, with emphasis on the consequences of the government dominating the funding of higher education. The papers were originally presented at the conference; most were revised afterward for inclusion in the volume.

INTRODUCTION

The book opens with an introduction by Sidney Hook, one of the most distinguished commentators on American higher education in this century. Professor Hook was asked to provide opening remarks on the general subject of intellectual freedom and government sponsorship of higher education.

Hook discusses the conflict inherent in complete freedom within universities when the universities rely on political institutions for support. He notes the critical distinction between academic freedom as anarchy versus responsible scholarship. Hook argues that faculty have a duty not to take undue license or to act irresponsibly with their privileged positions of tenure. On the other side, the government should not exploit universities to achieve political goals, or academic freedom will be perverted. As an example, Hook notes the impact of affirmative action, which distorts the idea of success in academia based on merit, not personal characteristics.

GOVERNMENT SPONSORSHIP AND INTELLECTUAL FREEDOM IN RESEARCH

The chapters in the next section of the book are the heart of the volume. They look at aspects of governmental involvement in specific disciplines. Some chapters examine the effect of government funding on the idea of freedom in research, others look at the impact of government funding on the conclusions of research, and others look for evidence of a political bias on the part of academicians; i.e., do academicians appeal to the state by becoming ideological promoters of the state?

Donald Erickson, a professor of education at UCLA (and formerly at the University of Chicago), presents a personal saga of intellectual distortion and dishonesty by federal bureaucrats who have political incentives to obtain the "correct" results from scholarship. Correct meaning that the results will promote their objectives. Erickson notes that his discipline is almost wholly oriented to serving the interests of public education and that the impact on research has been dramatic. The incentive of scholars in education is to curry favor in the governmental educational establishment by engaging in research that furthers the growth of the state system. Important questions, such as why do we observe radical differences in the output of private versus public elementary and secondary schools, are largely ignored.

There is little doubt that the existence of a large number of Departments of Agricultural Economics is due to the largess of the US Department of Agriculture. Without that federal support, the land grant universities would not have established agricultural economics. Professor E.C. Pasour of North Carolina State University (a land grant school) examines the impact of the federal funding of agricultural economics and the organization of that discipline. He demonstrates that agricultural economists have helped provide the intellectual justification for the agricultural policies that cost us tens of billions of dollars per year, but are politically popular.

Two distinguished professors of accounting, Ross Watts and Jerold Zimmerman, who have played an important role in the development of modern accounting scholarship, examine the impact of government regulation on research in academic accounting. The University of Rochester scholars explain that the accounting profession is greatly affected by state and federal regulations. Out of necessity, the teaching of accounting must include significant discussions about accounting standards mandated by governments. However, much research in accounting has been devoted to inventing "scholarly explanations" to justify political actions that impact accounting. While this rationalizing research is still commonplace, the authors note that academic competition has aided the emergence (in recent years) of accounting research that is more positive in focus.

Do the attitudes of legal scholars about what the law should be have a strong influence on legislators who write the law? Most scholars believe that expert opinions matter in the construction of policies that may benefit from intellectual competition. Fred McChesney, a law professor at Emory University, studies the popular belief that intellectual attitudes exert influence on legal change. Studying a period of dramatic economic change —going from the prosperous, conservative 1920s to the depressed, liberal 1930s—he finds no evidence that the great legal developments in the depression were influenced by the scholarly legal literature. This finding is consistent with the modern economic theory of government which demonstrates that government policies are determined by the interaction of political constraints and economic motives, not by elected officials and bureaucrats who seek to maximize "the public interest."

Many surveys have demonstrated that college professors are more liberal than the general population. The reason for this has been discussed, but never explained very well. Peter Aranson, a professor of economics at Emory University, who has a Ph.D. in political science and is a leading scholar in the field of public choice, looks for evidence that faculty have been "bought" by the government to support the government. He examines empirical evidence about the relative liberalism of faculty and the amount of federal funding received. There is evidence that political scientists are among the most liberal professors. Yet, they receive trivial federal research dollars in comparison to faculty in the sciences, who do not appear to be as strong in their political orientation. While federal research dollars may be politically directed, Aranson does not find evidence to support the notion that political scientists have become advocates of expanded government to justify support for their work.

The National Science Foundation is often casually viewed as a federal agency that seeks to support only the highest quality science removed from political concerns. John Sommer, who moved to the NSF after many years in academia as an economic demographer, reviews recent NSF policy in supporting academic research. Sommer documents how government policy and academic scientists have become intertwined. This intertwining reduces the incentives of academic researchers to work on topics they believe to be the most fruitful. Instead, by necessity, scholars must respond to the structure of funding determined by Congress and executed by its agents, such as the NSF. Political pressure for market-oriented science (applied research) is in conflict with notions of academic freedom (basic research) in the academy.

Most great scientific discoveries are the unintended consequences of projects directed toward other purposes. Michael Ghiselin, whose specific research has focused on certain marine organisms, but who has also written extensively on the process of scientific discovery, uses the history of the science of coral reefs as the basis of his chapter. Charles Darwin invented the modern theory of coral reefs. His work, and that of many other scholars who have studied reefs, was a by-product of a governmental enterprise that had little concern with pure science. Ghiselin shows how creative cooperation with governments can allow pure scholarship (basic research) to be accomplished at relatively low cost.

GOVERNMENT AND THE STRUCTURE OF HIGHER EDUCATION

The next major section of the book contains chapters that look at the historical origins of the structure of American higher education. Another chapter examines the economic rationale for government support and control of higher education. The last chapter in the section considers the purpose and effects of accreditation on the structure of universities and of specific programs within universities.

The structure of the modern American university system is largely at odds with most of its history, notes Leonard Liggio, a historian, and Roger Meiners, a lawyer-economist, in their chapter on the evolution of higher education in the US. From the beginning, colleges benefitted from a mix of public and private support, but they were primarily private and often had a strong religious orientation. Federal involvement in higher education began during the Civil War, but did not become significant until World War II. Public colleges now dominate the market, but the existence of state control rather than national control provides a measure of independence.

Edwin West, an economist who has written for years about the economics of education, argues that there is little economic justification for large scale government subsidization of higher education. West finds that governmental funding produces incentives for colleges to be inefficient and expand costs to attract more public funds. The result is an increasingly monopolistic higher education system in which many private colleges are squeezed for resources. West argues that there is little reason to be optimistic about academic freedom or responsibility in a higher education system that depends on the public purse for support. Education is a service that can be more responsive to students only if there is a more direct link between the purchasers (students) and suppliers (colleges) than there is under the present financing scheme.

Expanded federal control of higher education can be expected, argues Robert Staaf, a lawyer-economist who authored the chapter on the role of accreditation in higher education. The US Department of Education is working with accrediting associations to help cartelize the higher education market by restricting what can be offered at universities and still allow the universities to be accredited and be eligible for federal funds. Staaf finds little evidence that accrediting associations exist to insure quality; rather they are becoming indirect regulatory arms of the federal government. The result is less and less ability to compete in the higher education market by offering a different product. This cartelization has serious consequences for the ideal of academic freedom.

FURTHER THOUGHTS ON THE PRODUCTION OF KNOWLEDGE AND HIGHER EDUCATION

A major concern of epistemology is the growth of knowledge. William Bartley, a distinguished epistemologist at the Hoover Institution, presents an in-depth argument about the basic conflict between the organization of higher education and the free market in ideas. He argues that a part of the problem is economic: in universities the consumers (students) do not buy, the producers (faculty) do not sell, and the owners (trustees) do not control. The non-economic structure is largely responsible for the lack of intellectual growth that Bartley observes. Many intellectuals follow the sociology of knowledge posited by Thomas Kuhn, which reinforces the lack of intellectual development. Bartley calls for more attention to Karl Popper's economics of knowledge to break the intellectual stultification.

The final word in the book is had by Gordon Tullock. Tullock was asked to address the conference casually about some observations on higher education. Tullock's long, productive career has been marked by original insights in many disciplines. He is one of the few scholars who can converse successfully with scholars in diverse fields. In his remarks, Tullock posits that we have a limited notion of what constitutes higher education.

Tullock argues that modern higher education concentrates on training of practical value. Historically, higher education offered many subjects that may have been intellectually challenging but were not practical. The purpose of such education may be to screen for people who are bright and hard working. Further, higher education tended to provide those who obtained such education with a common basis of intellectual knowledge. This development of a common ground no longer occurs as college tends to be specific toward various disciplines. Tullock argues that if we wish for higher education to provide citizens with a common basis of higher knowledge, it may have to be mandated by the government; but there is little reason to trust the government to produce a quality result.

Tullock's point is that the current system has many defects. A major restructuring may be required to produce better results. Because there is no reason to presume the system that has evolved is the best we can have for the money invested, Tullock offers some innovative schemes for radically restructuring higher education.

Tullock's discussion at the conference spawned a heated debate among the participants. The debate underscored our purpose in organizing the conference, which was to stimulate scholarly work on the impact of government on the academy. We believe the papers in this volume help to fill the void and hope they will stimulate more scholarship on this increasingly important topic.

On July 12, 1989, Sidney Hook, author, thinker, and political philosopher passed away. We dedicate *Federal Support of Higher Education* to his fond memory.

ONE

INTELLECTUAL FREEDOM AND GOVERNMENT SPONSORSHIP OF HIGHER EDUCATION

Sidney Hook

There is something hopelessly vague and general about our theme unless we can specify the time and locus of our problem. I am assuming that we are dealing with the situation of the American system of higher education in the current period, the problems and tendencies that have developed, their likely outcome, and what, if anything, as educators we can do to make the outcome desirable.

I want to begin by making a few common sense observations which will save us from the besetting sin of deriving policy considerations from antecedently held commitments to either a free market or welfare state ideology. By intellectual freedom I assume we mean the uncoerced choice of professionally qualified scholars of the themes and projects of their research, their right to reach conclusions they deem warranted by the evidence, and their right to employ whatever methods of instruction they regard as necessary for effective instruction. These freedoms are involved in our conception of the autonomous university. Since universities are always an integral part of society, their autonomy cannot be absolute, their activities cannot be beyond the jurisdiction of the criminal and civil laws that obtain in the whole of society.

From a purely abstract point of view one might argue that there is no logical or necessary responsibility of government for the existence of universities and the presence or absence of intellectual freedom in their operation. One can conceive of a government setting up license requirements for certain professions whose practices affect the lives and safety of its citizens, and administering fair and objective tests to whoever applies. A series of institutions called universities or institutes are permitted to function operated by philanthropists or, as in the Philippines some years ago, as purely business organizations run for profit. The presence and absence of intellectual freedom in these "academic" institutions would be a chancy affair depending upon the principles or whims of their owners and directors. And if one believes that whoever pays the piper calls the tune the prospects of intellectual freedom would be bleak indeed. (It is well to remember that academic freedom in the sense of *Lehr-und Lernfreiheit* which is today a part of the law of the land in the United States was actually introduced in the University of Berlin in Imperial Prussia and not in the much more politically democratic regimes of England and the United States which barred religious dissenters and unbelievers from their staffs.)

Suppose we enjoyed complete intellectual freedom with respect to government needs and demands. Would that necessarily result in a desirable state of affairs? Not if it were at a cost of the degradation of educational quality. The simple point I am making is that when we stress intellectual freedom we are presupposing at least a minimal level of intellectual activity or achievement worth defending as a basis for further qualitative improvement. I can see no virtue in celebrating the intellectual freedom of an educational institution in which no standards are organized, and anything can be taught or professed to a point of intellectual idiocy. I do not want to be misunderstood. Institutions of this character should not be suppressed. They should be legally tolerated. But my primary concern as an educator is whether they are sufficiently educational to profit from the existence of intellectual freedom.

The main point I want to stress here is that in the conditions of our time, the educational quality or level of performance of a qualitatively acceptable university enjoying intellectual freedom depends upon the institutions of the society of which it is a part, that it cannot continue to function at an acceptable educational level without direct or indirect social support. Realism requires that a free university which is not a service station to some industry or special interest that follows its own autonomous course, enjoy some recognized support from society if it is to continue to function at an adequate educational level. Otherwise it is always at risk. Consider for example what would happen to our free university if it were denied tax exemption not only with respect to contributions but with respect to its buildings and grounds. Few private universities would survive for long without suffering adverse effects if deprived of this benefit which most other enterprises aside from churches and hospitals do not enjoy. No matter how autonomous the university is regarded or regards itself, government provisions for the entire community may affect its operation. Not only the requirement that goals and time schedules for minority employment be implemented but the clerical burden of detailed record keeping for each appointment and failure to appoint, adds to already burdensome costs. Since the non-academic staff that constitute the supply staff outnumber the academic teaching staff in almost all institutions, a multitude of regulations bearing on health and labor practices add to the costs of administration. Potentially most dangerous of all is the possible impact of the prohibition of mandatory retirement upon the research and teaching capacities of university faculties. At a time when they are at their top earning power and when their productivity is at its lowest, Federal law gives tenured faculty members the right to stay on indefinitely, thus blocking the advancement of their younger colleagues. Unless something is done to modify the operation of the non-mandatory provisions for retirement as it affects universities, we shall in time have fully tenured faculties, with the possibility of new appointments to tenure track positions a function only of the professorial death rate. Alternately, special inducements may have to be provided to induce early retirements.

If it is demonstrable that any conception of university autonomy inevitably requires sympathetic government or state support, it is just as clear that the purposes of our government require sponsorship of higher education. Today there is hardly any government function whether to provide for the common defense or establish public health and welfare that does not depend on the active cooperation of the universities. It is not necessary to elaborate upon the point that they need each other to survive. To be sure, some have suggested that for purposes of research, whether pure or applied, the government can forego the uses of the university and establish its own research institutes or contract out specific research tasks to industrial corporations. But in the long run unless there is an adequately functioning set of teaching institutions that prepare qualified candidates for research tasks through the continuous process of liberal and scientific education, these institutes could not function. Both our state and federal educational agencies recognize this and the recent emphasis upon strengthening linguistic, mathematical and scientific skills would be incomprehensible without reference to the larger national goals that seep into the curricular offerings of our schools.

I propose therefore that we drop all our ideological conceits and take our point of departure from the current American scene in which state and university are inextricably intertwined. We cannot do without government sponsorship of higher education and at the same time we cannot as scholars of integrity accept limitations on our academic freedom. An increasingly influential Marxist segment of academic opinion argues that the subordination of higher education to the dominant values and objectives of capitalist society flows from the corporate structure of most universities in the private sector and from the personnel of the Boards of Regents in the public sector. Although there have been some outrageous abuses of freedom of inquiry and teaching in some institutions, private and public, by and large the corporate structure of most universities was not established to market commodities or earn profit but in the private sector to function as public service institutions and in the public sector to ensure a relative autonomy that would provide some independence of the political parties that held executive and legislative power. By and large administrative intrusions into American university life in the colonial and early modern periods were more a consequence of religious than of economic or political intolerance. It would hardly be an exaggeration to say that in most American universities today, despite their formal legal structure, the actual decisions on tenure and promotion are made by university departments and faculty committees with administrators performing household functions. There are a great many additional and educationally adventitious services that have been tacked on to traditional curricular offerings, but where educational dissatisfaction exists any resolute faculty can get them modified. When these educational excrescences persist, it is easy to establish the presence of contributory faculty responsibility. The very fact that educational leadership in higher education seems to have lost the prestige it once enjoyed, and administrative presidential posts carry no promise of long tenure, speaks worlds about the evolution of the American university.

Of even greater significance in evaluating the influence of outside agencies, private and public, on intellectual freedom has been the complete indifference of the business community and of foundations established by the great business fortunes of the past to the widespread complaint about the pervasive hostility of the humanistic disciplines to the values of our economic system. The adversarial posture of the American academy to business civilization is notorious particularly with reference to disciplines engaged in the normative analysis of values. To be sure, some foundations have recently been established to counteract excessive bias, and universities have properly refused to accept any contributions that have ideological strings attached to them. Nonetheless, the record shows that there has been a continuous increase in educational benefactions to the universities by segments of American society closely tied to the business enterprise.

The sponsorship of educational activity in any university by a private or public agency, particularly if it is of a continuing character, requires the operation of some system of accountability. The danger here is that the requests for excessive detail in the administration of the grant especially of time consumed, overhead allocations, choice of personnel, evidence of fair practice and avoidance of discrimination as interpreted by government bureaucracies and the courts, may impose unnecessarily heavy burdens both on scholars and their institutions. These obligations are likely to be very much less onerous under private than public sponsorship but with respect to basic research in science, medicine and defense, the amounts involved are of such proportions that of necessity only government sponsorship is feasible. It is significant that the few educational undergraduate institutions that have bravely eschewed any kind of government support to insure their educational independence do not develop strong departments in the natural and biological sources.

In the nature of the case there are no ideal solutions to the problems generated by the inescapable necessity of massive federal support for higher education. The government, in regarding the university as a contractor for a wide range of specific services, has no alternative but to hold the university to the same basic criteria it employs in contracting with enterprises for non-academic services. The universities on the other hand, to the extent that they are faithful to their academic mission, owe their primary loyalties to the pursuit of intellectual excellence in the liberal arts and sciences regardless of the pressing needs of governments to administer a progressively more complex society in an increasingly interrelated and more dangerous world. One of the justifications for the university's acceptance of contractual agreement to provide particular educational services is the expectation that some of the support that comes with the grant will enable it to pursue the disinterested research, to add to the richness of the cumulative intellectual and cultural heritage that are constitutive to its capacity to undertake specialized tasks. Sometimes a generalist training, even if not essential, is the most effective way to mobilize intellectual resources for limited, particular goals. We may grant the insightful and well argued position of Edward Shils that when the government awards a grant to a university for a particular service, it receives as a free good the sustained benefit of academic cooperative tradition and the capital accumulation of intellectual habits and sensibility that have been built up over the generations. However, even if there were a way of determining a fair or reasonable price for what the government receives now as a free good over and above the costs of the specific project which it is funding, viz "the effect of the long tradition of the universities' devotion to the discovering, interpretation, and teaching of fundamental knowledge of serious things" (as Shils puts it), this would only add to the reasonable costs of the specific services contracted by the government. It would not obliterate or mitigate the difference between the multiform concerns of the government and the restricted mission of the university even if the enlightened government recognizes that mission as one among its plural concerns.

This is best illustrated today in the problems associated with the allocation of funds for basic and military scientific research. Let us assume the existence of an enlightened government policy that makes its allocations on the basis of autonomous and therefore voluntary intellectual interests of university faculty, whose applications for support of projects is evaluated by the traditional peer system of review and that grants of this character are uninfluenced on the federal level by narrow budgetary restrictions such as productivity criteria for the involved faculty members or purely quantitative student faculty teaching loads. Scientific achievement and the promise of significant findings are the overriding considerations. As legitimate as are the scientific interests of the academically free researcher so are the government decisions in a democratic polity of what the national needs in science are—what research projects to further the military safety or the national health of the nation. Where there are no unlimited resources, choices on priorities must be made. Within the limits of constitutional restraints, such choices, whatever their wisdom, are broadly political. They should be made with the consultation of the scientific community. But they obviously cannot be made only by the scientific community in any area since where alternative choices reflect strong differences about public policies and the nature of the threats to the survival of the free society, these differences are found among the scientists themselves.

When the nation finds itself engaged in war, differences are moderated to the common necessity of victorious survival. When the nation is at peace, but divided by differing estimates of the dangers of war, how best to avoid them, and how to limit the costs of disaster, the conflict becomes more acute. Most of these differences reflect divergent political analyses unrelated to the specific area of specialization.

However, as American history in the 20th century has shown, even in cases of war and national emergency, the federal support of research has not imposed, with respect to the freedom to engage in research, any sacrifice of the principles of academic freedom, except in the interests of classified research which wherever possible was channeled to special agencies off campus. Today most universities do not accept any kind of classified research. Nor has the American government, as far as I know, imposed any research project on any university which it was unwilling to undertake as a condition of support for other research projects universities were willing to sponsor. So long as the universities are free to decline proposals for research, whose conditions of acceptance are repugnant to its conception of the integrity of the educational process, without suffering any overt sanctions, I see no threat to academic freedom. It goes without saying that this may sometimes require courage to turn down research projects accompanied by overhead subsidies and other perks that ease its chronic burdens, resulting temporarily at least in some hardships. Interestingly enough, the problem of secrecy for a limited period raises fewer hackles in universities when they arise in research sponsored by industrial corporations. By and large the experience of Harvard with government-sponsored research reported to its faculties and governing boards in *Harvard and the Federal Government: A Report to the Faculties and Governing Boards at Harvard University* (September 1961, pp. 10-11) summarizes the general experience:

> The image of a coercive government dictating what shall and shall not be done in university laboratories and libraries simply does not fit Harvard's experience with Washington.... Communication and understanding between the University and the Government regarding the conduct of the research are generally satisfactory, and the impact of federal funds on a particular research project does not seem to differ basically from the impact of money in similar amounts from private sources.

The most dangerous threat to intellectual freedom from government sponsorship of higher education came from the ill-fated, misinterpreted Executive Order which outlawed discrimination on grounds of race, sex, religion or national origin. There was nothing in the literal text of the Order which justified the bureaucratic interpretation of its application which converted the Executive Order barring invidious discrimination into an instrument of reverse discrimination against white males. Now that the courts on the whole have upheld the use of racial and gender criteria allegedly to overcome racial and gender discrimination, it is not likely that despite the public opposition to the violation of the civil service principle based primarily on merit, that these educationally and morally illegitimate practices will disappear in the near future. The most effective way to resist their educational impact is to insist in the day-by-day practices of higher institutions upon the development and use of a common set of relevant and adequate principles of testing and evaluation in the selection and promotion of teachers.

There is no reason to believe that any diminution in the magnitude of federal aid to higher education will by itself make a substantial difference in the persistence of the current unhappy practices of the Presidential Executive Order since the courts can easily find ways of extending their jurisdiction. The role of the Federal government in extending educational opportunities to large segments of the population deprived of them, the long and consistent effort to overthrow the segregational policies of state educational systems has generated widespread popular support. And justifiably so. The remedial legal and educational measures to extend the areas of equal opportunity for those victimized by past practices of invidious discrimination should be encouraged and extended. Although it is unfashionable to believe and even more unfashionable to proclaim it, I believe it is possible to abolish the discriminatory practices of the past, to make special compensatory provisions for those who have personally suffered from such practices, and at the same time in the areas of educational teaching, research and scholarship operate with adequate standards of achievement universally and equitable applied.

TWO

GOVERNMENT DISTORTION OF THE STUDY OF EDUCATION

Donald A. Erickson

My assignment is to discuss possible government distortion of scholarship in the field known as education, with special attention to the effects of government funding of educational inquiry.

Educational inquiry is concerned with such questions as how people learn, especially within the context of schools; how the various subjects of study are, or should be, arranged and presented; and how various enterprises to foster learning are, or should be, staffed, financed, and organized. Though some analytic methods have been extensively honed in their particular application to educational problems, the study of education is best viewed, in my opinion, as having no investigative assumptions and methods peculiarly its own. Rather, the modes of inquiry of numerous established disciplines are used in attempts to unravel educational enigmas. We students of education represent a broad range of disciplines and sub-disciplines, including psychology, social psychology, sociology, anthropology, linguistics, philosophy, political science, history, and economics.

Most of us are located, as a matter of convenience, in graduate schools of education, where we assist with the training of teachers and school administrators, but many hold joint or exclusive appointments in other university schools and departments.

But whether scholars who inquire into educational phenomena are located in schools of education, or in other academic homes, all are subject to the self-interested impulses discussed by Bartley in Chapter 12. The distorting consequences of those impulses are particularly strong, I suspect, in fields like agricultural economics, discussed by Pasour in Chapter 5; accounting, discussed by Watts in Chapter 2; and my own field, education—fields in which government not only finances research but has a major, direct impact upon practice through extensive regulation or sponsorship.

In education, I believe extensive distortion of scholarship occurs because government sponsors the huge enterprise composed of public schools at elementary and secondary levels. Since much money and influence flows through that enterprise, there is much at stake when the winds of received wisdom shift, and thus the motives for preserving entrenched paradigms can be particularly strong. Though approximately 12 percent of the nation's youth attend private schools at elementary and secondary levels, for instance, it would be easy to demonstrate that scholars who study education concentrate almost exclusively on public school issues, often as if private schools did not exist, and most textbooks in the field exhibit a strong bias against private schools. The explanation for this distorted tunnel vision seems rather obvious. For scholars who play their cards well, public schools are a consultant's heaven. Public schools always need advice on something, and can pay for it. They always have a program which, as a matter of state or federal law, must be evaluated. They always have people who need "in service training." (Several of my scholar friends are millionaires.)

Scholars attached to schools of education may be especially vulnerable to such blandishments, since most of them spent long years as teachers or administrators in public schools before moving on to higher education, and thus are well attuned to the opportunities and requisite dogma, but some of the worst examples of academic self-seeking in my experience, as discussed below, involve scholars *not* thus affiliated. Whether in schools of education or not, most scholars seem to welcome the headlines and consulting dollars generated by educational programs sponsored by state and federal governments. But the notoriety and lucre come at a price. One must be an expert on matters relating to these *public* programs. One must cultivate the state and federal bureaucrats who oversee those programs—bureaucrats who nearly always have close connections and extensive experience in public schools. It helps if one is a public school advocate, with extensive friendly "contacts" in the public school world. It hurts if one produces conceptualizations or evidence at all critical of that world. To specialize in private schools, or to indicate sensitivity toward them, is the kiss of death. Something in this arrangement is reminiscent of the so-called "military- industrial complex."

As a consequence of such dynamics, the focus of scholarship in my field is dramatically different from what it would be if government were not running the schools which most children attend. Many school problems investigated extensively by scholars simply would not exist, or would take a notably different form, if the public school "system" did not exist, and many private school problems now largely neglected would receive attention instead. (As I argue in a book on educational privatism to be published soon under the aegis of The Independent Institute in San Francisco, publicly sponsored schools are different in numerous important respects from privately sponsored schools.) Furthermore, there would be little reason to slant educational research so as to favor public schools, as I believe is frequently done, if public schools did not dominate the scene.

My mandate, however, is to discuss a different though closely related aspect of government distortion of scholarship in my field—the distortion that occurs because government finances education research. In that regard, I suffer a serious handicap: Unable to uncover systematic studies of this topic, I am forced to rely upon personal experience, with all the subjectivity that implies. The lack of research along this line is itself interesting. Perhaps the topic is taboo. Since every educational researcher whom I know has either fed at the trough of government grants and contracts or attempted to do so, such researchers may have had little motivation to antagonize government agencies by investigating their foibles.

This chapter should be regarded, then, not as a firm statement of what is occurring, but as providing speculation and hypothesis based upon personal observations over the years. I will be saying, in effect, "Here are some ways in which government funding of research may be distorting scholarship in my field. Let us ponder these possibilities to see whether they warrant systematic inquiry." In support of my speculations and hypotheses, I offer nothing more than examples of possible distortion that I have encountered, sometimes through personal experience, and sometimes in the literature.

The examples drawn from personal experience could easily be warped by emotion and selective perception. Since I do not wish to damage reputations or invite lawsuits, I must disguise identities and omit details, thus making it impossible for the evidence to be checked. Some of this evidence would be regarded as hearsay in a court of law. Though my sources seem unimpeachable to me, I cannot identify them or summon them to testify on their own. Even if my readers assume my reports are accurate, one swallow does not a summer make, and a few examples do not substantiate a trend. Most of the evidence, furthermore, is suggestive and circumstantial. It falls short of demonstrating any causal connection. Educational research would be seriously biased even if there were no government funds for research, as I argue later, and as Bartley demonstrates well in Chapter 12. One cannot simply attribute to government all bias exhibited in the context of government grants. My personal opinion, for what it is worth, based upon considerable experience with the phenomenon, is that distortion often occurs as a consequence of government funding of educational research, and is powerful and pervasive.

I address this topic with trepidation and reluctance. At the 1986 meeting of the American Educational Research Association, I offered a few off-the-record comments along these lines in a small, obscure session, asking the counsel of trusted colleagues. These colleagues advised me to seal my lips, at least until retirement. (They will forgive me, I trust, for pondering their advice and deciding not to follow it.) They could be right. One's career can always be damaged, and in this era a lawsuit lurks at every corner. But I am induced to speak by the importance of the topic, and by the conviction that I may be the least vulnerable scholar with these convictions. Many scholars may be genuinely unaware of the tendencies I will discuss. If one is studying topics government agencies like to finance, one will probably think the funding decisions are a matter of simple logic. As with discrimination in other areas of life, the people likely to detect it are its victims, not the comfortable majority. As one who writes mainly on the topics government funding agencies seem to avoid, I may have an obligation to speak. With mounds of data as yet only partially analyzed, furthermore, I have little need of additional grants. If I antagonize government funding agencies, I have little to lose personally, in one sense. And I cannot sensibly be accused of a sour grapes mentality, for though long a certified maverick in my field, I have received more than my share of government money for research, and though threatened on occasion with dire career consequences for my views, I have been a tenured full professor at two universities of considerable repute—the University of Chicago and the University of California at Los Angeles (UCLA). Somehow, perhaps through some secret stellar or angelic sponsorship, I have escaped the punishment administered, as I see it, to the bulk of my like-minded peers, some of the best of whom have retreated from academic life. It may be my duty to speak, albeit cautiously.

My procedure in the passages that follow is to list, and later discuss, seven ways in which government domination of research funding may distort what is taken to be the truth about educational phenomena. This list of seven is not intended to be exhaustive. There are other important avenues of bias, such as the demand for practical outcomes at the expense of basic research, and the demand for geographic distribution of government grants, both discussed persuasively by Sommer in Chapter 7.

The seven possible avenues of government distortion of scholarship to be discussed below are as follows:

(1) Biasing the selection of questions to be asked and topics to be investigated;

(2) Slanting the interpretation of evidence;

(3) Selectively advancing the careers of scholars favorable to particular points of view;

(4) Selective dissemination of research findings, favoring particular points of view;

(5) Simple-minded dissemination of complex findings, fostering faulty conclusions and applications;

(6) Introduction of research rigidities that handicap and distort;

(7) Provision of inducements that exacerbate the human treachery which so often infects scholarship.

BIASING THE SELECTION
OF QUESTIONS AND TOPICS

It seems to me, as I have noted, that government funding of educational research may produce distortions by biasing the selection of questions to be asked and topics to be investigated.

Through systematic investigation it would be easy to demonstrate, I suspect, that topics favored by the political party in power, by powerful individual politicians, and/or by prominent scholars who serve as gatekeepers to government funds have been studied extensively and repetitiously under government grants and contracts, that unfavored topics have been ignored to a notable extent, and that the emphases shift with changes in the loci of power and shifts in popular ideology. Investigation would show, I predict, that studies concerning equality of educational opportunity have been funded far more frequently and liberally than studies concerning the education of the nation's brightest and best. For instance, studies of the negative effects of ability grouping have proliferated, while the negative consequences of slow-paced instruction on superior students are glossed over. We have bookshelves of data on the problems of disadvantaged students, but little on how the learning of talented youth is impeded in our schools.

Most procedures for the certification and credentialing of teachers and school administrators are, in my view, quite ludicrous, but since these procedures help fill the classrooms of scholars in my field, and help friends in teacher unions control access to the profession, it is not surprising that few scholars take the risks involved in scrutinizing the procedures for certification and credentialing and their purported effects on educational quality.

Similarly, federally financed studies of private schools and parental choice have been—beyond all reason, I suggest—few, far between, generally meager in scope, and when they are done, often deliberately slanted. Much of the opposition to disinterested research on private schools and parental choice, both in government and elsewhere, seems simple-minded, based upon the ludicrous assumption that to study something is necessarily to promote it. Thus, in major universities scholars will be rewarded for studying the Mafia, or cancer, or economic recessions, but even in an institution as renowned as the University of Chicago, a dean can reprimand a scholar (I speak from experience) for studying private schools. (Shortly after explaining that he wanted his institution to be noted for its "public school orientation," the dean quietly enrolled his own child in an elite private school.)

One example of possible government bias against funding studies of parental choice is found in a thick, federally funded evaluation, in 1976, of the widely publicized "alternative public schools" in Berkeley, California, an experiment with educational diversity into which the federal government had poured approximately six million dollars, ostensibly to learn what happens when educational alternatives are offered to parents.[1] Berkeley attempted to give families a free choice of diversified educational programs, to see how parents would respond and how students would fare. But astonishingly, in the study of the project financed by the National Institute of Education, nobody bothered to ask parents why they had chosen various alternatives, or how they made the decisions. If there was anything more important to discover in the Berkeley experiment, I cannot imagine what it was. Here again, a plausible explanation for the curious omission is not hard to find. In its early days, the National Institute of Education (NIE) fell on hard times because its first director neglected the political aspects of his job.[2] That mistake was so extensively publicized and analyzed that no successor was likely to forget the lesson. NIE was repeatedly exhorted to tend its fences in Congress and to cultivate the constituencies that would support its budget requests—especially the huge public school constituency. And the notion of parental choice has never been popular in such circles. As E.G. West has argued, it is in the interests of the school bureaucracy to make attendance of children as predictable as possible, not subject to parental preferences.[3] So if political realities forced support of the Berkeley program on NIE, NIE could minimize the damage by de-emphasizing parental choice in its evaluation of a program intended primarily to foster choice.

I should probably emphasize here a point that will be apparent at several junctures in this chapter: The political forces exhibited in Congress are not identical with those that affected the National Institute of Education, which for several decades was the major source of government funds (or funds in general, for that matter) for educational research. From time to time powerful congressmen have demanded research on private schools and taken a deep interest in parental choice, as promoted by voucher schemes and tuition tax credits. But since NIE's largest source of potential political support was the huge public school bureaucracy, NIE had special reasons to avoid the appearance that it was interested in schools outside the public sector, even to the point of seeming at times to defy Congress *sub rosa*.

An example of reluctance to sponsor studies of private schools is found in the way the rather recent congressionally mandated School Finance Project dealt with the statutory demand that it investigate financial issues in both public and private schools. I regarded the School Finance Project as an arm of NIE, for it was located in the NIE building, and its staff was studded with NIE personnel. Like other scholars, I attempted to monitor the work of that project. I testified before its advisory committee, suggesting that many school finance projects are rather silly in one important sense, since they assume that public school finances can be understood in isolation and that private school finances are not important enough to discuss. Since public school finances affect private school finances, and vice versa, most of the Project's studies should be comprehensive, I argued, involving both public and private schools, in such a way as to illuminate the fiscal relationships between them. Nothing of the sort happened. A series of finance studies began, focusing as usual on public schools as if private schools did not exist. Disappointed, I began to inquire about the second-best approach—supplementing the public school studies with private school studies. I inquired repeatedly, as did others, as to when investigations involving private schools would be conducted. Month after month, while the Project's research proceeded in public schools, no news emerged about private school studies. Eventually, when the Project's life was about to expire and its budget was almost depleted, project leaders contacted me by telephone for advice about a projected quick, small-budget study of parental choice making. There was little money and little time, they explained, so an almost instantaneous, limited, low-budget investigation would have to be done "in house." I heard from several sources that this study was done under duress, because members of Congress who had taken special pains to state in the enabling legislation that the research must include private schools were now angry to find that nothing of that nature had occurred. It was too late for the Project to assign the study to someone properly aware of the previous relevant literature and of the relevant peculiarities of private schools. What should have been a landmark national investigation, in the light of the total budget given to the School Finance Study, involved a sample of only 144-odd private school households, ridiculous as a purported representation of all areas of the country, all grade levels, and an enormous diversity of private schools, whose parents are known to attend for notably different reasons.[4] The choices made for each child were probed, on average, in a telephone interview of approximately 15 minutes. Thus, many of the most important differences among schools and family types had to be left unexplored. It is difficult to escape the suspicion that key figures in the Project deliberately subverted the intentions of the Congress in an effort to stay in the good graces of the public school establishment.

Another example, more extended, is drawn directly from my own experience. Late in November 1977, I learned that legislation had been passed in British Columbia to grant sizeable tax support to private schools (there known as "independent" schools) for the first time in that province's history. The private schools received, on a per pupil basis, 30 percent of the per pupil operating expenses of public schools in adjoining areas. Having been interested for years in the effects of public *versus* private funding on private schools, I decided to seek funds to permit a longitudinal study of the effects of the aid program in British Columbia. Fortunately, I knew that Senator Moynihan and others were sponsoring bills to provide education vouchers in the US, and had been complaining that the National Institute of Education, despite the millions it had spent on educational research, could provide not a shred of direct evidence on the topic. "Get us some evidence on vouchers," the congressmen were demanding. I also knew that one of NIE's key officers at the time, viewed by some people as a misfit in the institute, and soon to leave (as it turned out), had a long-standing interest in vouchers. Needing more money than I believed I could get from any private source, I decided to try to capitalize on these special circumstances in an agency that I viewed as generally unreceptive to such ideas. I rushed an unsolicited proposal to NIE, pleading for rapid action on a grant that would permit me to start the work at once by gathering base line data on conditions in B.C. private schools before any of the tax money began to flow. As one does in such proposals, I used the currently important words—such as "education vouchers"—liberally, though the aid was never generally regarded as a voucher scheme in B.C. My terminology was not dishonest. I have heard E.G. West argue persuasively that the B.C. aid, properly understood, is a voucher arrangement.

The bet paid off to a notable extent—largely, I believe, because of the above-mentioned special circumstances in NIE.[5] Even so, key officials in NIE informed me that it was politically impossible at the time for them to give a large grant for a study of private schools. Under the law, they were forbidden to negotiate a fundamental shift in the focus of an unsolicited proposal, so they simply indicated that if I rearranged the study to focus equally on public and private schools, it might be fundable, but otherwise definitely not. They were "apprising me of facts," and "not demanding anything," or "negotiating." It seemed wiser to me to do the study with public schools included than to abandon the effort altogether. In the light of later events, which I cannot discuss here, I regard the inclusion of public schools as a serious error that compromised the work enormously. The idea of including public schools was at no point suggested in my unsolicited proposal, which is available for anyone to examine. I would definitely not have made the drastic shift in research focus apart from the government coercion (read "advice"). (The officials also informed me, understandably, that they would deny, if the issue ever arose, doing anything to influence the research focus.)

Toward completion of the B.C. study, in the fall of 1981, there was more dramatic evidence suggesting how NIE responded to its political context in determining the topics on which it would and would not finance research. We were proceeding in terms of a research design, approved by the NIE officer in charge of overseeing the grant, that called for a final major survey and other extensive work in the spring of 1982. Without that final work, much of the effort and expense devoted to earlier surveys would be rendered useless, since the anticipated comparisons at different points in time would be impossible. By the fall of 1981, however, we were experiencing stiff opposition from the teacher union in British Columbia, whose leaders apparently thought our evidence might damage their cause. They had circulated memoranda to all the union locals in B.C., urging them to block the aspect of our work that involved public schools. Perhaps because that did not stop us, the B.C. teacher union, according to information given to me by our NIE officer, contacted both the American Federation of Teachers and the National Education Association in Washington, urging them to protest our study at the major source of our funds—the National Institute of Education. NIE reportedly paid little heed to the American Federation of Teachers, which had refused to lend its backing to the recent campaign to elect

President Carter. However, the NEA and its locals had poured enormous effort into the Carter campaign. Shortly after the election, President Carter personally visited the NEA head-quarters to express his appreciation. Political commentators began discussing the NEA's unprecedented influence in the White House.[6] I began to hear immediately from our NIE officer that there were "noises in the front office" about my B.C. study, and within a very short period of time our budget was cut and we were told no further support would be possible beyond that fiscal year. The decision had nothing to do with politics, we were assured, but merely reflected financial shortages at NIE. The study was vitiated, because several key components of the longitudinal design had to be abandoned. Happily for our pur-poses, President Reagan's NIE appointees eventually took over, and under their aegis, much more favorable to private enterprise, the direction of government bias shifted in that regard, and I was able to obtain a final modest NIE grant to bring the study to a reasonably decent, but still mutilated, conclusion.

SLANTING THE ACQUISITION AND INTERPRETATION OF EVIDENCE

It seems to me that government funding of educational research may often produce distortions by slanting the acquisi-tion and interpretation of evidence. I suspect that this type of government-induced bias occurs mainly through the strategy of giving grants and contracts deliberately to scholars deemed likely to favor particular points of view. Sometimes, of course, the selection of scholars, like the selection of Supreme Court justices, fails to produce the intended consequences.

Ironically, I myself was the scholar selected to bias the acqui-sition and interpretation of evidence, as I now see it, in the incident that I find most convincing in this regard. Then still a relatively new assistant professor in the Department of Educa-tion at the University of Chicago, I received a telephone call in 1968, from an acquaintance at the now-defunct Office of Economic Opportunity (OEO). OEO, along with other public and private money givers, had been pouring large sums into a "demonstration school" on the Navaho reservation, and needed someone to conduct a comprehensive evaluation of the enterprise. Would I like to do it? I expressed surprise, opining that the task should be performed by an anthropologist who knew a lot about American Indian education. I was unqualified on both counts, having never studied anthropology systematically, and having never entered a school for American Indian youngsters. Furthermore, my existing commitments would make it well-nigh-impossible, I said, to give a major evaluation proper attention.

Not to worry. OEO (for which I had consulted on numerous occasions) was impressed with my grasp of policy issues, he said, and with the sensitivity I had demonstrated in my writings on the Old Order Amish. He thought I would approach the school with a special sympathy for minorities and a fresh viewpoint, both of which were important. Furthermore, OEO would provide ample funds for a research staff, and to secure the advice and help of anthropologists and experts on American Indian schooling. I could guide the enterprise without investing a tremendous amount of time. He mentioned several people I should consider as advisors. Describing an utterly fascinating school, he urged me not to say "No" before doing a "site visit" to the school at OEO's expense. I weakened and made the trip.

The walls of the school were festooned with magnificent Navaho artifacts. Silversmiths wrought their magic in full view. Navaho parents roamed the halls like inscrutable wraiths, and staffed the dormitories in place of the Bureau of Indian affairs personnel so often ridiculed in the literature. Navaho language and culture were revered and taught. Medicine men came, chanted, and were honored. An all-Navaho board had full legal control. The school's director, a white anthropologist married to a Navaho, declared with eloquence and deep conviction that this school would prepare Navaho children to be competent and comfortable in *both* Navaho and mainstream cultures. There would be no denigration of Navaho people and Navaho ways in this school! Captivated by the noble concepts, the stunning landscape, the reservation's healing silence, I was loath to leave. I suppose my enchantment showed.

Back in Chicago, I heard immediately from OEO that the school's director felt, as did OEO officials, that I was exactly the right person to do the evaluation. I could perform an important service by documenting the promise of this unusual educational approach to the needs of oppressed people. (I concluded later that OEO had granted the director unofficial veto power over the choice of an evaluator.) Quite unable to resist at this point, I assented. There was one small detail, the OEO official then observed. OEO was required to invite proposals from all people who might be interested in conducting the evaluation. I would need to submit one myself. But it was quite unlikely that anyone would match my special qualifications. Subsequently, under unreasonable time constraints, I submitted a hastily constructed proposal. As had been predicted, I "came out on top" in the "competition." Enormously overcommitted and preoccupied, I concentrated on getting started, and gave little thought to the way the contract was awarded. The temptation to believe my competence had carried the day was obviously quite strong.

I assembled a rather large advisory committee, formed mostly of scholars suggested by OEO, plus two Navahos and experts on Indian education, scrutinized books about Navahos and American Indian education during well-nigh-sleepless nights. I appointed as my associate a scholar with extensive anthropological training.

As the first step in starting the work, I spent a day with the advisory committee, discussing my evaluation design. The meeting ended with the committee's assurance that if I gathered and analyzed the evidence as planned, the committee would have confidence in the findings. Everything looked encouraging. OEO was enthusiastic. The school's director was enthusiastic. The advisory committee was enthusiastic. I was enthusiastic.

When we began to compare that nationally renowned demonstration school with three other schools serving the same area of the reservation, however, we found much below the surface that appeared to contradict the school's claims. I assembled the surprising data in various forms, called another day-long meeting of the advisory committee, and said to the members, in effect: "I gathered the evidence exactly as we agreed I should. It is full of unanticipated tendencies. Help me be sure I am not misinterpreting." One particularly renowned scholar, whom OEO had insisted must be a member of my advisory committee, seemed instantly belligerent. He argued that my evidence was almost totally misleading, a product of my "culture shock" as a person who encountered Navaho culture without proper preparation. Too bad a naive, inexperienced person like Erickson had been trusted to do the study. At the end of the day, after everyone else left, he threatened to discredit me completely and ensure that I would never gain tenure at the University of Chicago if I did not agree to report the data very selectively, in a manner he described in considerable detail. I need not *change* any data, he observed, but simply *omit* most of it. My investigation, he said, had been unnecessarily comprehensive. If I reported only part, that would certainly be enough. All would then be well, and he would see that I was honored for my contribution. To follow his suggestion would have been to reverse the central tenor of the evidence. With deep misgivings, I refused.[7]

After the conference, everything seemed to go wrong. My associate was ordered by reservation officials, on the basis of charges which later proved entirely false, never to return to the scene of our research. Bereft of her help, and under seemingly impossible time demands, I made a hurried visit to the reservation for a final round of critical data. Just before I left for that visit, a graduate student turned up, as if by divine intervention, to offer his assistance on an aspect of the study where he claimed considerable competency. Sighing relief, I hired him on the spot. A few days later, one fragrant moonlit evening in the romantic shadow of the monoliths, he confided to one of my female Navaho field workers that he had infiltrated my staff at the behest of the scholar who had threatened me. If he had blackmail in mind, he found nothing to use, but he significantly damaged the cause by "accidentally losing" the entire file of the most telling data gathered on the trip. When I returned from the reservation, I learned that a scurrilous secret paper, full of inaccurate claims, which came to my attention mostly by accident, had been circulated in the halls of power in Washington, in an obvious attempt to discredit our report before it was even written. Upon OEO's erstwhile cordiality there dropped a thick mantle of silence. In a small American Indian publication, an article was published in my defense, stating that Indian observers themselves, who could hardly be accused of culture shock, thought my picture of the school was accurate, but no one gave that comment much attention.[8]

In later months, I gravitated to the view that I had been selected to do the evaluation, not because OEO and the school's director were convinced of my wizardry as a scholar, or because my proposal was the best submitted, but because the people with the most at stake thought my initial glowing enthusiasm for the school, my lack of anthropological training, my naivete about American Indian schooling, my relative inexperience in research, and my grossly overburdened schedule would all work together, abetted by advice from powerful members of my advisory committee, to ensure a superficial, naive study, gushing with poetry about the school's accomplishments. I would be agog at the school's impressive show-window material, as on my initial visit, and notice little else. But my fascination produced an unintended consequence. I spent much time on the reservation, during a period of six months, at the expense of other commitments. I insisted that I, and all members of my staff, must be housed in the student dormitories, not in guest apartments. We ate in the student dining room. We haunted the classrooms and playgrounds. We attended board meetings. We assembled reams of notes on first-hand observations, in addition to data from interviews in school and community, school board minutes, achievement test evidence, student cumulative records, and questionnaires. When my findings proved mostly negative, it was as if I had violated a sacred trust. Previously lionized in these circles, I was suddenly an outcast. Fortunately, though the consulting pipeline dried up at OEO, the episode rendered no significant permanent damage to my career that I can discern.

In retrospect, the politics of the situation seem obvious. The school in question and its director had powerful congressmen behind them, such as Robert Kennedy. OEO could not afford to override the school's director in the choice of an evaluator, or alienate the congressmen by producing a negative report that would complicate their well intentioned efforts to help American Indians. A Robert Kennedy, for instance, who had visited the school himself, would probably trust his own impressions far more than someone's dull research, wonder why OEO was nit-picking one of his favorite enterprises, and be less enthusiastic about OEO's budget requests the next time around. The scholar who threatened me had spent much of his career articulating and advocating the ideas the school embodied. His own research on approaches of this kind—research which I now regard as suspect—had produced glowing results. He was winning grants in steady sequence, for continuing work along this line. He was a well-paid consultant to practically anything that was pertinent and important. My findings, he candidly told me, could nullify much that he and others had accomplished over several de-cades. Much had been riding on the assumption that I, like he, would produce a confidence- inspiring chronicle of educational success. When I did not, the anger and attempts to discredit were virtually inevitable.

My point in all this is that government biasing of research may often occur by means of a biased selection of the scholars who are given the government grants and contracts. My inter-pretation of the incident cannot be proven accurate, but I think it warrants consideration. It would be interesting to determine how many scholars have similar stories to tell.

I regard Bridge's analysis of data from the Alum Rock "voucher" experiment as another possible example of the po-tential for government distortion of research through a biased selection of the scholars who will receive grants and contracts.[9] Picture the situation.[10] The Office of Economic Opportunity, which was bursting with enthusiasm about the education voucher concept at the time, had made an extensive, widely publicized effort to launch one experiment that would yield firsthand evidence on how the concept might work in practice. Only one public school system in the entire nation had proven willing to stage the experiment in exchange for millions of federal dollars. The central concepts of the experiment proved too threatening to Alum Rock teachers and administrators, and thus were never put into practice. Nevertheless, Alum Rock did provide a number of educational alternatives, in the form of "mini-school" programs within existing public schools. The programs were well publicized among parents, and serious steps were taken, including the provision of free busing, to encourage parents to choose the programs they thought would suit their children best.

The plan was for every participating public school to offer between three and five alternative programs, known as "mini-schools," involving different curricular emphases, instructional styles, or approaches to discipline. Parents of all eligible children were given vouchers each spring, along with information about each mini-school, and were asked to decide where their children would go to school in the coming fall. Unfortunately, close scrutiny showed that the Alum Rock mini-schools represented something less than met the eye.[11] Beneath the trappings of diversity, unfortunately, almost all the programs proved, upon close examination, to be pretty conventional and similar. But even in this disappointing context, where parents were not allowed to apply their vouchers to private school alternatives, and where public school alternatives were mostly conventional and similar, tendencies were found that I regard as encouraging. Initially, parents of higher social status knew considerably more about the program than did parents of lower social status, but the information disparity declined notably over a period of time. Though the community as a whole was rather disadvantaged and impoverished, parents developed an impressive interest in their schools. In 1972, over one third of the parents said they wanted a voice in teacher hiring and firing, and the proportion rose to over half in 1973. Even higher proportions of parents wanted to participate in decisions about spending, and in the hiring and firing of school principals. The proportions of parents who could specifically identify the mini-programs in which their children were enrolled were 84 percent in 1972 and 97 percent in 1973 for Anglos, 80 percent in 1972 and 82 percent in 1973 for blacks, 72 percent in 1972 and 89 percent in 1973 for Hispanics who could be interviewed in English, and 76 percent in 1972 and a dramatically improved 96 percent in 1973 for members of other ethnic groups.[12] Having encountered in my own research a surprising number of parents who, in the absence of significant opportunity for choice, cannot even name the *schools* which their children attend, I find these proportions impressive.

At the beginning of the Alum Rock program, proximity—the distance of a minischool from one's home—was mentioned as a significant factor in the choices of over 81 percent of parents who were aware of the voucher program. I do not find that figure surprising, partly because a fair percentage of parents were not aware of the free busing, partly because it seems likely that many parents, especially at this early stage, would be skeptical of the benefits of sending their children to distant schools, and partly because it makes good sense to keep young children in schools close to home. In fact, the interest of parents in the program is impressive in the light of the alienation that 75 percent of them expressed by agreeing with the statement, "In general, teachers and principals do not want the advice of parents."

By the second year of the program, when information about various mini-schools had been more adequately disseminated, the proportion of parents choosing programs in schools other than the one closest at hand rose to 18.5 percent. Black parents exhibited a particular propensity to bypass the closest school; about 41 percent of black parents did this.

Opponents of education vouchers had insisted, as opponents of parental choice still do, that parents, given freedom to select their children's schools, would segregate themselves racially. In fact, that did not happen in Alum Rock. Other opponents of education vouchers argued that parents would make choices on superficial grounds, handicapping their children academically. But academic achievement scores stayed as high as ever. In some respects, the achievement scores may even have risen, but two key members of the Alum Rock team have informed me that much of the relevant evidence was lost.

Bridge, in keeping with a popular Marxist interpretation, lamented the fact that parents of lower social status were more likely than parents of higher social status to choose programs that seemed more highly structured. The consequence of this, according to Bridge, might be to handicap the low-status students, thus contributing to social stratification. The low-status students would learn, in highly structured programs, to be obedient and master facts, thus equipping themselves to be hewers of wood and drawers of water. The high-status students would learn, in structures providing more scope for student choice and imagination, to be creative and self-reliant, thus equipping themselves to be professionals and executives. What an impressive body of research on teaching suggests, however, is that the low-status parents were making wiser choices than experts like Bridge apparently would make for them, for their children *needed* highly structured programs in order to acquire the basic academic skills without which they could never move on to the creative, self-directed activities that might help them become professionals and executives.[13]

When Bridge noted that, at the beginning of the Alum Rock experiment, low-SES parents were handicapped by possessing less knowledge than high-SES parents of the available choices, he argued that, since low-SES parents would not have their fair share of the freedom to choose, schemes to maximize parental choice would work to the disadvantage of low-status parents and their offspring, and therefore should be minimized. When Bridge realized that the information disparities tended to disappear over time, he argued, flying in the face of voluminous evidence about resistance to change in public schools,[14] that educational arrangements would constantly shift, thus continually reinstating the information disadvantages of the disadvantaged, who apparently take longer to find things out. Anyhow, even if the disadvantaged are given an equal opportunity to choose, they would simply handicap their children by selecting highly structured programs. I think it is obvious that Bridge was determined to argue against parental choice schemes *regardless* of the evidence. If low-income parents suffered an information disparity, that was a reason to argue against choice schemes. If low-income parents had equal freedom to choose, that was a reason to argue against choice schemes. Bridge's decision-making rule in reaching conclusions and recommendations apparently was something like, "Heads I win, tails you lose." Whatever the evidence, parental choice should be lamented.

I think the evidence from Alum Rock is generally encouraging as to the outcomes of parental choice. Here, in a community of generally disadvantaged people, in a school system that has inspired little parental trust, in an arrangement of educational alternatives that are mostly alternatives only in name, a notable proportion of parents take a rather deep interest in school affairs, information about the available programs seeps rather quickly to all social strata, eventually in rather equal proportions, a surprising proportion of parents, especially black parents, choose options not available in the closest school (thus indicating some depth of conviction), and parents apparently make wiser choices than the educational experts would be inclined to make in their behalf. Despite alarming predictions to the contrary, there is no decline in academic achievement, and no tendency toward greater racial segregation.

I submit, in fact, that virtually any scholar without a settled predisposition to denigrate parental choice would draw conclusions radically different from Bridge's conclusions. By the time Bridge began his analysis, the Office of Economic Opportunity was dead, and the National Institute of Education, with its well publicized need to cultivate the support of the public school constituency, was in charge of the Alum Rock experiment. It would have been easy at the time to identify scholars less prejudiced against the concept of parental choice. The possibility warrants thought, then, that NIE was protecting its political frontiers in its choice of the scholar to do the analysis. Faced with a study of parental choice which it inherited from OEO, which had no such need to cultivate the public school constituency, NIE could minimize the damage by producing an analysis which condemned parental choice schemes in the face of evidence which, in my view, virtually defies Bridge's interpretation. Here again I emphasize that my interpretation of these events, though it seems to fit them well, cannot be proven accurate. The evidence is circumstantial.

I have had experiences even more directly to the point, but for obvious reasons do not wish to discuss them in much detail.

On one occasion, a friend in NIE informed me of an exceptionally large award of funds for research on a sensitive subject to a group headed by a scholar who had little or no experiential background for conducting such studies and whose writings identified him, in the eyes of many people, as exhibiting a strong bias toward the interests of the public schools in that regard. I expressed consternation. I could not have undertaken the research myself, but knew numerous scholars who were appropriate for the task. The conversation that followed convinced me that NIE had deliberately selected a scholar with those views. If forced by congressional pressure to finance work on a taboo subject, NIE could protect itself against the anger of the public school constituency by being in a position to say: "Rest assured. Notice who got the money. The studies that result will be entirely sympathetic to your point of view." In fact, they were.

SELECTIVELY ADVANCING SCHOLARLY CAREERS

It seems to me that government funding of educational research may distort scholarship through selective advancement of the careers of scholars who favor particular points of view.

I suppose few people would argue with the contention that scholars who manage to acquire government grants and contracts for their research have a definite career advantage over those who do not, especially in fields, such as the study of schooling, where little research money is available elsewhere. In many universities, obtaining a government grant or contract is, in and of itself, enough to provide the scholar with "brownie points" toward tenure, promotion, and "merit" salary increments. The grants and contracts have the further effect of permitting research which could not otherwise be done. (As an example, I was singularly unsuccessful in obtaining money from private sources to initiate my above-mentioned British Columbia study; the research was so costly I would not have attempted it if the National Institute of Education grant had not come through.) The research which government money makes possible leads, in turn, to the articles, chapters, books, and papers at professional meetings that are so critical to tenure, promotion, and professional reputation.

In addition, the state and federal bureaucrats who manage the flow of research funds use some of the money from time to time to sponsor conferences on various topics. In choosing the scholars who will make presentations at these conferences, they provide important opportunities for visibility, thus affecting careers. The same bureaucrats are often called upon to recommend scholars deemed to be experts in various areas. In my years of observation, I have frequently thought such scholars were recommended, not because they were the people best qualified to contribute, but because they exemplified points of view favored by the bureaucrats, because they had ingratiated themselves with the bureaucrats one way or another, or because they were favored by people whose goodwill the bureaucrats wished to curry. (Often, after all, the bureaucrats need to find employment elsewhere, and thus have reason to develop their own "connections," or need the friendship of influential people who will help them protect and advance their careers in government agencies.) I have little reason to complain of my personal treatment in this regard, but believe several highly capable colleagues have been treated most unfairly, while others have been accorded undue privileges. The result, I fear, is to distort the direction of scholarship. Here again, it would be interesting to discover how many scholars have similar observations to make. It should be feasible in careful investigations, further, to document concrete instances of this possible trend.

SELECTIVELY DISSEMINATING RESEARCH FINDINGS

It seems to me that government funding of educational research may produce distortions by producing selective dissemination of research findings. When legislative bodies create government agencies that sponsor research, they normally demand that those agencies disseminate the findings that result. I think any scholar who has watched this dissemination process would agree, however, that it is done very selectively; some findings being given far more attention than others, with little regard to the quality of the supporting evidence.

The first example that occurs to me concerns my evaluation

of the Navaho school, discussed above. As I have already observed, if the intent of the Office of Economic Opportunity was to produce an evaluation biased in favor of the school, it apparently failed. That failure did not make OEO powerless to influence the impact of the study, however, at least insofar as media coverage and Washington halls of power were concerned. Shortly after the report had been submitted to OEO, I received a telephone call from Philleo Nash, who, as a member of my advisory committee, had expressed his indignation, but not the least surprise, concerning the attempt to induce me to report the data selectively. A former Commissioner of the Bureau of Indian Affairs, he was "well connected" in Washington, D.C. Officials of OEO, he reported, were angry that my findings were the opposite of what they anticipated, but were managing the situation by "releasing the report a hundred feet underground." There would be none of the usual OEO releases to the press, he predicted, and copies would prove exceedingly difficult to obtain. Whatever the explanation, I saw not the smallest item on the study in the media, the copies we provided for the school's library at the request of teachers whom we interviewed all disappeared, and I received many inquiries from people, both on the reservation and off, who had been completely frustrated in their efforts to obtain a copy. Fortunately, OEO's subterranean dissemination did not prevent the report from becoming a matter of common knowledge among scholars. I distributed many copies myself in response to inquiries, and apprised many scholars of the availability of microfilm copies from the federal agency then responsible (before creation of the current "ERIC" system) to make federally funded studies accessible. Nonetheless, the report might have had a larger impact if OEO had so desired, especially among the money-givers.

Perhaps even more important is the question of the research findings that federal agencies see fit to push. One current notable example concerns the so-called "effective schools" research, which has been given tremendous notoriety by the decision of the National Institute of Education, and more recently, after the death of NIE, by the federal Department of Education more directly. Few bodies of educational research have been more extensively and powerfully disseminated, mostly, if my observations are at all accurate, by these federal agencies, though certainly by numerous state agencies as well. In its final months, the National Institute of Education established two major research centers devoted to further "effective schools" research. As of September 1984, it was reported that 1,750 school districts and 7,500 schools across the United States had introduced "effective schools" programs.[15] Mississippi was incorporating "effective schools" findings into its accreditation standards. South Carolina was requiring every public school in the state to develop an action plan based upon "effective schools" findings.

Unfortunately, the main body of research on which this vast movement is based is seriously flawed.[16] Its main strategy has been to determine the characteristics that distinguish school "outliers"—generally schools in which achievement test means in reading and mathematics are considerably higher than one would predict in the light of the socioeconomic characteristics of the school constituency.

But there are several serious problems with such an approach: (a) This strategy isolates only the characteristics that distinguish the "effective" schools from other schools. Just as the blond hair associated with Norwegians cannot be assumed to cause the Norwegian accent, the widely publicized correlates of "effective" schools cannot be assumed to cause school effectiveness. (b) Even if some of the correlates are causal—something we do not know—they have not been identified in schools in general, but in a few schools deemed unusually effective, and thus, reflecting the special competencies of scarce, unusually competent people, they may not be generally applicable. (c) Several correlates thus identified are conceptualized at such a high level of abstraction that it is impossible to determine what concrete strategies they represent. (d) This method of identifying "effective" schools is highly unreliable, since schools thus identified as "effective" in one year have little more than a random chance of being so identified in another year. (e) Since achievement test gains may be produced in some schools by hazarding the physical and mental well-being of students and teachers, and by sacrificing important attitudes and values, achievement test scores are unacceptable as global indices of school effectiveness.

Nevertheless, the very notoriety of the "effective schools" findings seems to lend them legitimacy, and I have noticed, as have several colleagues, that scholars who should know better are beginning to assume, without reading the research itself, that the "effective schools" findings are well established, and are quoting them widely and building upon them.

I have little doubt that the findings in question would have had a considerable impact even apart from the government decision to disseminate them with unusual emphasis. The findings provide a welcome antidote against the widespread pessimism that apparently resulted from Coleman's widely publicized (but generally misunderstood) 1966 finding to the effect that fluctuations in school structure and policy were far less strongly associated with student learning than were fluctuations in the socioeconomic status of the students' homes.[17] I seriously doubt, however, that the "effective schools" movement would have gained anything like its current momentum without the powerful impetus of dissemination by government agencies that sponsor educational research. Careful studies could be designed to test the validity of this perception. It might be feasible, for example, to determine where many influential leaders first obtained their awareness of the "effective schools" findings and recommendations.

In contrast, I think of the recent investigations by Barr and Dreeben into the causes and consequences of variable pacing of instruction in elementary schools.[18] Barr and Dreeben discover, in some of the most meticulously, persuasively documented evidence I have yet encountered, that the assignment of students to groups distinguished by various rates of instructional pacing is an exceptionally telling determinant of how much students learn. Thus, surprisingly independent of student ability, how much a student learns depends, in their sample, upon how rapidly the teacher presents the material. I consider this to be trail-blazing research, with profound implications for the organization of instruction in American schools, but no government agency, to my knowledge, has taken the slightest step to disseminate it, perhaps partly because the findings would be unpopular in the current era.

I find little awareness of the work of Barr and Dreeben among my colleagues. I believe the work will eventually have a major impact as a consequence of its sheer salience and persuasive power. A few scholars will begin to discuss it, thus bringing it to the attention of others, and the word will spread. But in the meantime, at least in the short run, the pervasive attention being paid to the "effective schools" literature, in contrast to the general unawareness among scholars of the best evidence on instructional pacing, may be to a significant extent attributable to selective dissemination on the part of government agencies that fund educational research.

DISSEMINATING RESEARCH FINDINGS SIMPLE-MINDEDLY

Not only, in my opinion, do government research-sponsoring agencies tend to disseminate research findings selectively. They often disseminate simple-mindedly, glossing over the complexity of research findings, ignoring research limitations, and thus encouraging conclusions, recommendations, and actions that reflect a distorted view of how children learn and how schools work.

I will cite just one instance in this regard: dissemination of findings about the importance to learning of student time on the task. The best-known findings in this regard were produced by a large California research effort known as "BTES"—the Beginning Teacher Evaluation Study.[19] Competently done, the study showed, among many other things, that the amount students learned, particularly as reflected in achievement test scores in reading and mathematics, was strongly associated with the amount of time students spent actively engaged in learning activities that were so paced and structured that the students experienced high rates of success. The amount of this "academic learning time," in turn, was of course dependent upon several other factors, such as the amount of time allocated to instruction in specific areas, the extent of classroom interruptions, and the teacher's ability to make smooth transitions from one subject to another.

The BTES findings on "academic learning time," like Barr and Dreeben's on teacher pacing of instruction, can easily be misinterpreted. Thus, merely stepping up the pace or increasing allocated instructional time in a given area cannot be assumed to lead, under all conditions, to greater learning. Student time on task could be judged only indirectly in the BTES study; researchers coded a student as "on task" if he or she *appeared* to be attending to the assigned material. But who has not had extensive experience feigning attention? If instruction were inferior, or if students were unmotivated, or if students had reached a saturation point in a given area of instruction, an increased quantity of instruction might easily lead to less learning rather than more. Nevertheless, frequently in the face of protests from the researchers, the National Institute of Education (which had helped finance the study) and the California State Department of Education began an almost unprecedented dissemination effort, widely and repeatedly emphasizing the importance of allocated instructional time and student time on task without properly emphasizing the limitations of the findings. Apparently as a consequence of this dissemination effort, one sees virtually everywhere in the United States various programs being instituted, many of them highly questionable, to maximize instructional time and student time on task. It would be interesting to determine, in addition, how much writing and teaching in schools of education reflect a grossly misleading and simple-minded understanding of this forcefully disseminated body of research.

INTRODUCING INFLEXIBILITIES INTO EDUCATIONAL RESEARCH

It seems to me that government funding of educational research may often produce distortions by introducing serious inflexibility into the research itself. Recently, I happened to discuss with a colleague the modest track record, in her view and mine, of a university which has received what may easily be an unprecedented amount of federal money for research on educational administration and educational policy. The record, I observed, was difficult to comprehend, since scholars whom I regarded as exceptionally capable had been involved in the research during the period in question. My colleague, who had more firsthand acquaintance with that university than did I, then made what I regard as an apt observation: The flow of government funds for research had done much to divert the attention of the scholars from their most productive ideas. One had to secure approval of the federal agency in order to pursue a particular line of inquiry. Once the approval was secured, one was "locked into" that line of inquiry until the project was finished. The freedom to abandon an idea when it proved fruitless was lost, and the freedom to shift research strategies in keeping with developing ideas and changing research conditions was drastically curtailed. Furthermore, much energy that should have gone into research was diverted into writing progress reports, completing forms, preparing for site visits by the funding bureaucrats, and cultivating the political support on which the flow of money depended.

I resonated to this observation because I had experienced the same constraints in often-galling form in my own British Columbia research, mentioned earlier. At several points in the study, for example, logic would have dictated abandonment of our effort to trace the effects of the government aid program on public schools, but it became clear that I could not do so without losing the federal grant. Even more galling was the realization, again and again, of the power of the "Contracts and Grants" office, within the National Institute of Education, to prevent the very shifts in methodology that seemed most important to the effectiveness of the study. Essentially, I learned, there are two branches in federal agencies that allocate funds. At NIE, for example, one branch was in charge of ideas. Key personnel in that branch decided what research ideas had the most promise, and thus should be funded, and supervised the research, in an important sense, to help ensure that it would be done properly. The other branch at NIE, "Contracts and Grants," was in charge of the arcane, Byzantine craft of federal procurement. Presiding over thick rule-books, personnel in this branch sought to ensure that research budgets were not padded, that funds were not questionably diverted from one major budget category to another, and that scholars did not in other ways put the money to unsavory use. In order to make significant shifts in research strategy, I discovered, one made oneself vulnerable to serious consequences if one did not secure Contracts and Grants approval of the necessary budgetary reallocations. Virtually without exception, obtaining approval of a budget reallocation turned out to be an extremely frustrating, draining, time-consuming process. After personnel in the "idea" branch of NIE approved the shift, the papers would go to Contracts and Grants, where they would sit, unprocessed, for lengthy periods of time—more than nine months on one occasion—while our work ground to a halt and our trails of evidence grew cold. The general assumption in Contracts and Grants, in the light of my perceptions, was that when a researcher sought a budgetary allocation, he or she was normally "up to something shady," and thus that it was best, as a general policy, to do everything possible to discourage such shifts. Inaction was the strategy of discouragement in most instances in my experience. On other occasions, when I would succeed, after what seemed innumerable letters and long distance calls, in getting the attention of a Contracts and Grants Officer, I would encounter questions which I regarded as demonstrating a total lack of understanding of how research was conducted. I have no hesitation in stating that the B.C. study was drastically marred by these rigidities resulting from government financial sponsorship. At several critical junctures where circumstances demanded a shift in strategy, we were forced to proceed ineffectively, in keeping with the plan mapped out months before on the basis of limited information.

I remember that President Reagan, early in his first term, announced that he was looking for people "as mean as a junk-yard dog" to prevent waste and fraud in government expenditure. It has often occurred to me that he found ample people of that type, but that the result is not what he intended. Junk-yard dogs are as likely to bite customers as thieves, and the labyrinthine procedures created to prevent waste often foster it instead by making efficiency impossible.

EXACERBATING HUMAN TURPITUDE

I have suffered my share of disillusionment during my career as I have encountered instances of dishonesty and "career blackmail" in academe. I have come sadly to the conclusion that much educational research may be misleading because of it. Perhaps one should expect some of this. The history of science is strewn with stories concerning the suppression of unconventional ideas and the persecution of unconventional scholars, as Bartley indicates in Chapter 12. This hoary tendency can hardly be regarded as springing entirely, or even primarily, from government funding of research. In the modern era, however, I suspect its strength and frequency has a lot to do with money and power in the context, not only of research funds, but as I noted at the beginning of this paper, of the money and power that flow through the vast enterprise known as public education. (Shades of Lord Acton!) In this sense, government's intervention into education in general and into educational research specifically may tend to enhance the human turpitude that has always infected and impeded the search for knowledge.

I think, for example, of a study that impressed me enormously when I encountered it. It opened up possibilities which, if explored systematically, might have done much to discredit the over-emphasis of past decades upon an educational equality that is almost always left ambiguous and loosely defined. The study report indicated that the two authors were contemplating further, more carefully structured inquiry along that line. When no further studies by the authors were reported over a period of many months, I asked one of them, then a colleague at one of the universities where I have served, for an explanation. This colleague reported doing extensive further work that established even more clearly the tendencies shown in the initial study. He or she then moved to the present location, however, and asked to be relieved of further responsibility for the research. Subsequently, the collaborator in this research was visited by senior colleagues whose consulting activity was then extremely lucrative in the context of government funds being expended in pursuit of "equality of educational opportunity." Apparently fearing their consulting activities could be undercut by the findings, they threatened dire career consequences, according to my friend who had helped produce the evidence, if the data were not buried. The burial was quickly arranged. I doubt that the evidence will ever appear. It would have drawn into serious question much that now passes for knowledge in our textbooks.

CONCLUDING COMMENTS

The present chapter has suggested several ways in which government funding of educational research may distort scholarship. The suggestions, supported only by examples that are subject to conflicting interpretations, should be regarded merely as hypotheses that may warrant investigation. Nevertheless, it appears that the possibility of notable, widespread distortion of scholarship, at least partly through government funding of research, must be seriously entertained.

Probably the most difficult aspect of inquiries along this line would be to unravel the consequences of government funding from the distortion that would happen in the absence of such funding. The history of science, as I have noted, suggests that suppression of unorthodoxy frequently occurs. If government were to abandon its role in sponsoring research, for instance, one would still expect most foundation executives to follow prevailing ideas in the various fields of scholarship. My observations of the Ford Foundation, to cite one example, suggest that its emphases in the field of education have rather faithfully echoed the emphases in the National Institute of Education. Even so, a particular malevolent long-range potential may loom whenever government intervenes to influence systems of belief and commitment.[20] Thus, while the Constitution forbids government to favor one religion over another, it does not forbid private agencies to do so. Government activity has a special tendency to foster corrupting concentrations of power.

My own leaning, in conclusion, obviously not substantiated by the evidence except perhaps in a very loose suggestive sense, is to believe that scholarship would be considerably less biased if government were not sponsoring research, especially in an era when little money for educational research is available from other sources, and much less biased if government were not sponsoring a vast schooling enterprise. But much bias in favor of currently popular views would no doubt survive, as it always has. I would love to see a foundation or two devoted exclusively to the support of inquiry that scholars can show to be discouraged and suppressed, to investigations of academic skulduggery, and to the legal defense of those who dare discuss it.

NOTES

1. Scientific Analysis Corporation, *Educational R & D and the Case of Berkeley's Experimental Schools*, Vols. I and II, Final Report to the National Institute of Education (San Francisco Scientific Analysis Corporation, 1976).

2. Lee Sproul, Stephen Weiner and David Wolf, *Organizing an Anarchy: Belief, Bureaucracy, and Politics in the National Institute of Education* (Chicago: University of Chicago Press, 1978), especially chapter 4.

3. E.G. West, *Education and the State: A Study in Political Economy* (London: The Institute of Economic Affairs, 1965).

4. Mary Frase Williams, Kimberly Small Hancher and Amy Hutner, *Parents and School Choice: A Household Survey*, School Finance Project working paper (Washington, D.C.: Office of Educational Research and Development, US Department of Education, 1983); also reported in Joel D. Sherman *et al.*, *Congressionally Mandated Study of School Finance: A Final Report to Congress from the Secretary of Education, Vol. 2: Private Elementary and Secondary Education* (Washington, D.C.: Office of Educational Research and Development, US Department of Education, 1983).

5. The research, done under two grants from the National Institute of Education, supplemented by grants from the B.C. government, is discussed in two final reports: Donald A. Erickson, *The British Columbia Story: Antecedents and Consequences of Aid to Private Schools*, final report to the National Institute of Education and the British Columbia Ministry of Education (Los Angeles: Institute for the Study of Private Schools, 1982); and Donald A. Erickson, *Victoria's Secret: The Effects of British Columbia's Aid to Independent Schools*, final report to the National Institute of Education and the British Columbia Ministry of Education (Los Angeles: Institute for the Study of Private Schools, 1984).

6. Stephen Chapman, "The Teachers' Coup," *New Republic*, October 11, 1980, pp. 9–11; George Neill, "NEA: New Powerhouse in the Democratic Party," *Phi Delta Kappan* 61, October, 1980, pp. 85–86.

7. The results of the study are reported in full in Donald A. Erickson and Henrietta Schwartz, *Community School at Rough Rock: An Evaluation for the Office of Economic Opportunity* (Chicago: Midwest Administration Center, University of Chicago, 1969); available as Document PB 184471, Scientific and Technical Information Office, US Department of Commerce, Springfield, Virginia. The controversy over the

study was discussed in several articles in *School Review* 79, November, 1970.

8. "Bad Day at Rough Rock," *Guts and Tripe*, 1 Yellow Leaf Moon, 1969, no pages. Also see a series of articles on this topic in *Navaho Times*, beginning December 4, 1969.

9. R. Gary Bridge, *Family Choice in Schooling: Parent Decision-Making in the Alum Rock Voucher Demonstration*, A working note (Santa Monica, California: Rand, 1974); R. Gary Bridge and Julie Blackman, *A Study of Alternatives in American Education: Vol. IV: Family Choice in Schooling* (Santa Monica, California: Rand, 1978); P. Gary Bridge, "Information Imperfections: The Achilles' Heel of Entitlement Plans," *School Review* 86, May, 1978, pp. 504–527.

10. The history of the Alum Rock experiment is discussed at some length in several chapters in James A. Mecklenburger and Richard W. Hostrop, eds., *Education Vouchers: From Theory to Alum Rock* (Homewood, Illinois: ETC Publications, 1972).

11. Bridge and Blackman, *A Study of Alternatives in American Education*, Vol. II (Santa Monica, California: Rand, 1978).

12. I am omitting the data for the Hispanics who had to be interviewed in Spanish, since the sample was far too small to provide reasonable frequency estimates.

13. Jere Brophy and Thomas L. Good, "Teacher Behavior and Student Achievement," in M.L. Wittrock, ed., *Handbook of Research on Teaching*, A Project of the American Educational Research Association, 3rd edition (New York: Macmillan Publishing Company, 1986), pp. 328-375; Barak Rosenshine and Robert Stevens, "Teaching Functions," *ibid.*, pp. 376–391.

14. For one of the best-known treatments of this topic, see Seymour Sarason, *The Culture of the School and the Problem of Change*, revised edition (Boston: Allyn and Bacon, 1982).

15. Lynn Olson, "Effective Schools," *Education Week* 5, January 15, 1986, pp. 11–21.

16. Brian Rowan, Stephen T. Bossert and David C. Dwyer, "Research on Effective Schools: A Cautionary Note," *Educational Researcher* 12, April, 1983, pp. 24-31; Brian Rowan, "Shamanistic Rituals in Effective Schooling," *Issues in Education* 2, Summer, 1982, pp. 76–87; Linda F. Winfield, "Are Successful Schools Successful?", paper presented at annual meeting of American Educational Research Association, New York, New York, March, 1982.

17. James S. Coleman *et. al.*, *Equality of Educational Opportunity* (Washington, D.C.: US Office of Education, 1966).

18. Rebecca Barr and Robert Dreeben, *How Schools Work* (Chicago: University of Chicago Press, 1983).
19. See the several chapters in C. Denham and A. Lieberman, *Time to Learn* (Washington, D.C.: National Institute of Education, 1980).
20. Stephen Arons, *Compelling Belief: The Culture of American Schooling* (New York: McGraw-Hill Book Company, 1983).

THREE

SOURCE OF FUNDING AND FREEDOM OF INQUIRY IN AGRICULTURAL ECONOMICS

E.C. Pasour, Jr.

> It is true even in the United States that the more heavily the
> university is dependent on the patronage of government, the less is
> the freedom of inquiry.[1]

There are only two ways of coordinating economic activity in
agriculture and in other areas—the market and central direction.
The decision concerning which activities should be public and
which private has important implications both for productivity
and individual freedom.[2] Moreover, the problem of improving
institutional performance is important in agriculture, just as it
is in all other areas. However, as shown below, agricultural
economists have helped to rationalize government enforced
restrictions on competition in agriculture.

The problem of financing economic analysis in the most effective manner is closely related to freedom of inquiry.[3] Government-sponsored work in agricultural economics differs from that in nonagricultural disciplines, since in the former both the organization of research and educational work and funding are more highly structured and centralized. Agricultural economists in land grant universities are supported in large measure by either US Department of Agriculture (USDA) or state experiment stations. The funding is quite different for nonagricultural disciplines in the same universities where classroom teaching is the primary institutional commitment.

Schultz warns that work by some economists has supported special interest legislation to restrict competition.[4] This raises an important issue of whether work in agricultural economics has contributed to the special interest fragmentation of the economy. The nature of funding work by agricultural economists and the heavy treasury outlay on farm programs would appear to make agricultural economics, among the economic disciplines, uniquely susceptible to this problem. The agency that administers farm programs, the USDA, also is heavily involved in the planning, administering, funding, and evaluation of agricultural research and educational activities.

The purpose of this paper is to analyze the relationship between funding method and size of profession and work agenda of agricultural economists and to explore the implications for freedom of inquiry. First, development of public funding of research and education in agriculture and development of agricultural economics as an academic discipline is traced. Second, the effect of farm programs on the market for agricultural economists is described. The role of agricultural economists in the development of federal farm programs and the influence of the programs on the agricultural economics discipline are analyzed. Third, "market failure" is contrasted with "rent seeking" as an explanation of government intervention in agriculture. Finally, implications of funding method and organization of research for scientific progress and freedom of inquiry are explored.

PUBLIC FUNDING OF RESEARCH AND EDUCATION IN AGRICULTURE—THE EARLY YEARS

Publicly financed research and educational activities in US agriculture were begun more than 100 years ago.[5] The USDA was created as an information agency for farmers in 1862. The enabling legislation for the system of land-grant colleges, the Morrill Act, was enacted the same year. The Hatch Act of 1887 encouraged development of a system of state agricultural experiment stations that has played a dominant role in agricultural research in land grant universities.[6]

From 1862 to 1932, USDA activities were limited mainly to research, education, and some policing activities such as food safety. Government expenditures in agriculture during this period were small and seldom directly affected the individual farmer. However, the nature of USDA activities changed dramatically with the advent of the Roosevelt Administration and the Agricultural Adjustment Act (AAA) in 1933. The host of price support and other New Deal "action programs" had important implications not only for the USDA but also for work by agricultural economists in the USDA, and in land grant colleges.[7]

EARLY DEVELOPMENTS OF AGRICULTURAL ECONOMICS

Agricultural economics as an organized body of knowledge is relatively young. It did not emerge at once as a clearly defined area of study and did not exist as a field of specialized study either within general economics departments or in colleges of agriculture prior to 1900. Early work in agricultural economics reflected interests of people trained in agricultural disciplines whose primary interests were either in cost of production or farm management. The formation of the American Farm Management Association (AFMA) in 1910 was the beginning of agricultural economics as an organized discipline.[8] An Association of Agricultural Economists (AAE), formed in 1916, was consolidated with the AFMA into the American Farm Economics Association in 1920.[9] Thus, the decade prior to 1920 was a pioneering period when a new field, the application of economics to agricultural problems, was being staked out.[10]

The period from 1920 to 1933 was a time of consolidation and broadening in scope of work by agricultural economists. The Purnell Act in 1925 was designed to facilitate research in newer agricultural disciplines—primarily agricultural economics. Early in the 1920s, several agencies of the USDA were consolidated into the Bureau of Agricultural Economics (BAE). By 1930, there were fewer than 800 professional agricultural economists in the United States, with the BAE and land grant colleges and universities each having about the same number.[11]

The emergence during the Great Depression of agricultural economics as a major academic discipline had important implications. Many prominent economists at that time favored central economic planning, holding that classical economic doctrines were no longer relevant.[12] Opinion was widespread that "scientific management" must replace "the clumsy mechanisms of unregulated price determination" in agriculture and in other sectors.[13] Even before the passage of the AAA, Roosevelt authorized reorganization of USDA to make it an instrument of national planning.[14]

The New Deal farm programs reflected "...virtually full acceptance, for agriculture, of most of the techniques of monopolies, trusts, and cartels."[15] In the prevailing economic climate, price supports, marketing orders, and other restrictions on competition were considered necessary to strengthen the "bargaining power" of farmers. The policy of *laissez faire* was to be replaced by a corporate one in which large scale organizations would plan for the production and distribution of goods and services.[16] In this view, which considered the trusts of the late 19th and early 20th centuries as a model of the new order, the cartelization of agriculture clearly was beneficial.[17]

As leaders in the "scientific management" movement, agricultural economists played a major role in increasing government action in agriculture. Some of the leading agricultural economists of that era, including Bushrod W. Allin, John D. Black, J.S. Davis, M.J. Ezekiel, E.G. Nourse, H.R. Tolley and M.L. Wilson, were staunch advocates of central planning in agriculture.[18] In furthering this objective, M.L. Wilson proposed that schools of "agricultural social engineering" be developed.[19] Although many agricultural economists were opposed to the New Deal initiatives in agriculture, after 1933 "almost every agricultural economist" was engaged, directly or indirectly, in the development, administration, or appraisal of these agricultural programs.[20]

FARM PROGRAMS AND AGRICULTURAL ECONOMICS

The New Deal action programs in agriculture dramatically affected the demand for agricultural economists. From 1929 to 1939, the number of agricultural economists in land grant colleges increased from 364 to 597 and the rate of increase in the BAE was about the same.[21] However, the BAE was not the only agency in the USDA contributing to the increased demand for economists. The total number of agricultural economists in the USDA in 1939 was about four times higher than in 1929.[22] The large increase in demand for agricultural economists induced an increase in college enrollments. The number of undergraduate agricultural economics majors increased from 642 in 1929 to 1517 in 1939, while the number of graduate students increased from 243 to 555.[23]

Post-New Deal Growth in Agricultural Economics

Although agricultural economics as a discipline of study has grown considerably since 1940, the increase has not been as fast as during the 1930s. The number of agricultural economics researchers in land grant colleges increased 171 percent from 1940 to 1970 and there was another 30 percent increase from 1970 to 1980.[24] The rate of increase for extension personnel after 1940 was relatively less rapid, with numbers in land grant colleges increasing by 117 percent from 1940 to 1970.[25]

The number of economists in the USDA-ERS has varied considerably since 1940, depending upon the prevailing political winds.[26] The large increase during the 1930s was documented above. The reduction during the 1940s was just as pronounced.[27] Comparable data are not available for the entire period since World War II. However, available data suggests that although the number of economists in the USDA-ERS is lower now than it was in the early 1940s, the number of agricultural economists increased by 25 percent from 1967 to 1982.[28]

This growth over time in numbers of agricultural economists employed in the USDA-land grant system can be viewed in two ways. In one sense, it is ironic that numbers of agricultural economists in the USDA and universities have been increasing as numbers of farms and farmers and the value of farm output relative to total output have been decreasing. On the other hand, Halvorson and Smith found it paradoxical that agricultural economics budgets did not increase relative to other agricultural disciplines from 1940 to 1975, in view of the Purnell Act and other federal laws enacted to encourage social science research.[29]

Federal funding has been decreasing in relative importance and is not the dominant source in funding agricultural economics work at the state level. In 1980, 28 percent, on the average, of the budget of agricultural economics departments for research, teaching, and extension work came from the USDA, whereas 58 percent came from the state.[30] The comparable figures in 1970 were 34 and 58 percent, respectively.

Farm Programs and the Agenda of Agricultural Economists

Federal farm programs have been changed numerous times since the 1930s, but after eight years of the Reagan "Revolution," US farm policy remains firmly in the New Deal mold. It now appears that USDA expenditures under the 1985 farm bill will be the highest ever. It is no coincidence that growth of government in agriculture has been accompanied by increased numbers of agricultural economists. Indeed, the 1985 farm bill so compounds the complexity of farm programs that it has been labeled a full employment act for agricultural economists.[31]

Agriculture has been the victim of more than its share of bad economics—and most of it during the past 50 years has been related to farm programs. And, agricultural economists have played an important role in rationalizing these programs. For example, agricultural production control as a way to increase product prices was a brainchild of agricultural economists.[32] Further, although "parity" prices for farm products based on 1910–1914 relative prices is a "vulgar economic concept,"[33] the

parity approach to setting price supports persisted in farm legislation for 45 years with USDA economists providing the key
data. The parity approach was followed by cost of production,
also economically indefensible, as the primary guide in determining price support levels in the 1977 Food and Agriculture
Act.[34]

Even more fundamental for public policy, the inherent
incompatibility between price supports and efforts to reduce
trade barriers is seldom addressed. Indeed, the AAA of 1933, as
amended, *requires* that the US Government impose quantity
restrictions whenever imports would "materially interfere"
with the operation of US farm programs.[35] Without rigid import
controls, consumers would substitute lower priced imports for
price-supported products including sugar, butter, cheese, and
peanuts, thereby undermining domestic price support programs.
To address the contradiction between price supports and free
trade is to question the whole system of price supports, export
subsidies, marketing orders, and other restrictions on competition
in agriculture. And, it is easy to be constrained by considerations of
political realism in evaluating policy alternatives.[36]

There is another reason why analyses of farm programs by
economists in the USDA-land grant system often do not include
healthy criticism of the programs. The lack of competent economic criticism of production and marketing cartels, land-use
planning, nutrition planning, parity and cost of production as a
basis for farm price supports, two-price plans, and other faulty
economic programs quite likely is related to the method of
funding agricultural economics.[37] USDA funds both the action
programs and ERS economists' salaries—a situation that mili-
tates against objective analyses of program effects. ERS, like
other administrative agencies of government, is restricted to
research that will support its particular policy mandate, and it is
not within its domain to finance competent economic criticism
of the agency's activities.[38] Advancement in a bureaucracy generally is not achieved by advocating positions that would result
in budget cuts.[39] Economists in land grant universities are
much less subject to the whims of federal policy-makers. However, as described below, the method of funding research and

educational activities, there too, is likely to mute criticism of harmful farm policies.

These comments do not imply a lack of conscious objectivity in the sense that policy analysts fudge their results. There is no objective procedure for determining when "market failure" in agriculture warrants government action, and it is easy to rationalize that what is one's own interest is in the "public interest."[40] Moreover, it is likely that agricultural economics continues to attract analysts who begin with premises that lead to interventionist farm policy recommendations.

Action Programs and Political Pressures

Political pressures affecting agricultural economists have been especially pronounced in USDA.[41] From time to time the economics section of USDA has been reorganized in response to political pressures. In 1938, for example, the BAE was reorganized and became the central planning agency for USDA.[42] BAE agricultural economists welcomed the planning mandate and were in the vanguard in development of production controls, land use planning and other programs to "...bring scientists and other people together in the planning process."[43] The BAE became heavily involved in state and county land use planning before this planning program was abolished under political fire in 1942.

The BAE "Conversion Plan for the Cotton South" at the end of World War II also resulted in political constraints on economic activity in the USDA. The plan proposed to restrict cotton production to the best suited lands, reduce the number of people and amount of land in farming, diversify Southern agriculture, and encourage industrial development.[44] Pressure from Southern Congressmen, who considered the proposal a threat to prevailing social customs, led to abolition of the BAE in 1953.[45]

In ERS activities, there is a problem of maintaining objectivity because of the bureaucratic desire to use economic analysis to legitimize program activity. USDA publications extolling export subsidies disguised as Food for Peace is but one example.[46] The ERS review and publication process generally is unlikely to disseminate results that are contrary to stated policy. Recognizing that the political constraints on policy research in the USDA cannot be eliminated by reorganization, a former ERS official suggests establishment of a privately funded national agricultural policy research institute.[47]

Political pressures affecting the agenda of agricultural economists may come from within or outside agriculture. Policy research at the state level frequently confronts pressures by commodity groups from within agriculture.[48] Various interest groups may also attempt to increase the amount of economic research and education activities, sometimes by special legislative appropriations. Indeed, the intrastate pressures by commodity, farm organization, and other groups may well provide the most significant influence upon agricultural research and extension activities.[49]

Agricultural economists in land grant universities generally place higher priorities on economic problems at the state level when compared with work of economists in other disciplines.[50] Incentives in schools of agriculture typically are structured to encourage a state or regional orientation of research and extension activities. Consequently, these activities frequently focus on tobacco, peanuts, wheat and other commodities important to individual states. The funding method thus promotes provincial research and extension work, thereby creating a conflict between the incentive and reward structure relevant in schools of agriculture and those accepted as relevant for other parts of the university, where only limited state funds are available to support research and extension activities.[51]

FARM PROGRAMS—"MARKET FAILURE" VERSUS "RENT SEEKING"

Administrators and employees in publicly funded agricultural agencies face incentive and information problems similar to those confronted by decision-makers in other government agencies. Thus, as shown below, administrators in the USDA land grant system cannot achieve an "optimal" level of funding because of implementation problems inherent in the collective choice process—whatever the agency.

Informational Problems, Incentive Problems, and Rent Seeking

The *separation of power and knowledge* contributes to information problems in the collective choice process. Even if completely imbued with altruism, the bureaucrat cannot acquire the information on resources, production opportunities, and individual preferences required to determine the "public interest" pattern of expenditure.[52] Moreover, the collective choice mechanism provides no reliable guidelines to determine the efficiency of government agencies. That is, there are no signals in public agencies comparable to profits and losses in the market process. Thus, because of limits on information, even the most selfless research or extension decision maker cannot determine the "public interest" and must choose some other feasible goal such as budget maximization.

In reality, of course, few people are motivated mainly by altruism, and an incentive problem is likely to arise in public agencies because individuals in positions of authority do not bear important costs of their actions. The *separation of power and responsibility* means that administrators and employees have economic incentives to use the system for their own purposes, regardless of whether the actions taken are generally consistent with sound public policy.

Collectively provided goods and services, for example, generally are priced too low to cover the cost of provision. This is predictable, since the lower the price, the larger the quantity of service demanded and the larger the budget, number of jobs, and amount of influence by the agency providing the service. Information provided by Agricultural Extension Service agents and specialists to farmers, for example, is usually "free." Thus, it is not surprising that typically there is a "shortage" of extension services of all types.

Incentive problems in agriculture also manifest themselves in "rent-seeking" activity—the term used to describe attempts by individuals and groups to use the political process for economic gain.[53] Agricultural rent seeking may be engaged in by farmers, agribusiness firms, Congressmen, research and extension workers, or the bureaucracy. As an example, Schultz notes an increasing tendency for affected government personnel to marshall statistics in support of particular USDA programs— e.g., statistics designed to make the case for further expansion of food stamp programs.[54]

Market Failure and Economic Efficiency

Leading agricultural economists during the 1920s and 1930s believed that competition as conceived by Adam Smith cannot work in the modern business world.[55] Though economic theory and economic conditions in agriculture have changed dramatically since the 1930s, many agricultural economists continue to justify price supports, subsidized credit, subsidized water, subsidized exports, marketing orders and other farm programs on "market failure" grounds. Numerous examples could be cited, but the following are illustrative.

In an analysis of the government-sanctioned and -enforced dairy program, a quasi cartel, the conclusion was: "The relatively small implied consumer-to-producer transfers of the late 1970s resulting from classified pricing may be a small price to pay for the stabilizing aspect of classified pricing."[56]

Marketing orders for fruits, vegetables, and specialty crops ostensibly were provided to achieve "orderly marketing" conditions under the Federal Marketing Agreement Act of 1937. Oranges and other affected crops are subject to quantity and/or quality controls that reduce the amounts available for sale. A comprehensive USDA analysis of marketing orders provided the following rationale for these restrictions on competition: "These regulations are designed to compensate for or overcome certain characteristics of agricultural markets—imbalances in marketing power, instability, incomplete information...that prevent free trading from being fully efficient."[57]

Economic efficiency, however, is not an objective approach to public policy. The agricultural sector will *always* fall short when measured against the widely used norm of "perfect competition."[58] Not only is perfect competition, which assumes away information problems, useless as an efficiency standard, there is no other norm that can be used to measure the efficiency of actions of individuals in the real world in which decisions always involve uncertainty and costly information.[59] In assessing the efficiency of group actions, there is the additional problem that costs and benefits are subjective and noncomparable from person to person.[60] When the economic analyst takes these problems seriously, it follows that "net social benefit" is an artificial concept of little or no use for policy purposes.[61]

The existence of uncertainty and the subjective character of economic data mean that the agricultural economist cannot use marginal analysis to determine "optimal" farm policies.[62] Indeed, once transaction costs are included in the constraints on individual and government behavior, it cannot be analytically demonstrated that any particular policy is inferior to an *attainable* alternative.[63] On the other hand, it cannot be shown that "market failure" problems do *not* exist.

There is a great deal of casual evidence that publicly funded research and extension work in agriculture is consistent with the theory of bureaucratic productivity, which implies that services provided through the public sector tend to be oversupplied.[64] Public funding for these activities continues to increase as the agricultural sector declines in relative importance. Moreover, in the classic expansion pattern predicted by bureaucracy theory, economists in the USDA-land grant system have moved into tangential areas such as rural recreation, community facilities, and so on. It can be argued, of course, that this work merely reflects the interests of new clientele groups that have been successful in moving their concerns higher on the public policy agenda. The implication of the above discussion of economic efficiency is that economic analysis cannot be used to determine conclusively whether "market failure" or "rent seeking" is the correct explanation for any particular observed institutional change.

ORGANIZATION OF RESEARCH, FUNDING METHOD, AND FREEDOM OF INQUIRY

Freedom of inquiry is enhanced if there are as many independent centers of work as possible.[65] However, central funding is likely to support the ideal of a unified and centralized direction of scientific efforts. Indeed, recent reviews of the

USDA-land grant system have stressed the importance of having national goals for agriculture and agricultural research.[66] However, Hayek argues persuasively that the advance of knowledge is likely to be impeded when scientific pursuits are determined by some unified concept of social utility.[67] Are Hayek's concerns justified in the case of work in agricultural economics?

Funding and Planning of Agricultural Research

Despite the central planning thrust of the New Deal, there was little attempt at centralized long range planning of agricultural research and educational activities prior to World War II. The first major national planning effort occurred in the mid-1960s and planning efforts intensified in the 1970s.

As efforts to achieve more effective planning and coordination of the USDA-land grant system increased during the past two decades, there was increased pressure to give less weight to commodity production and marketing and to place more emphasis on rural development, environmental issues such as pesticide use, nutrition, food stamps, and other consumer concerns. Thus, planning objectives became more diverse as planning activity increased.

Nutrition Planning

Comprehensive planning, at least on paper, peaked during the Carter Administration in the concept of "nutrition planning." As described by Secretary of Agriculture Robert Bergland:

> We intend through research to build a constructive nutrition program from the facts...we want to know how much animal fat, how much sugar, how many eggs it's wise for a person to eat. Then we're going to build a new farm policy based on these truths.[68]

Dietary requirements can be met in a variety of ways and people's tastes differ. Consequently, there is no way for the planner to determine how much of which food everyone *should* eat. If the planner were *given data* on consumer tastes, prices, food nutrients, and nutrient requirements, nutrition planning would be reduced to a complicated but tractable mathematical problem. The relevant data for nutrition planning are, of course, *not* for the whole society given to a single mind.[69] Furthermore, when individual preferences are considered, nutrition data provide little guidance about which foods to promote through public policy.

Problems confronted in nutrition planning are fundamentally the same as those identified in the "market socialism" debate of the 1930s.[70] There is no way for a planner to determine optimal diet for 240 million people—or to "translate nutritional needs into production terms" successfully while maintaining individual freedom of choice. Yet, the "nutrition planning" concept has not been debunked by agricultural economists—in or out of Washington, D.C.

Current Research Information System (CRIS)

The federal-state system of agricultural research and educational activities as organized on paper is premised on the advantages of unified direction of scientific efforts by agricultural economists and other agricultural scientists. The system consists of a large set of federal and state organizations cooperating in planning and coordinating program activities.[71]

An elaborate reporting and monitoring system was begun in 1966 to provide feedback to funding sources and prevent duplication of efforts.[72] The Current Research Information System (CRIS) is a computerized reporting system of experiment stations and USDA research operated for the USDA and state agricultural research services in which projects are classified by activity, commodity, science, and research problem area.[73]

Too Little Planning and Organization?

Despite the centralized reporting and monitoring system, there is *relatively* little federal direction of agricultural research and educational activities at the state level. However, as suggested above, pleas for establishment of national goals and priorities for agricultural research are common. And, the Food Security Act of 1985 mandates increased planning and coordination of agricultural research and educational programs.[74]

Although there is strong sentiment within the states to maintain separate identity and localized control of the experiment stations,[75] the ideal of central direction of scientific effort in agriculture is shared by many scientists. In this view, it is only by establishing national priorities for agricultural research with control vested in the federal government that science can make its maximum contribution to agriculture.

Schultz, in sharp contrast, holds that the tendency to over-organize and centralize is the most serious problem related to the funding of agricultural research.[76] Central planning of agricultural production has been a disaster throughout the world and central control of agricultural research faces similar information and incentive problems. Agricultural production is exceedingly heterogeneous, being soil specific, product specific, and market specific. The idea that a highly competent administrator can determine the "optimal" pattern of agricultural research throughout the United States is merely "wishful thinking."[77]

CONCLUSIONS AND IMPLICATIONS

Agricultural economists can be highly useful in analyzing alternative institutional arrangements. And, the theory of markets rather than that of resource allocation should occupy center stage in this work.[78] In this approach, attention is focused on the market process and its relationship to the institutional setting within which people choose, rather than on constrained optimization procedures to determine the efficient pattern of resource use.

The nature and effectiveness of institutional critiques by agricultural economists hinge in large measure on who holds the purse strings. There is a basic distinction between decisions made under private ownership *versus* those made through the collective choice framework within which there is no residual claimant. It is fully predictable, then, that distortions will arise in publicly funded research because of implementation problems. Employees and administrators of federal and state agencies, constrained by information and incentive problems from pursuing the "public interest," are highly likely to select goals relating to factors such as job protection, size of budget, and agency growth. Thus, it would be surprising if there were no discernable harmful effects of the funding system on the agricultural economics discipline.[79] It should be emphasized that this analysis is *not* a criticism of particular individuals making funding and other administrative decisions—the problem is inherent in the collective choice process.

Various interest groups within agriculture—tobacco, milk, sugar, oranges, wheat, credit, and so on—seek protection from competition through programs created and administered by the USDA. The demand for agricultural economists has been greatly increased by implementation of these programs. The programs also create or intensify commodity group pressures affecting funding decisions at state levels. Thus, there are economic incentives for agricultural economists to rationalize the programs. It is unlikely that the publicly funded economist will take the position that a program of the funding agency is an inappropriate function of government.[80] It makes no difference in this regard whether the agency is the NSF or the USDA.[81]

Agricultural economists have played an important role in rationalizing the network of cartelistic farm programs that has persisted in the United States for the past 50 years. USDA-land grant economists not only were key personnel in the development of programs to restrict competition during the 1930s, they have helped maintain these policies during the past half century. Economic studies that support restrictions on competition in agriculture are harmful because they contribute to the special interest fragmentation of the economy. Support by agricultural economists for detrimental policies is difficult to avoid, however, when the government agency designing, administering, and analyzing the effects of the programs also plays an important role in funding and coordinating research and educational activities in agricultural economics.[82]

Agricultural economists have devoted very little attention to the consequences of past and current funding methods of agricultural economics research and educational activities for freedom of scholarly inquiry. Why is this? It is not just that there is a lack of incentive to do so. Although, as Schultz suggests, this is surely the case.[83] This paper shows that there are strong institutional incentives *not* to do so. Almost all of the studies cited that examine the implications of funding methods for freedom of inquiry were written by analysts outside the land grant university-USDA complex. This fact is evidence that the problem identified by Professor Schultz at the beginning of this paper remains unresolved for agricultural economists.

Acknowledgment

The author is especially indebted to Professor T.W. Schultz for direction, reference materials, and manuscript review. J.B. Bullock, D.B. Gardner, D.M. Hoover, M.A. Johnson, R.R. Rucker, and W.N. Thurman also provided many helpful ideas in revising the paper. The usual disclaimer applies.

NOTES

1. T.W. Schultz, "Distortions of Economic Research," *Minerva* 17, 1979, p. 464.
2. Friedrich A. Hayek, *The Constitution of Liberty* (Chicago: University of Chicago Press, 1960).
3. *Ibid.*, p. 390.
4. T.W. Schultz, "Distortions of Economic Research," *op cit.*, p. 467.
5. Agricultural education and research long had a unique characteristic in the United States—virtually all work was conducted under government sponsorship. Charles M. Hardin, *Freedom in Agricultural Education* (Chicago: University of Chicago Press, 1955), p. viii. By the 1970s, however, about two-thirds of the outlays on agricultural research and development broadly defined, were by private firms. Vernon W. Ruttan, *Agricultural Research Policy* (Minneapolis: University of Minnesota Press, 1982). For agricultural research narrowly defined, however, outlay amounts by private firms were much less—about 25 percent. T.W. Schultz, "Markets, Agriculture, and Inflation," in Lowell D. Hill, ed., *Role of Government in a Market Economy*, (Ames, Iowa: Iowa State University Press, 1982), p. 65.
6. H.C. Knoblauch, E.M. Law, and W.P. Meyer, *State Agricultural Experiment Stations: A History of Research Policy and Procedure*, Miscellaneous Publication No. 904 (Washington, D.C.: US Department of Agriculture, 1962).
7. Action programs depend for results on means other than or in addition to education—on inducements that are remunerative or punitive. Iowa State College Faculty Committee, *Education for Action Programs in Agriculture*, Iowa State College Bulletin 38, 1939, p. 7.
8. Vernon W. Ruttan, *Agricultural Research Policy*, *op cit.*, p. 299.
9. The AFEA was the precursor of the current American Agricultural Economics Association (AAEA).
10. T.W. Schultz, *Training and Recruiting of Personnel in the Rural Social Studies* (Washington, D.C.: American Council on Education, 1941), p. 3.
11. *Ibid.*, pp. 244–245.
12. The "market failure" explanation of the Great Depression is being increasingly questioned. There is a great deal of evidence that government intervention in the form of high tariffs, high taxes, restrictive monetary policy, and policies to maintain high wages and prices either caused or greatly exacerbated the economic chaos at that time. Christian Saint-Etienne, *The Great Depression, 1929–1938*

(Stanford, California: Hoover Institution Press, 1984). There also is increasing evidence that public choice theory is more plausible than market failure as an explanation of US farm programs that have persisted for 50 years. E.C. Pasour, Jr., "Rent Seeking and Farm Commodity Programs: Is Education the Solution?", *The Cato Journal* 5, 1986, pp. 263-270. Whatever the original rationale for the New Deal initiatives in agriculture, the programs have had a profound effect on the development of the agricultural economics profession, affecting both job opportunities and types of work.

13. Richard S. Kirkendall, *Social Scientists and Farm Politics in the Age of Roosevelt* (Columbia, Missouri: University of Missouri Press, 1966), p. 44.

14. *Ibid.*, p. 70.

15. M.R. Benedict, *Farm Policies of the United States 1790–1950* (New York: The Twentieth Century Fund, 1953), p. 514.

16. Lawrence Busch and W.B. Lacy, *Science, Agriculture, and the Politics of Research* (Boulder, Colorado: Westview Press, 1983), p. 14.

17. *Ibid.*

18. All except Tolley were later named AAEA Fellows, the highest honor bestowed by the association. In 1930, the Christgau national agricultural planning bill, prepared by M.L. Wilson and H.R. Tolley, was introduced by Minnesota Congressman Victor Christgau—the first agricultural economist to serve in Congress. The Christgau bill called for the use of scientific procedures to increase profit in farming, land use, and serve the interests of consumers and producers of farm products. Richard S. Kirkendall, *op. cit.*, p. 11. There is no evidence that agricultural economists of that era were aware of the implications of the economic calculation debate of the 1920s and 1930s for central planning in agriculture. Friedrich A. Hayek, *Individualism and Economic Order* (Chicago: University of Chicago Press, 1948).

19. M.L. Wilson, "New Horizons in Agricultural Economics," *Journal of Farm Economics* 20, 1938, p. 3.

20. O.V. Wells, "Agricultural Planning and the Agricultural Economist." *Journal of Farm Economics* 20, 1938, p. 753.

21. T.W. Schultz, *Training and Recruiting Personnel, op. cit.*, p. 183. The largest increase in land grant colleges was in the number of extension workers. Peterson found that the rate of growth in extension workers in agricultural economics from 1930 to 1935 "remains unsurpassed." Willis L. Peterson, "The Allocation of Research, Teaching, and Extension Personnel in US Colleges of Agriculture," *American Journal of Agricultural Economics* 51, 1969, p. 44.

22. T.W. Schultz, *Training and Recruiting Personnel, op. cit.*, p. 183. Even this figure considerably underestimates the effect of the New deal

programs on the demand for agricultural economists. The Farm Security Administration (FSA), forerunner of the Farmer's Home Administration, which helped individual farmers plan their operations, had more than 6,000 employees in 1939. While only a small number of FSA employees were professional agricultural economists, the FSA did recruit many of its workers from students majoring in agricultural economics. Some colleges had all available seniors in agricultural economics taken by the FSA. One-third of the agricultural economics graduates in land grant colleges in 1938 accepted positions with the USDA, of which FSA took the largest number. *Ibid.*, p. 101.

23. *Ibid.*, p. 123. The undergraduate figures include a small number of rural sociology majors.
24. Glenn R. Smith, "Has Social Science Research at the Experiment Stations Increased in Line With Society's Needs and Congressional Intent?", *American Journal of Agricultural Economics* 55, 1973, p. 668. Wallace E. Huffman, and L.J. Connor, "A Perspective on the Market for Agricultural Economists: Background, Trends, and Issues," *North Central Journal of Agricultural Economics* 8, 1986, p. 200.
25. Willis L. Peterson, *op. cit.*, p. 43.
26. In recent years, the Economic Research Service (ERS) has been the major economics agency of the USDA.
27. Charles M. Hardin, *Freedom in Agricultural Education, op. cit.*, p. 156. The role of the BAE in economic planning led to political reprisals, as explained in the following section.
28. Wallace E. Huffman and L.J. Connor, *op. cit.*, p. 200. Charles M. Hardin, *Freedom in Agricultural Education, op. cit.*, p. 156.
29. Lloyd C. Halvorson, "A Quarter Century of Agricultural Economics in Retrospect and in Prospect," *Southern Journal of Agriculture Economics* 7, 1975, pp. 17–24. Glenn R. Smith, *op. cit.*
30. B.F. Stanton and K.R. Farrell, "Funding for Agricultural Economics: Needs and Strategies for the 1980s," *American Journal of Agricultural Economics* 63, 1981, p. 798.
31. Vernon W. Ruttan, "Toward a Liberal Program for US Agriculture," *Forum for Applied Research and Public Policy* 1, 1986, p. 81.
32. Richard S. Kirkendall, *op. cit.*, p. 24.
33. T.W. Schultz, "Tensions Between Economics and Politics in Dealing with Agriculture," Agricultural Economics Paper No. 84:24, Department of Economics, University of Chicago, August 10, 1985, p. 5.
34. E.C. Pasour, Jr., "Cost of Production: A Defensible Basis for Agricultural Price Supports?", *American Journal of Agricultural Economics* 62, 1980, pp. 244–248. Indeed, some economists in the US and Canadian Departments of Agriculture defended the theoretical basis of cost of production as a guide in setting price supports. John

R. Groenewegen, and K.C. Clayton. "Agricultural Price Supports and Cost of Production." *American Journal of Agricultural Economics* 64, 1982, pp. 271–275.

35. E.C. Pasour, Jr., "On Free Trade's Price: US Farmers Can't Have Free Access to World Markets and Price Supports, Too." *Choices* 1, 1986, pp. 33–35.

36. Clarence Philbrook, "Realism in Policy Espousal," *American Economic Review* 43, 1953, pp. 846–859.

37. The conflict between New Deal action programs and institutional integrity was recognized early at Iowa State College "...it becomes a matter of great delicacy to show...how the land-grant college can make a significant contribution to the success of a program and yet avoid loss of the perfect detachment and objectivity which, under all circumstances, it should maintain." Iowa State College Faculty Committee, *The Role of the Land-Grant College in Government Agricultural Programs*, Iowa State College Bulletin 38, 1938, p. 6.

38. T.W. Schultz, "Distortions of Economic Research," *op. cit.*, p. 468.

39. R.L. Stroup and J.A. Baden, *Natural Resources: Bureaucratic Myths and Environmental Management* (Cambridge, Massachuttes: Ballinger Publishing Co., 1983), p. 49.

40. See the section in this paper entitled "Farm Programs—Market Failure *versus* Rent Seeking."

41. Charles M. Hardin, "The Bureau of Agricultural Economics Under Fire: A Study in Valuation Conflicts," *Journal of Farm Economics* 28, 1946, pp. 635–668.

42. Richard S. Kirkendall, *op. cit.*, p. 150.

43. *Ibid.*, p. 29.

44. *Ibid.*, p. 227.

45. Don F. Hadwiger, *The Politics of Agricultural Research* (Lincoln, Nebraska: University of Nebraska Press, 1982), p. 134. A successor agency, the Economic Research Service was established in 1961.

46. T.W. Schultz, *Economic Growth and Agriculture* (New York: McGraw-Hill Book Co., 1968), p. 284.

47. Vernon W. Ruttan, *Agricultural Research Policy, op. cit.*, p. 326. James Bonnen, former President of the AAEA, contends that this finding can generalized to all USDA research activities. "The USDA is no longer capable of sustaining a coherent science research mission. The USDA research agenda is...explained...by the problems USDA political leadership faces in making its way in the political jungle in which it lives. Research should be removed from the USDA to an environment that is capable of supporting national research leadership." James T. Bonnen, "Historical Sources of US Agricultural Productivity: Implications for R&D Policy and Social Science Research," *American Journal of Agricultural Economics* 65, 1983, p. 961.

48. The Iowa margarine incident is a good example. In 1943, an agricultural economist at Iowa State College wrote a pamphlet on dairy policy. It contended that margarine "compared favorably" with butter in nutrition and palatability and argued for changes in federal and state legislation that impeded consumption of margarine. Following attacks on the pamphlet by dairy groups and the recommendation by a review committee that the pamphlet be retracted and revised. Professor T.W. Schultz and several other agricultural economists resigned. Charles M. Hardin, *Freedom in Agricultural Education, op. cit.,* pp. 119–125. The Iowa incident is not unique. Agricultural economists who have questioned government sanctioned and enforced restrictions on competition in milk, tobacco, and other products have also faced political pressures from within agriculture.

49. *Ibid.,* p. 93. Political pressures from consumer, poverty, and environmental groups outside agriculture have also had a dramatic impact on the research and education agenda in agricultural economics during the past 20 years. Low food prices, food assistance, poverty, environmental protection, and rural development are among the concerns of people contributing to this new USDA "agenda." Don Paarlberg, "A New Agenda for Agriculture," in D.F. Hadwiger and W.P. Browne, eds., *The New Politics of Food* (Lexington, Massachusetts: D.C. Heath & Co., 1978).

50. T.W. Schultz, *Economic Growth and Agriculture, op. cit.,* p. 273.

51. Vernon W. Ruttan, *Agricultural Research Policy, op. cit.,* p. 316.

52. William A. Niskanen, Jr., *Bureaucracy and Representative Government* (Chicago: Aldine, Atherton, 1971), p. 39.

53. James M. Buchanan, Robert D. Tollison, and Gordon Tullock, eds., *Toward a Theory of the Rent-Seeking Society* (College Station, Texas: Texas A & M University Press, 1980).

54. T.W. Schultz, "Markets, Agriculture, and Inflation," *op.cit.,* p. 64.

55. Mordecai Ezekiel, *$2500 a Year from Scarcity to Abundance* (New York: Harcourt, Brace and Co., 1936), p. 35.

56. D. Hee Song and M.C. Hallberg, "Measuring Producers' Advantage from Classified Pricing of Milk," *American Journal of Agricultural Economics* 64, 1982, p. 7.

57. Agricultural Marketing Service, *A Review of Federal Marketing Orders for Fruits, Vegetables and Specialty Crops,* Ag-Econ. Report No. 477 (Washington, D.C.: US Department of Agriculture, 1981), p. 81.

58. E.C. Pasour, Jr., "Economic Efficiency: Touchstone or Mirage?", *The Intercollegiate Review* 17, 1981, pp. 33–46.

59. Harold Demsetz, "Information and Efficiency: Another Viewpoint," *Journal of Law and Economics* 12, 1969, pp. 1–22.

60. Lionel Robbins, "Economics and Political Economy," *American*

Economic Review 71, 1981, pp. 1–10.

61. S.C. Littlechild, "The Problem of Social Cost," in L.M. Spadaro, ed., *New Directions in Austrian Economics* (Kansas City: Sheed Andrews and McMeel, Inc., 1979), p. 192. Nobel Laureate Friedrich A. Hayek makes this point even more strongly: "The childish attempts to provide a basis for 'just' action by measuring the relative utilities or satisfactions of different persons simply cannot be taken seriously...the whole of the so-called 'welfare economics,' which pretends to base its arguments on inter-personal comparisons of ascertainable utilities lacks all scientific foundation." Friedrich A. Hayek, *Law, Legislation, and Liberty*, Vol. 3 of *The Political Order of a Free People* (Chicago: University of Chicago Press, 1979), p. 201.

62. Dean A. Worcester, Jr. "On the Validity of Marginal Analysis for Policymaking," *Eastern Economic Journal* 8, 1982, pp. 83–88.

63. C.J. Dahlman, "The Problem of Externality," *Journal of Law and Economics* 22, 1979, p. 154.

64. William A. Niskanen, *op. cit.* Ruttan contends that the implications of the theory of bureaucracy do not apply in the case of agricultural research. Vernon W. Ruttan, "Bureaucratic Productivity: The Case of Agricultural Research," *Public Choice* 35, 1980, pp. 529–547.

65. Friedrich A. Hayek, *The Constitution of Liberty, op. cit.*, T.W. Schultz, "The Productivity of Research: The Politics and Economics of Research," *Minerva* 18, 1980, pp. 644–651.

66. Office of Technology Assessment (OTA), *An Assessment of the United States Food and Agricultural Research System* (Washington, D.C.: Office of Technology Assessment, 1982). Rockefeller Foundation, *Science for Agriculture: Report of a Workshop on Critical Issues in American Agricultural Research* (New York: Rockefeller Foundation, 1982). Kenneth A. Dahlberg, ed., *New Directions for Agriculture and Agricultural Research* (Totowa, New Jersey: Rowman and Allanheld, 1986). "The lack of a coherent national agriculture policy, relating productivity goals and domestic and international policies with an explicit understanding of the value of agriculture to this country greatly hampers efforts to establish national goals and priorities for agricultural research." Rockefeller Foundation, cited above p. 9.

67. Friedrich A. Hayek, *The Constitution of Liberty, op. cit.*, p. 392.

68. Robert Bergland, as quoted in *The Progressive Farmer*, February, 1978.

69. Friedrich A. Hayek, *Individualism and Economic Order, op. cit.*

70. Don Lavoie, *National Economic Planning: What is Left?* (Cambridge, Massachusetts: Ballinger Publishing Co., 1985).

71. Alex F. McCalla, "Politics of the Agricultural Research Establishment," in D.F. Hadwiger and W.P. Browne, eds., *The New Politics of Food* (Lexington, Massachusetts: D.C. Heath & Co.1978), p. 89.

72. Most of the federal support for agricultural research is allocated to each state by a formula based on the number of farms and size of rural population. Vernon W. Ruttan, *Agricultural Research Policy, op. cit.*, p. 254. The formula requires the states to match the federal support for state research. However, states contribute much more than the required amounts for matching—in fiscal 1985, federal funds accounted for 20–30 percent of total research and educational programs at land grant universities. US General Accounting Office, *University Funding: Federal Funding Mechanisms in Support of University Research* GAO/RCED-86-53 (Washington, D.C.: General Accounting Office, 1986), p. 183.

73. US Department of Agriculture. *Manual of Classification of Agricultural and Forestry Research*, Revision IV (Washington, D.C.: US Department of Agriculture, 1982).

74. Lewrene K. Glaser, *Provisions of the Food Security Act of 1985*, AIB Number 498 (Washington, D.C.: ERS, US Department of Agriculture, 1986).

75. John Patrick Jordan, P.F. O'Connell and R.R. Robinson, "Historical Evolution of the State Agricultural Experiment Station System," in Kenneth A. Dahlman, ed., *New Directions for Agricultural Research* (Totowa, New Jersey: Rowman and Allenheld, 1986).

76. T.W. Schultz, "Markets, Agriculture, and Inflation," *op. cit.*, p. 66.

77. T.W. Schultz, "Agricultural Research, Canada and Beyond." in K.K. Klein and W.H. Furtan, eds., *Economics of Agricultural Research in Canada* (Calgary, Alberta, Canada: University of Calgary Press, 1985), p. 16.

78. James M. Buchanan, *What Should Economists Do?* (Indianapolis: Liberty Press, 1979), p. 19.

79. Admittedly, this distortion problem is not unique to agricultural economics but is present in all publicly funded research and educational activities.

80. Milton Friedman, "The Economics of Free Speech," in Bernard H. Siegan, ed., *Regulation, Economics and the Law* (Lexington, Massachusetts: D.C. Heath & Co., 1979).

81. "Caesar is not renowned for providing funds that best serve the knowledge activities of universities. Caesar wants policy support." T.W. Schultz, "Are University Scholars and Scientists Free Agents?" Franklin Lecture, Auburn University, April 30, 1986, p. 9.

82. Ludwig von Mises, in a closely related argument, suggests that support for detrimental policies follows when the discipline of economics is divided up by sector of the economy: "Economics does not allow of any breaking up into special branches. It invariably deals with the interconnectedness of all the phenomena of action.... There are no such things as 'economics of labor' or 'economics of

agriculture.' What these specialists deal with in their lectures and publications is not economics, but the doctrines of various pressure groups. Ignoring economics, they cannot help falling prey to the ideologies of those aiming at special privileges for their group." Ludwig von Mises, *Human Action*, 3rd edition (Chicago: Henry Regnery Company, 1966), p. 874. I am indebted to E.G. West for bringing these comments by von Mises to my attention.

83. T. W. Schultz, "Distortions of Economic Research," *op. cit.*, p. 466.

FOUR

GOVERNMENT REGULATION AND ACCOUNTING RESEARCH

Ross L. Watts and Jerold L. Zimmerman

$\mathbf{P}$apers at this conference examine the effects of government regulation on education and research. This paper describes the effects of government regulation on accounting research and education, with primary emphasis on the research effects. Government regulates the accounting disclosure of publicly traded firms and entry into the public accounting profession. The Federal Securities Acts empower the Securities and Exchange Commission (SEC) to regulate corporate accounting disclosures. The SEC has relied on non-profit, quasi-public organizations, most recently the Financial Accounting Standards Board (FASB), to promulgate most of the accounting disclosure rules which are then sanctioned by the SEC. Individual states regulate the practice of public accounting via state licensing laws of CPAs.

Government regulation has had a substantial affect on accounting research. The first academic accounting debates were generated by government regulation. The United Kingdom (UK) railroad depreciation debates of the 1840s were caused by government regulation of railroads and the general debate over depreciation in the UK in the 1880s is associated with income tax law changes. In this century, the US Securities Acts which regulated corporate disclosure were the principle government regulations affecting accounting research. From the mid 1940s to the late 1960s the leading accounting research journals were dominated by papers advocating particular accounting policy prescriptions.[1] We argue that the dominance of prescriptive writings was the direct result of the Federal Securities Acts. Despite the disappearance of prescriptive papers from the leading journals in recent years, regulation still influences the topics addressed by research papers.

The relation between regulation and accounting research arises because accounting influences firms' cash flows. Accounting procedures and the firms' published financial statements are integral parts of firms' contracting technology. Restriction of the available technology via government regulation of corporate disclosure imposes costs on firms and encourages them to argue for elimination of those restrictions. Accounting theories are demanded to support those arguments. The existence and form of government regulation can be influenced by accounting numbers. Large reported accounting profits are often cited by those proposing to regulate or tax firms (e.g. those arguing for taxation of oil firms in the late 1970s described the oil corporations' profits as "pornographic"). Vested interests on either side of regulatory controversies argue for the allowance or disallowance of accounting procedures that influence reported profit numbers. And once an industry's prices are regulated using accounting numbers, various interests argue over the accounting methods used to calculate those numbers. All these vested interests demand accounting theories to support their positions.

Regulation also has a large impact on accounting education. The prime influence is the state licensing laws that prescribe the educational requirements for certified public accountants, (CPAs).

We begin by discussing the cash flow effects of accounting procedures in Section II. Section III describes the Securities Acts' overwhelming effect on accounting research this century. Section IV presents the demand for and supply of accounting theories. Section V analyzes the effects of railroad regulation and income tax laws on accounting research. The effect of government regulation on education is investigated in Section VI and Section VII contains a summary and conclusion.

ACCOUNTING PROCEDURES' EFFECTS ON FIRMS' CASH FLOWS

Before the recent federal income tax bill a firm's choice of accounting procedures had little direct effect on its income taxes. With the exception of the LIFO/FIFO inventory valuation choice and some accrual choices (e.g., bad debt expense), firms were allowed to choose different accounting procedures for income tax and financial reporting purposes. Tax law influenced accounting procedure choice only to the extent that it is costly to keep two sets of books and to the extent that accounting practice could influence the tax law. Hence, with the exception of the LIFO/FIFO choice, the tax code did not have an overwhelming influence on the choice of accounting procedures. Under the new tax code different procedures are still allowed for the different purposes. But, beginning in 1987 a corporation's minimum tax calculation is based on its reported income. Given this linkage between reported profits and the minimum tax, all financial accounting procedure choices and accounting standards that affect reported income have cash flow effects via their influence on Alternative Minimum Taxes. Those tax effects will certainly influence the firm manager's choice of accounting procedures and lobbying on accounting standards. The manager has a demand for an accounting theory to support his position.

Reported accounting numbers are used in various corporate contracts (e.g. debt agreements, management compensation contracts, sales contracts, etc.). Regulations that affect the accounting procedures available for calculating numbers in the firm's published financial statements affect the set of contracts available to the firms. Those regulations can also change existing contract provisions defined in terms of reported numbers (e.g. debt agreements). Hence, regulation of accounting procedures, such as that under the Securities Acts, affects firms' cash flows and induces managers to lobby on a particular accounting procedure. And, managers demand accounting theories to support their positions.

Anecdotal evidence suggests that federal securities legislation and administration of the Securities Acts by the Securities and Exchange Commission (SEC) create a demand for normative accounting prescriptions justifying particular accounting procedures. That is, corporate accounting procedures such as straight line or accelerated depreciation methods affect corporate cash flows via extant bond covenants, management compensation plans, and various types of regulations impacting the firm. These cash flow effects of accounting create incentives for corporate managers, potentially affected by changes in mandated accounting procedures, to lobby on the proposed accounting procedures. Normative accounting theories are often useful excuses in this lobbying process thereby creating a demand for prescriptions.

This section sketches how private contracts and government regulations cause accounting procedures to affect cash flows.

Cash Flow Effects Due to Private Contracts

Agency theory and the theory of regulation provide insights into the cash flow effects of accounting disclosures. Agency theory predicts that parties to the firm (managers, stockholders, and debtholders) devise contracts that reduce the sum of the contracting costs and the costs of opportunism resulting from the conflicting interests.[2] Corporate by-laws, charters, bond indentures and management compensation plans are major contractual devices that appear to reduce agency costs.[3] Accounting numbers are used in these contracts.

Bond Covenants. The ratios of reported net income to interest expense and debt to stockholder equity play a key role in most debt arrangements. Managers promise to keep the ratio of income to interest above a specified minimum and the ratio of debt to equity below a specified maximum. If these constraints are violated, the repayment of the debt is accelerated or certain activities (e.g., mergers) are restricted. These ratios are designed to prevent stockholders from increasing the firm's leverage and expropriating debtholder wealth.[4] Dividends and share repurchases are also constrained to a fraction of accounting profits preventing shareholders from altering the risk of the debtholders' claims or paying liquidating dividends and leaving the debtholders with a worthless shell.

Management compensation plans. The total payouts to management from bonus plans are constrained by reported earnings. If earnings are below a specified amount, no bonus payment occurs. Accounting earnings are used in these contracts to encourage managers to increase shareholder wealth.

Debt and bonus contracts rely on externally reported accounting earnings, the same numbers regulated by the Securities and Exchange Commission. These accounting reports are audited annually by a CPA. Since debt and bonus contracts are private agreements, the parties can use any set of accounting or non-accounting based numbers in the contracts and hence avoid using the SEC regulated numbers. The fact that most contracts rely on the regulated numbers suggests that they are still the efficient procedures for private contracts.

Changes in the regulated set of accounting procedures used in external reports cause reported earnings to change. This can cause firms to violate debt covenants or alter the payout under bonus contracts. Wealth transfers and/or dead weight losses accompany these changes. Contacts are either renegotiated or wealth transfers result.

The evidence is consistent with the preceding predictions.[5] Stock prices of firms forced to change accounting procedures are decreased when the FASB of SEC unexpectedly restrict accounting rules. Cross sectional variation in the stock price changes are a function of the type of contract affected. Managers' accounting procedure and their lobbying on proposed accounting regulations are related to their existing debt and bonus contracts.

Cash Flow Effects Due to Regulation

Besides the foregoing agency cost/contractual effects of accounting numbers, there is evidence that accounting earnings affect the extent of government regulation imposed on firms.

Large firms systematically choose accounting procedures that *reduce* reported earnings. Large firms are more likely to choose accelerated depreciation methods over straight line depreciation than smaller firms. If changes in reported profits increase government scrutiny of these firms and if large firms are greater targets of government intervention than small firms, then managers of large firms will choose accounting procedures that report smaller profits, *ceteris paribus*.[6]

Public utility commissions base regulated rates on reported accounting numbers: operating expenses and a return on the rate base. This form of regulation creates incentives for utility managers to elect expense increasing (and hence rate increasing) accounting procedures, *ceteris paribus*. Accounting procedures such as deferred taxes and allowance for funds used during construction are accounting devices designed to increase regulated rates by affecting the accounting-based numbers used in the regulatory process.

Agency theory and the theory of regulation have been used to develop and test hypotheses about the cash flow effects of alternative accounting numbers. Cash flow effects create incentives for managers to lobby on proposed regulatory changes in financial accounting procedures. These incentives exist even when capital markets are efficient (unbiased) with respect to publicly available information.

THE REGULATION OF ACCOUNTING DISCLOSURE

Prior to the 1933 and 1934 Federal Securities Acts, corporate disclosure was unregulated except for state "blue-sky" laws.[7] Listing requirements of the New York Stock Exchange (NYSE) mandated annual financial disclosures. Benston reports that in 1926, a hundred percent of the NYSE firms disclosed net income and 82 percent were audited by a CPA.[8] Managers were free to contract on the amount of disclosure and in particular on the accounting procedures used in their external reports.

The Federal Securities Acts

The 1933 and 1934 Federal Securities Acts created the SEC and empowered it to regulate the issuance of securities in interstate markets and the trading of securities on national security exchanges. These acts also vest with the SEC broad powers to determine the accounting procedures used in preparing corporate financial reports filed with the SEC. These reports are to be certified by "independent public accountants."

One of the goals of the securities legislation was to prevent future stock market crashes. "Inferior" accounting and reporting practices, alleged to create overvalued assets, were cited as a contributing factor of the 1929 crash.[9] Alleged frauds and misrepresentation in financial statements justified the securities legislation. Prior to 1929, firms used a wide variety of accounting procedures making interfirm comparisons difficult. Benston found that about 40 percent of the firms listed on the NYSE did not disclose sales prior to the Securities Acts.[10] These alleged abuses were to be corrected by the SEC. After more than 50 years, accounting procedures remain diverse and security analysts continue to complain about the difficulty of making interfirm comparisons because procedures are non-uniform.

Accounting Series Release Number 4

Between 1934 and 1938, the SEC debated how to regulate and standardize accounting practice in reports filed with the Commission and issued to investors.[11] Two commissioners, both lawyers, wanted the SEC to promulgate a set of uniform accounting procedures and require all firms to comply in their reports filed with the Commission. At one point, the SEC instructed their Chief Accountant to prepare a series of accounting procedures by industry. This would be very difficult due to the existing diversity in company accounting practices, and trying to uniquely classify firms by industry. Other Commissioners preferred, instead, that the accounting profession develop accounting procedures and reduce the diversity among current practice. In 1938, the Commission issued SEC Accounting Series Release Number 4 (ASR 4) stating that "financial statements ...(which) are prepared in accordance with accounting procedures for which there is *no substantial authoritative support...* will be presumed to be misleading or inaccurate. [emphasis added] The SEC has never defined what constitutes "substantial authoritative support," but more than "general acceptance" was implied. "Unless a source of authority satisfactory to the Commission were created, the determination of accounting principles and methods used in reports to the Commission would devolve on the Commission itself. The message to the [accounting] profession was clear and unambiguous."[12]

The Commission could not rely on general acceptance of an accounting procedure because current practice was blamed for contributing to the crash. Prescribing detailed accounting procedures across all industries is a huge and costly task and one that might not avert future accusations that faulty accounting numbers caused stock price declines. One hypothesis is that not directly promulgating accounting procedures was the least cost solution for the SEC. ASR 4 partially shifts the onus of blame for future accounting misrepresentations from the Commission to the accounting profession. An alternative hypothesis is that the accounting profession captured the rights to set accounting procedures. This capture hypothesis holds that auditors, who certify the reports, can increase the demand for their services and/or lower the cost of providing services by mandating the content and accounting procedures used in the financial reports filed with the Commission.[13]

Private Sector Accounting Boards

The accounting profession responded quickly to ASR 4. The American Institute of Certified Public Accountants (AICPA) empowered its Committee on Accounting Procedure (CAP) to "promulgate rules of practice and procedure."[14] Between 1938 and 1959, the CAP issued 51 Accounting Research Bulletins that dealt with such topics as inventory pricing, depreciation, pensions, and leases. Following a series of much publicly disclosed financial and auditing "crises," the AICPA abolished the CAP in 1959 and replaced it with the Accounting Principles Board (APB). Between 1959 and 1973, the APB issued 31 Opinions, four Statements, and a series of "unofficial" interpretations. In 1973, again amid a number of financial and auditing "crises," the APB was abolished. A new non-profit foundation was established to govern the Financial Accounting Standards Board (FASB). Funded by the private sector, primarily accounting firms and industry, the FASB is a seven member, full-time board that issues Financial Accounting Standards. To date, the FASB has issued over 87 standards and numerous technical interpretations.

Accounting pronouncements are issued to solve a perceived "crisis" or to standardize accounting after a regulatory, tax or technological innovation. For example, after passage of the Investment Tax Credit (ITC) in 1960, firms were accounting for the ITC in various ways. Some firms were taking the entire ITC into income, others spreading it over the life of the associated asset.[15] The APB issued an accounting opinion stating the ITC must be taken into reported income over the life of the asset. This position was reversed after intense lobbying efforts. In most cases, accounting practices are devised before a regulatory method is promulgated. The regulators then narrow managers' discretion by outlawing certain procedures or by delineating the conditions under which the various methods are appropriate.

The accounting pronouncements by the CAP, APB, and FASB have the effect of administrative law because the SEC chooses to follow them. In ASR 150, the SEC formalized this relation by stating that "principles, standards and practices promulgated by the FASB will be considered by the Commission as having substantial authoritative support, and those contrary to such FASB promulgations will be considered to have no such support." ASR 150 goes on to state that "the Commission will continue to identify areas where investor information needs exist and will determine appropriate methods of disclosure to meet these needs." Typically, the SEC allows the FASB or its predecessors to take the lead in setting accounting procedures. The SEC issues an opinion letter on proposed FASB drafts. If the FASB does not move fast enough or in the direction the SEC desires, the Commission issues an *Accounting Series Release* which preempts and calls into question the viability of the FASB. For example, during the inflationary 1970s, the SEC pushed for price level or current value accounting to disclose the effects of inflation. The FASB could not agree on the appropriate action. The SEC then issued ASR 190 calling for supplemental disclosure of replacement costs of inventory, plant and equipment. The FASB responded with Statement 33 which required additional disclosures of general price level adjustments.

Effect on Accounting Research

Besides involving private sector accounting standards boards in the regulation of accounting procedures, the SEC's ASR 4 also changed the nature of accounting research. Three effects are observed:

(1) Following the Security Acts and up until the late 1960s, the accounting literature became decidedly more normative. The major accounting "classics" prior to the Acts described how accounting is done. Following the Acts, the "important" research (i.e., that which is taught in doctoral programs) prescribed how accounting should be done.

(2) Accounting writers began adopting the SEC's objective for accounting. The SEC's objective has been described as:

> The theory of the Securities Act is that if investors are provided with sufficient information to permit them to make a reasoned decision concerning the investment merits of securities offered them, investor interests can be adequately protected without unduly restricting the ability of business ventures to raise capital.[16]

Prior to the Acts, accounting writers described the reasons for calculating profit and loss as maintaining management's stewardship over firm resources, profit sharing schemes between capital and labor, and administering bank loans.[17] Following the Acts, accounting writers began to emphasize reporting to the "ordinary investor." The literature's emphasis shifted from corporate reports which are to primarily serve the private parties to the firm (shareholders, managers, and creditors) to accounting for the "public interest" (investors in general, government officials, the public). For example, financial accounting is "to facilitate the operations of an organized society for the welfare of all."[18] This "public interest" orientation continued in even the leading academic journals until the late 1960s.

(3) Following the Acts the accounting profession began searching for an underlying theory. Prior to the 1930s, most accounting writers described current practice with little effort

devoted to developing an accounting theory. In the 1940s, accounting organizations began sponsoring research to find a "complete philosophical system of thought." Such normative theories not only help provide the "substantial authoritative support" the SEC wanted in ASR 4, but searching for an underlying theory helps justify the private sector boards' existence in an environment where these boards have no legislative mandate. In the United Kingdom, where there was no government body with statutory power to prescribe accounting procedures, there was little interest in formulating a normative accounting theory.[19]

The specific form of regulation of accounting procedures (i.e., ASR 4) affected academic research for over 30 years. It created a demand for normative accounting theories which prescribe practice. It also affected the objective function assumed by the theory. Since the Securities Acts affected the nature of accounting research, did other types of regulation have a similar impact on accounting research? The next sections generalize the preceding example and examine the demand for and supply of accounting theories under other regulatory interventions.

THE DEMAND FOR AND SUPPLY OF ACCOUNTING THEORIES

The preceding sections have described how external accounting reports are regulated and how these reports are used in agency cost reducing contracts and in the government's regulation of the firm's activities. By involving the private sector in the regulation of accounting procedures *vis-a-vis* the FASB, the SEC has created a demand for accounting theories (i.e., "excuses") to justify and rationalize various mandated accounting procedures. This section generalizes these observations by examining other uses of accounting theories.

Demand for Accounting Theories

Watts and Zimmerman hypothesize that accounting theories serve three functions.[20] First, there is an *information demand*. The parties to the firm's contracts (shareholders, debtholders, managers, and auditors) seek to understand how different accounting procedures affect the various parties' incentives to engage in opportunistic behaviors. The demand for external auditors depends on their ability to reduce contracting costs (including agency costs). Hence, auditors want a positive theory of how alternative accounting procedures affect agency costs.

Second, the *pedagogic demand* for theories is to help accountants and auditors learn the various alternative accounting procedures. Accounting practice includes a large number of alternative accounting methods. A positive accounting theory helps teachers structure the variation found in practice, thereby assisting learning. Authors of 19th-century accounting textbooks reviewed current practice and attempted to distill general principles from the diversity found in practice.

Third, the *justification demand* for theories provides auditors arguments to be used against managers attempting to use accounting procedures to increase profits and thereby their compensation. Early textbooks provide auditors with ready-made arguments to counter managers attempting to avoid under depreciating assets to show higher profits.

These three demands for accounting theories existed prior to federal regulation of corporate disclosure. Court-developed case law "regulated" accounting practice by codifying the best practices and by ruling against those practices that were ex post determined to have violated prior contracts. Both auditors and the courts had incentives to adopt conservative accounting procedures to counter managers' incentives towards optimistic procedures. For example, the rule of thumb "recognize expenses when accrued but revenues when received" is a conservative device to counter managers' optimism. Bonus plans and management performance evaluation create incentives for managers to overvalue assets and to recognize income early. Courts and auditors have incentive to focus on these overvaluations and to adopt conservative accounting procedures. This creates informational, pedagogic, and justification demands for theories that expound conservative accounting procedures.

Government regulation increases the demand for justifications because wealth can be redistributed via mandated changes in accounting procedures. For example, adoption of an accounting procedure that increases the reported costs of a public utility without a concomitant increase in cash outflows (e.g., the allowance for funds used during construction) allows the utility to argue for higher rates. An accounting theory that argues that such an accounting procedure is "correct" or is in society's interest will increase the likelihood such an accounting procedure is adopted. Moreover, such a procedure is more likely adopted by the state regulatory commission, if the SEC or FASB mandates it for all publicly traded firms.

Accounting theories that justify an accounting procedure using public interest rationales are more useful to politicians and bureaucrats than are self-interest rationales. A public interest rationale argues everyone is better, most are better off, or a regulation is "fair." Public interest rationales also argue that a market failure exists and that government regulation can remedy the failure. Politicians, bureaucrats, and even special interests find public interest rationales more useful than special interest rationales because public interest rationales help justify their regulatory proposals.

Since it is costly for voters to become informed and to form coalitions to lobby elected representatives, parties seeking wealth transfers do not want to identify who will be harmed by their proposed political actions. Such information will lower the coalition costs of their opposition. Proponents will choose theories that justify their actions using public interest rationales thereby raising the opposition's lobbying costs and lowering the amount of competing lobbying.

The demand is not for just one accounting prescription, but rather for numerous theories. Because there are both potential winners and losers on any given policy issue, each side will demand a theory to buttress its arguments. Hence, a diversity of competing prescriptive theories will be observed.

As long as it is costly for individuals to differentiate among competing theories, several can coexist. For most proposed wealth transfers, the majority of individuals have little incentive to investigate the validity of competing rationales. No one is being "fooled" by the accounting theories because, given the costs of becoming informed, rational individuals prefer to remain ignorant.

Supply of Accounting Theories

Special interest groups demand accounting theories and will determine the production of theories. Since there are no barriers to entry on producing accounting theories, a potentially large number of individuals can supply such theories and the supply will respond to demand.[21] Accounting professors, economists, CPAs, and executives are potential suppliers of theories. The value of a particular theory will depend on its author's prestige and ability to articulate the theory. The greater the theory's value, the greater the flow of resources (in terms of prestige or dollars and students) to the author's institution. Researchers may never have intended their prescriptions to be used by vested interest groups. But once a theory is in the public domain, authors cannot prevent special interests from quoting the study. The ability of the theorist to write on current controversies further enhances the resource flows to the writer's institution. For example, when Congress mandated the SEC to limit oil and gas accounting alternatives in the 1970s, a demand was created for theories justifying the various accounting methods. Justifications were produced for the alternative accounting methods for treating exploration costs ("full cost" and "successful efforts").

Researchers have an incentive to be consistent in their assumptions and approach across issues because such consistency enhances their reputation and integrity. Academic criticism and evaluation create incentives for researchers to be consistent over time. While any given theorist is consistent over time, the rationales of the existing policies need not be consistent. The existing policies depend on the winning coalition; who wins depends on the costs and returns the various coalitions face on each issue. Since the costs and returns likely vary across issues, different coalitions will win on different issues. The rationale for the existing policy is the winning coalition's rationale. Hence, rationales are likely inconsistent across time. In accounting, the extant accounting standards are rationalized using a variety of often inconsistent justifications. Some mandated accounting standards rely on historical costs and others rely on market values. We hypothesize that the economic rationales justifying the series of banking regulations (or farm policies) also would be inconsistent from one regulation to another.

EXAMPLES OF REGULATION'S EFFECT ON ACCOUNTING RESEARCH

The preceding sections described accounting disclosure regulation and argued that an important market for accounting research is the market for "excuses" to be used in justifying accounting procedures in the political process. If the demand for justifications is important in directing the output of accounting researchers, then accounting theories should be produced around the time that regulations are being introduced which have accounting implications.

Railroad Regulation

US and UK railroad regulation around 1840–1850 contained provisions tying freight rates to accounting profits.[22] These regulations created incentives for railroads to reduce reported earnings by writing off (i.e., depreciating) their assets very quickly. In some cases, railroads wrote off against profits the entire cost of the rolling stock in the year of acquisition.

Prior to the railroads, firms did not treat depreciation of assets as an annual charge to earnings. Dividend covenants in corporate articles and case law required that dividends could not be paid out of the firm's fixed capital. Firms recorded depreciation of fixed assets periodically (usually in profitable years) as a charge to a capital account and not a charge to annual earnings. These procedures were consistent with reducing the conflicts of interests (i.e., agency costs) between the debt-holders and shareholders.

But railroad managers had incentive to charge depreciation every year to earnings. The public policy issue of railroad profits was raised in both the US and UK in the 19th century.[23] Since regulations tied railroad rates to profits, managers had incentive to write-off assets to profits. The accounting literature discussed the "proper" role of depreciation as either an annual charge to earnings or as a periodic charge to capital. Thus, there was a demand for justification of these alternative accounting procedures. The accounting literature began debating the pros and cons of treating depreciation as an annual charge to profits. Articles and books were written and theories of depreciation were produced.[24]

Income Tax Acts

While most railroads and public utilities adopted depreciation as an annual charge to earnings, non-regulated firms continued to treat depreciation as an occasional charge to capital. This all changed with the income tax laws. "In 1878 the [UK tax] law was modified to permit deduction of a reasonable amount for the diminished value of machinery and plant resulting from wear and tear."[25]

The UK accounting literature began discussing treating depreciation as an annual charge to income. But the US accounting literature did not discuss annual depreciation charges for all corporations until after 1900 when the first US income tax laws were enacted (e.g., the Excise Tax Act of 1909). Thus, the US and UK difference in the timing of the accounting debates over depreciation for all corporations can be explained by the timing of the passage of the income tax laws in the two countries.

The UK and US income tax acts had a major impact on accounting practice and in particular on depreciation accounting.

> [The 1909 Act] levied a 1% tax on net income of corporations in excess of $5000. This net income was said to be the figure resulting after deducting ordinary and necessary expenses and all losses, including an allowance for depreciation, from gross profit. Depreciation expense was made an allowable deduction and was universally deducted by those corporations affected by the act. The effect of this act on the growth of the use of depreciation cannot be overemphasized. It was the first instance in which the writing off of depreciation as an expense was definitely advantageous. That fact alone insured its general application.[26]

REGULATION'S EFFECT ON ACCOUNTING EDUCATION

State licensing laws prescribe the higher education requirements necessary for certification to practice as a certified public accountant (CPA). Besides passing a written exam and meeting experience requirements, certification requires completion of an accounting program registered by the state board on public accountancy. In New York State, this board reports to the Board of Regents.

College and university accounting programs are registered if they include minimum numbers of credit hours for accounting theory, auditing, business law, taxes and other general business topics such as economics, finance, computers, and statistics. Minor exceptions to the guidelines are allowed. The education requirements are extensive and preclude most course elective choices by the students.

State licensing laws directed at CPA education requirements have inhibited the development of accounting education. The orientation of most accounting programs towards preparing students to pass the CPA exam and the educational requirements cause accounting courses to contain relatively large amounts of institutional details on current accounting, auditing, and tax procedures to the exclusion of training students how to analyze problems. The CPA educational requirements reduce faculties' ability to experiment with new courses and more conceptual material and constrain students' choices of electives outside accounting.

Recently, some states have moved towards a five-year baccalaureate education requirement to further expand the institutional knowledge required of CPAs. The net effect of the CPA educational requirements is to reduce the attractiveness of majoring in accounting *vis-a-vis* other majors, such as finance and marketing. Several leading business schools such as Chicago, Harvard, and Stanford no longer offer registered accounting programs and no longer train students for public accounting. These train students for other, more lucrative, fields than public accounting; fields that do not have the costly restrictions of the CPA educational requirements.

CONCLUSION

Government regulation has had a major impact on accounting education, practice, and research. State licensing laws of CPAs have affected the content of the accounting curriculum. Accounting practice has been affected by legislation and regulation. Accounting research has been affected by political processes because accounting writings provide useful "excuses" in justifying various accounting procedures demanded by vested interest groups. The analysis of this paper is not limited to accounting education and research, but likely extends to other social science fields such as economics.

There has always been a demand for positive accounting theories due to their pedagogic and information values. Following the 1933 and 1934 Securities Acts, normative writings came to dominate the accounting literature because such writings are useful excuses in lobbying before accounting regulatory boards. Since the mid-1960s, the production of new normative accounting theories diminished and positive research re-emerged. The re-emergence of positive research appears to have resulted from a change in both the supply side—a reduction in the cost —and demand side for positive research.

The appearance of machine-readable databases (such as CRSP and Compustat) and the reduction in the cost of computing have lowered the relative cost of positive research. Also, partly from the reduction in the relative cost of empirical research, finance and economic theories are now available for use by accounting researchers (e.g., capital asset pricing model, theories of regulation, agency theory). These positive finance and economic theories further reduce the relative cost of producing positive accounting theories by providing useful underlying analyses for accounting researchers. These cost reducing devices for producing accounting research increased the quantity produced relative to the quantity of normative research.

Besides supply side shifts, demand side shifts occurred. Business schools compete to produce managers and accountants valued by employers. This means they train their graduates to understand and predict the consequences of their actions, that is to construct positive analyses of business problems. The construction of positive theories is important in business school research agenda. The strictures of CPA educational requirements cause leading business schools to produce fewer CPAs. Hence, the demand for normative accounting theories is relatively less important to these schools. The rewards for producing normative theories in leading business schools are likely lower today because of the shift away from producing CPAs. Tenure and promotion processes at leading business schools are under greater control of finance faculty than in the past when accountants played a relatively larger role. Finance faculty value positive research higher than normative work because it is more consistent with training managers. This has caused some accounting departments to seek autonomy from their business schools by establishing separate schools of accounting.

While there has been a relative shift in accounting research back towards positive studies, accounting research is still affected by the demands for "excuses" to justify political actions. Accounting faculties at primarily state schools with large undergraduate CPA programs continue writing on current accounting controversies and seek to influence the political process which regulates accounting procedures.

NOTES

1. T.R. Dyckman and S.A. Zeff, "Two Decades of the Journal of Accounting Research," *Journal of Accounting Research* 22, 1984, pp. 225–297.
2. M.C. Jensen and W.H. Meckling, "The Theory of the Firm: Managerial Behavior Agency Costs and Ownership Structure," *Journal of Financial Economics* 3, 1976, pp. 305–360.
3. See Ross L. Watts, "Corporate Financial Statements: A Product of the Market and Political Processes," *Australian Journal of Management* 2, 1977, pp. 52–75; C.W. Smith, Jr. and J. Warner, "On Financial Contracting: An Analysis of Bond Covenants," *Journal of Financial Economics* 7, 1979, pp. 117–161; C.W. Smith, Jr. and Ross L. Watts, "Incentive and Tax Effects of US Executive Compensation Plans," *Australian Journal of Management* 7, 1982, pp. 139–157.
4. Smith and Warner, *op. cit.*
5. Ross L. Watts and Jerold L. Zimmerman, *Positive Accounting Theory* (Englewood Cliffs, New Jersey: Prentice-Hall, 1986), chapters 11 and 12.
6. *Ibid.*, chapter 10.
7. Many states had laws regulating issuing securities, including the disclosure of information. However, some states either did not regulate such security sales or had very lax laws. Federal security laws were needed, it was argued, to prevent firms from avoiding restrictive legislation by organizing in states with lax incorporation and security laws.
8. G.J. Benston, "The Value of the SEC's Accounting Disclosure Requirements," *Accounting Review* 44, 1969, pp. 515–532.
9. *Ibid.*, pp. 517–518.
10. See *supra* note 8.
11. S.A. Zeff, *Forging Accounting Principles in Five Countries: A History and Analysis of Trends* (New York: Stipes, 1972), pp. 132–133.
12. *Ibid.*, p. 134.
13. Entry of new auditors would dissipate any rents. The existence of entry restrictions by state certification boards would allow rents to be earned. Also, super-marginal auditors or those with brand-name capital would still earn rents even with entry.
14. Zeff, *op. cit.*, p. 135.
15. Financial accounting for the ITC has no affect on taxes paid. ITC accounting only determines when the tax benefits of the investment are reflected in reported income.

16. R.H. Mundheim, "Foreword: Symposium on Securities Regulation," *Law and Contemporary Problems,* Summer, 1964, p. 647.
17. Ross L. Watts and Jerald L. Zimmerman, "The Demand for and Supply of Accounting Theories: The Market for Excuses," *Accounting Review* 54, 1979, p. 296.
18. American Accounting Association, Committee on Basic Accounting Theory, *A Statement of Basic Accounting Theory* (New York: American Accounting Association, 1966), p. 5.
19. Zeff, *op. cit.,* p. 310; K. Shackelton, "Government Involvement in Developing Accounting Standards: The Framework," *Management Accounting,* January, 1977, United Kingdom, pp.17–21.
20. See *supra* note 17.
21. George H. Stigler, "Do Economists Matter?", *Southern Economic Journal* 42, 1986, pp. 347–254.
22. E.M. Dodd, *American Business Corporations Until 1860* (Cambridge, Massachusetts: Harvard University Press, 1954), p. 260.
23. L.E. Nash, *Anatomy of Depreciation* (Washington, D.C.: Public Utlilties Reports, 1947), p. 3.
24. See H. Pollins, "Aspects of Railway Accounting Before 1868," reprinted in A. Littleton and B. Yamey, eds., *Studies in the History of Accounting* (Homewood, Ill: Richard D. Irwin, Inc., 1956), pp. 332–335; J.L. Boockholdt, "Influence of Nineteenth and Early Twentieth Century Railroad Accounting on Development of Modern Accounting Theory," unpublished working paper 31, University of Alabama, July, 1977; W. Holmes, "Accounting and Accountants in Massachusetts," *Massachusetts CPA Review,* May-June, 1975, pp. 18–21.
25. E.A. Saliers, *Depreciation: Principles and Applications,* 3rd edition (New York: Ronald Press, 1939), p. 255.
26. *Ibid.,* pp. 17–18.

FIVE

INTELLECTUAL ATTITUDES AND REGULATORY CHANGE
LEGAL SCHOLARS IN THE DEPRESSION

Fred S. McChesney

It seems generally believed that, as a group, intellectuals are able to influence legal and political change. But no convincing theoretical rationale has been offered for this proposition. Nor has any empirical evidence been produced in support of it.

This essay examines the role of intellectuals in legal change, both theoretically and empirically. It analyzes and attempts to measure the influence of law-school academics on the various regulatory changes enacted during the Depression collectively known as the New Deal. Legal academics' influence is tested by analyzing their attitudes toward law, government and business, as evinced in their law journal publications.

The essay compares those writings for two periods: 1921–1925 and 1931–1935. As shown in Section II, the former was a period of prosperity and tranquility, when the existing order of laissez faire apparently functioned well. In contrast, the years 1931–1935 were a period of crisis and upheaval, when regulation increasingly supplanted the free market system. The issue of intellectual influence is tested by comparing the writings of those two periods to see if lawyers' attitudes were becoming more tolerant or even encouraging of government intervention in economic affairs, at a time when regulation itself was evidently becoming more popular politically. If intellectual attitudes were in any way responsible for the great popular and political acceptance of greater regulatory intervention, one should find that lawyers' writings were increasingly hospitable to the economic intervention of the New Deal and opposed to the regime of comparative laissez faire that preceded the Depression.

As explained in Section III, the popular belief that intellectual attitudes exert an important influence on legal change appears unwarranted, *a priori*. Under a public-interest model of regulation, disinterested intellectuals might well strive to better the world; altruistic politicians might truly be interested in what intellectuals had to say. But for the most part, public-interest models are of little help in explaining political events. Regulatory change is driven by the political play of private interests who stand to gain or lose from regulation. Academic intellectuals may themselves constitute an interest group, but they do not necessarily gain from the sort of economic regulation imposed during the New Deal.

Section IV then reports the results of comparing legal academics' publications under a variety of headings that encompass attitudes toward regulation. Lawyers' writings on legal education, government and corporations are contrasted, as are law journal reviews of two controversial works from the time periods studied that advocated greater regulatory intervention into corporate affairs. The findings are revealing. Overall, they lead one to conclude that the attitudes of law-school academics cannot have played much of a role in the New Deal regulatory upheavals of the Depression.

INTELLECTUALS AND LEGAL CHANGE: HISTORICAL BACKGROUND

Historical Setting

In attempting to analyze the role of intellectuals in political change, one could hardly find a better natural experiment than that afforded by a comparison between the early 1920s and early 1930s. As shown in Table 5-1, the former period was one of growing affluence, the latter just the reverse. Total and per capita gross national product (Table 5-1A and 5-1B) were growing through the 1920s, and unemployment (Table 5-1C) falling. Though the "Roaring Twenties" began with a brief, sharp recession in 1921:

> [T]he 1920s were a period of relative prosperity, marked by substantial growth, rising real wages of the worker, growing incomes, and particularly, expansion of the consumer durable goods industries. This was the decade in which the refrigerator, the radio, the gas or electric stove, and most notably the automobile became a part of most households in America.[1]

Analysts like Friedman and Schwartz note other trends that manifested growth in personal wealth, such as the "bull market in stocks [that] mirrored soaring American optimism about the future."[2] The 1920s, Galbraith concurs, were a time of "boundless hope and optimism."[3] The short-term trends in production and unemployment in 1921–1925 apparently justified that buoyant outlook.

There was a general reversal of attitudes between the 1920s to the 1930s, however, from confidence to uncertainty. The figures in Table 5-1 explain why. Total and per capita gross national product fell substantially in the 1930s, and unemployment rose precipitously to a full quarter of the work force. "Fear of losing things, of property, is one legacy of the Thirties."[4] From 1929 to 1933, about 80 percent of the total value of stock owned by the public evaporated—indeed, "it was not until the 1950s that stock prices recovered to the level they had been in 1929."[5] Attitudes toward business were especially shaken. Almost 10,000 commercial banks, over one third of the total number, failed between 1930 and 1933. "If the Depression had one overriding

Table 5-1
Comparisons Of Economic Performance
1921–1925 Versus 1930–1935

A. Real Gross National Product (billions of 1958 dollars)

1920	$140.00	1930	$183.50
1921	127.80	1931	169.30
1922	148.00	1932	144.20
1923	165.90	1933	141.50
1924	165.50	1934	154.30
1925	179.40	1935	169.50

B. Per Capita Real Gross National Product (1958 dollars)

1920	$1315.00	1930	$1390.00
1921	1177.00	1931	1490.00
1922	1345.00	1932	1154.00
1923	1482.00	1933	1126.00
1924	1450.00	1934	1220.00
1925	1549.00	1935	1331.00

C. Unemployment (percentage of civilian labor force)

1920	5.20%	1930	8.90%
1921	11.70	1931	16.30
1922	6.70	1932	24.10
1923	2.40	1933	25.20
1924	5.00	1934	22.00
1925	3.20	1935	20.30

D. Government Budget Expenditures (billions of dollars)

1920	$6.36	1930	$3.32
1921	5.01	1931	3.58
1922	3.29	1932	4.66
1923	3.14	1933	4.60
1924	2.91	1934	6.64
1925	2.92	1935	6.50

Source: US Department of Commerce, Historical Statistics of the United States (1975), pp. 224 (Series F-5 and F-4), 126 (Series D-9), and 1104 (Series Y-336).

effect, it was to create a profound sense of insecurity, a sense that no firm ground existed between economic order and chaos."[6]

The economic uncertainty caused many to abandon faith in the existing economic system of laissez faire, and to seek alternatives to the dominance of the marketplace. For some, the shift in attitudes included the more radical alternative of government ownership of the means of production, realized in part through establishment of government enterprises like the Tennessee Valley Authority. Others embraced a more thorough-going American totalitarianism. Walter Lippmann, for example, urged President Roosevelt that he had "no alternative but to assume dictatorial power."[7]

For the most part, though, the Roosevelt administration instituted a vast system of regulation that inaugurated or increased government control over private business in almost every sphere, rather than foster outright government ownership. Rabin notes that prior to the New Deal, the "widely shared philosophical and political perspective...stressed the limited responsibility of government for economic well-being; essentially this perspective was premised on an autonomous market-controlled economy."[8] There was "a deep-seated aversion" to government intervention. In this sense, "the New Deal was a watershed in the development of the federal regulatory system;" it established:

> ...a commitment to permanent market stabilization activity by the federal government. Along with this market-corrective model of economic regulation, the New Deal developed the framework for a transformed federal responsibility to assure individual economic security, and, more generally, triggered a substantial shift in traditional conceptions of the separate spheres of public and private activity.[9]

As shown in Table 5-1D, government spending was declining throughout the early 1920s, but rose substantially in the 1930s. Between 1930 and 1934 alone, the government budget doubled.

Because the role of government and the extent of regulation were changing profoundly from the 1920s to the 1930s, that era furnishes a natural experiment useful for appraising any relationship that might exist between lawyers' intellectual attitudes and legal change. To what extent, I shall ask, were lawyers' intellectual attitudes also changing with respect to the appropriate role of government in economy? Was legal intellectual opinion becoming more interventionist at a time when legal policy clearly was? If so, were lawyers' intellectual attitudes in any way responsible for the growing role of government in the 1930s?

THE ROLE OF INTELLECTUALS IN LEGAL CHANGE

I begin by defining a lawyer-intellectual as an attorney who earns his living primarily by teaching, writing, lecturing or otherwise communicating ideas. For the most part, this limits "intellectual" status to professors. This is somewhat narrower than the dictionary definition of "intellectual," but corresponds better to the ordinary usage of the term.[10] It defines the subjects of the inquiry occupationally, excluding lawyers like bureaucrats and private practitioners whose professional tasks are admittedly cerebral but who are not commonly included in the category of intellectuals.

Claims for Intellectual Roles in Regulation

Statements that intellectuals exert an important influence in political and legal events are not hard to find. Historian Paul Johnson believes that "The practical influence of intellectuals has expanded enormously.... As Lionel Trilling put it, 'Intellect has associated itself with power as perhaps never before in history and is now conceded to be itself a kind of power.'"[11] The power is thought by some to operate indirectly by molding public opinion, which then causes legal change. Perhaps the most famous exposition of this thesis is Dicey's celebrated 1898 lectures at Harvard, which postulated a "close dependence of legislation...upon the varying currents of public opinion" in nineteenth-century England.[12]

> [T]he beliefs or sentiments which, during the nineteenth century, have governed the development of the law have in strictness been public opinion, for they have been the wishes and ideas as to legislation held by people of England, or, to speak with more precision, by the majority of those citizens who have at a given moment taken an effective part in public life.[13]

More recently, in perhaps the most quoted assertion of intellectuals' influence, Keynes claimed that:

> [T]he ideas of economists and political philosophers, both when they are right and when they are wrong, are more powerful than is commonly understood. Indeed, the world is ruled by little else. Practical men, who believe themselves to be quite exempt from any intellectual influences, are usually the slaves of some defunct economist. Madmen in authority, who hear voices in the air, are distilling their frenzy from some academic scribbler of a few years back.[14]

Other economists subscribe to the thesis of intellectuals' influence. Milton Friedman, in comparing the laissez faire development of the 19th-century Japanese economy with the statist policies of 20th-century India, finds that the "difference in policies reflects faithfully the different intellectual climates of the two eras."[15]

Upon more careful consideration, however, the proposition that intellectual attitudes account for political and legal change is far from obvious.[16] Those who believe in intellectuals' power do not explain, first, how their influence is actually brought to bear on the process of legal change. The exact mechanism by which opinion influenced law is not clear in Dicey.[17] Keynes is a prime case in the difficulty of establishing intellectual influence in changing government policy. Despite the enormous academic influence that *The General Theory* had, the Roosevelt administration had already inaugurated Keynesian deficit-spending by the time the book appeared in 1936. Keynes' friend and biographer, Roy Harrod, did not believe Keynes had influenced economic policy,[18] a position given additional support in a recent statistical study, by Gordon Tullock, of deficit policies before and after the appearance of *The General Theory*.[19]

Models of Intellectual Participation in Legal Change

More important than the failure to explain how intellectual attitudes alter legal outcomes, however, has been the absence of a model explaining why intellectuals would attempt to influence outcomes and what positions they would adopt in trying to do so. As the concern here is the role of intellectuals in regulatory change specifically, one might look to the more specialized literature on economic regulation for systematic treatment of intellectuals' influence. But the intellectual is largely absent from the various models of regulation.

The Public Interest Model

The two most popular models are the competing public-interest and interest-group hypotheses. The former postulates that regulation is undertaken to correct some sort of market failure (public goods, externalities, monopoly) and inures to the general welfare of society. No explicit role is assigned to the intellectual in the public-interest model. Rather, the focus of the model is on politicians and bureaucrats and the way they respond to popular demand for correction of market failure.[20]

Implicit in the public-interest model, however, one might discern a special role for the intellectual. Both natural and social scientists in principle subscribe to the scientific method, a rigorously logical system for separating truth from falsehood by deductive reasoning and empirical testing.[21] As one with a comparative advantage in analyzing problems, as well as a specialty in imparting ideas to the wider public, the intellectual therefore might take the lead in recognizing market failure and communicating its existence and effects to the public. If so, the problems that arose in the Depression should have led to a substantial increase in intellectual attention to those problems, and a shift in attitudes toward new policies designed to solve the problems. These propositions are testable.

Provisionally, however, it is questionable whether the model of the intellectual as dispassionate truth-seeker corresponds to reality. It is doubtful, for example, whether scientific method in fact explains intellectuals' political and regulatory attitudes. Certainly, resort to scientific method cannot explain intellectuals' attitudes and political activities concerning questions outside their disciplines (e.g., Physicists Against the War). And even within their own disciplines, there is considerable evidence that scientific method often (normally?) does not explain the conclusions intellectuals reach.[22]

In addition, it is commonly believed that intellectuals are biased against markets and in favor of regulation, though for no particularly scientific or intellectual reason. "The intellectual has never felt kindly toward the marketplace: to him it has always been a place of vulgar men and base motives."[23] This appears true of many legal academics in particular. If biased against markets to begin with, intellectuals cannot fulfill the role assigned them under the public-interest model, recognizing and analyzing true market failures.

Finally, the public-interest view of academics as discovering and communicating the need for substantive legal and political change hardly corresponds to the observed activities of law-school academics, for whom substance has always been less important than method. With the adoption of Langdell's "case method" at Harvard in the 1870s, which emphasized the process of winnowing law from cases, legal method began to dominate substance in academe.[24] Succeeding movements aimed at dethroning the case method necessarily have been process-oriented as well. In the 1930s, for example, Legal Realism increasingly challenged the case method, especially at the more prestigious law schools.[25] The Realists emphasized the need to combine other disciplines, especially social science, with traditional legal studies in the law-school curriculum. Thus, in combating Langdell, the Realists urged the replacement of his methodology with theirs, in what was essentially a process-oriented debate. To one of its major proponents, Karl Llewellyn, Legal Realism was "merely a methodology."[26]

This emphasis on method sets law apart from the social and natural sciences, where scientific method is commonly agreed upon and whose histories thus are dominated by substantive debates.[27] The history of legal education, however, is a never-ending reexamination of pedagogical processes. Following the decline of Realism, the Association of American Law Schools (AALS) Curriculum Committee undertook to articulate the rationales underlying legal education, apparently the first time this subject had been approached systematically by the academic establishment. The Committee's report concentrated on distinguishing the different skills that comprised "thinking like a lawyer," and criticized the case method as inadequate for developing them.[28] Analysis of the substance of a legal curriculum was of secondary importance.

Intellectual developments in the legal academy since World War II demonstrate repeatedly the concern with method rather than substance. The "process approach" of Henry Hart and Albert Sacks suggested a unified system for approaching all areas of law, and had considerable influence on the research agenda of legal academics of the time. But as the name would suggest, the "process approach" was essentially methodological: the "essential method," Hart and Sacks admitted, "is nothing more than an application of the method of teaching law first popularized by Christopher Columbus Langdell in the 1870s."[29] The growing inclusion of clinical courses in law schools in the 1960s and 1970s was a methodological innovation for learning law, one obviously and explicitly designed to get away from three full years of the case method.

By contrast, the one truly substance-based criticism of legal education, the "Law, Science and Policy" (or "policy-science") approach of Yale professors Harold Lasswell and Myres McDougal,[30] has been the least successful. The Lasswell-McDougal approach had its methodological side; seminars were thought particularly useful in inculcating policy-science. But the principal aim of policy-science, unlike most other innovations urged upon law teaching, was substantive and quite political. Of all those innovations discussed here, however, policy-science had the least impact on the legal academy.[31]

In short, the public interest model predicts that as economic crises such as the Depression arise, academics will respond with increasing efforts to understand and solve the problems. Provisionally, however, the implications of the public interest model seem questionable. The model does not correspond to the way academics appear to choose their policy positions, and ignores what appear to some to be systematic biases by intellectuals in economic affairs. And in law schools particularly, one finds that intellectuals have always been driven more by process than by substance.[32]

The Interest Group Model

In addition to its shortcomings in this particular context, the public interest model has been of diminishing persuasiveness in analyzing regulatory change generally. Academicians of all sorts have increasingly repudiated the notion that regulation arises to correct market failure, in favor of the interest-group model (sometimes referred to as the economic model) of regulation.[33] Under this model, regulation is not supplied to rescue a public suffering from market failure, but to benefit well-organized private interest groups (e.g., producers) at the expense of the larger public (e.g., consumers). Indeed, the economic theory seems strongly confirmed by the generally pro-business

New Deal regulations established in the period 1931–1935.

Intellectuals might play a role in the interest-group model, to the extent that they were organized and had relatively homogeneous interests that could be advanced by regulation affecting them.[34] Our interest, however, is the role of intellectuals in the sorts of legal change directed primarily at others, such as the broad regulatory changes affecting private business enacted during the Depression. It is not immediately obvious how intellectuals could expect to gain from such legal change; as consumers, of course, they would lose as prices rose. As producers, however, they might gain if the demand for their services was a positive function of regulatory change. This could happen, for example, if intellectuals had a comparative advantage in identifying regulatory opportunities of benefit to others and were able to sell the information to those beneficiaries, who then would press for regulation. Intellectuals could also gain as producers if their outputs (e.g. articles) were effective in changing voters' attitudes about regulation, and the beneficiaries of regulation compensated them for their outputs.

Neither of these potential benefits to intellectuals as suppliers of ideas and published output appears of much importance. The most prevalent form of intellectual output, the journal article, normally entails no direct compensation at all. True, indirect benefits (e.g., outside consulting) may result. Intellectual ideas and articles, that is, might be lower-cost inputs that the ultimate beneficiaries of regulation would purchase to help achieve beneficial regulation for themselves. Empirically, however, relatively few legal academics have important outside income sources, and most of those earn it in strictly case-related matters.

For most academics, the most important source of gain is the teaching contract with one's university. Intellectuals might benefit if the demand for their service as teachers rose with regulatory changes. But here also, it is difficult to see why an increasing governmental role in the country's economic affairs would result in greater demands for a teacher's services. Indeed, if regulation is harmful to the economy as a whole, and if education is a normal good (i.e., one whose demand increases with rises in income), then regulation actually would be harmful to academics.

It might be objected that, while academics in general would have no particular self-interest in advancing increased regulation, legal academics are different. Regulation increases the number of laws, which would arguably increase the demand for (and so the return to) lawyers, which in turn might raise the demand for places in law schools, and so boost the demand for law teachers. The hypothesis cannot be dismissed *a priori*, but seems controverted by the facts. In a careful statistical analysis, Pashigian found that "the economic status of the legal profession is closely tied to the performance of the economy and not to the scale of government regulation."[35] The 1920s, he discovered, were a period of greater prosperity for lawyers than the 1930s.

Finally, under the interest-group model, legal academics might become more politically involved if economic crises like the Depression caused the primary demanders of their services, students, to seek law schools with more politically-minded professors. But this does not appear to be the case, either.[36] Except perhaps for the most elite, law schools are essentially trade schools. Law students by and large are interested in being able to practice, not change the world. Unlike graduate students in social or natural sciences, law students want to practice, not teach. Ideologies (of the left or the right) are largely irrelevant, as student indifference to both the now defunct Antioch Law School and the Maharishi International University's College of Natural Law attest. Students' vocational bent means that a law faculty interested in attracting students is unlikely to structure itself on advocacy of substantial legal change.[37]

In summary, the public-interest model of regulation would treat intellectuals as specialists in solving problems and communicating the solutions to the public and politicians. In times of difficulty, such as the Depression, intellectual activity would increase and should favor changes in the status quo to remedy the ills. Under the interest-group model, however, there is no particular reason to expect intellectuals to respond to widespread problems unless they themselves are benefited. It is hard to see how the demand for intellectuals' principal activities, teaching and writing, would be stimulated by a crisis like the Depression. Nor is it clear that, to the extent economic crises did cause intellectuals to react, they would favor the sorts of regulatory change enacted with the New Deal. But the issue can be resolved empirically: did legal intellectuals' attitudes change with the Depression?

LEGAL SCHOLARS AND THE DEPRESSION: EMPIRICAL EVIDENCE

Methodology

Data

In order to measure and then compare legal academics attitudes toward regulation, the entire corpus of law journal[38] articles for 1921–1925 and 1931–1935 under four different headings was analyzed. The categories were "Law Schools," "Legal Education," "Government," and "Corporations," headings under which the *Index to Legal Periodicals* (ILP) reports articles germane to the present inquiry. Over 2000 articles under these four headings were considered. In addition, as explained further below, I compared law journal reviews of two highly controversial works advocating increased government intervention in corporate affairs, one written in the halcyon days of the 1920s and the other appearing in the midst of the Depression crisis.

The articles under each category were characterized along a continuum according to their themes, from interventionist to noncommittal to laissez faire. Articles classed as noncommittal discussed the issue of governmental intervention but did not take a stand on the issue. Also noted were articles that did not even mention the issue, which for purposes here were classified as irrelevant. Of course, different readers might at the margin characterize the theme or message of an article differently. This is a lesser problem for our inquiry, however, which seeks to measure change. It compares two different time periods, rather than attempting to characterize a single period as interventionist or laissez faire. As long as the criteria applied to the articles in the two time periods are the same, useful comparisons of the two can be made.

Causation

Another problem in analyzing intellectuals' roles in political change is the difficulty of establishing causation, a point mentioned above in connection with both Dicey and Keynes. Throughout the period under study here, government became more interventionist and less protective of laissez faire. To have caused this switch in any way, intellectuals themselves must have become more interventionist advocates in their writing and teaching. But mere demonstration that intellectual attitudes became more interventionist would not prove that intellectuals helped cause the governmental change. The coincidence of the two phenomena could be no more than that: mere coincidence.

A shift toward more interventionist attitudes, in other words, is a necessary but not sufficient condition for causation. Merely comparing intellectual attitudes during the 1921–1925 period with those of 1931–1935 cannot prove causation. But a showing of strong changes in intellectual opinion simultaneous with changing regulation, if not conclusive evidence, may nevertheless be suggestive. Further, because a shift to more interventionist attitudes is necessary for causation, lack of causation can be shown. Logically, if intellectuals' attitudes were either becoming less interventionist or were not changing as increased regulation became the political agenda, intellectuals cannot have played an important role in the regulatory shift.

The inferences that one legitimately can draw thus depend on the data. Causation cannot be proven conclusively, but may be suggested by a demonstration that intellectuals became more interventionist as popular and political attitudes did also. Conceptually, lack of causation can be proven more convincingly, if intellectual attitudes were not changing in the interventionist direction that government regulatory policy increasingly took.

Empirical Evidence

Law Schools and Legal Education

If the attitudes of law-school academics were becoming more interventionist throughout the period under study, one change should have been manifested in their writings about their own institutions and about what they were or should be teaching.

This is particularly true, given the changes in legal education taking place in late 1920s and early 1930s. In the early 1920s, admission to law schools, even the most prestigious, was generally open to all high-school graduates willing to pay.[39] By the 1930s, slots in entering classes had been limited, making admissions competitive. The case method of instruction was increasingly challenged by Legal Realism, as discussed above.

Did law teachers' ideas about the role of the academy and about what they taught and wrote in fact become more pro-government during this time? Tables 5-2 and 5-3 indicate they did not. Table 5-2 summarizes the 176 American law review articles listed under the ILP heading "Law Schools" for 1921–1925 and the 56 under that heading for 1931–1935.[40] The articles are divided according to their interventionist or laissez faire stance.

Table 5-2
Articles on Law Schools
1921–1925 and 1931–1935

		1921–1925	1931–1935
Total Articles	176	56	
Interventionist	0	1	
Non-Committal	0	0	
Laissez-Faire	4	3	
Irrelevant	172	52	

As shown, there was almost no interest among legal intellectuals in the question of government intervention in the economy as it applied to the work of law schools, either before or during the Depression. Fully 98 percent of the articles in 1921–1925 and 93 percent of those in 1931–1935 simply ignored the question. Of the few articles that considered the appropriate role of government in the economy, the prevailing sentiment was non-interventionist both before and during the Depression. In short, there is no evidence of increasingly interventionist attitudes in the distributions of articles from 1921–1925 to 1931–1935.[41]

It is perhaps not surprising that so few persons considered the question in 1921–1925, and that the attitudes of those who did were laissez faire. But it is surprising that as the Depression set in and the regulatory law was becoming much more interventionist, so few legal academics apparently thought that this had implications for legal education. Only one author, writing in 1934, adopted a strongly interventionist position, though his was hardly a call for further change. Rather, he noted the changes that had occurred in American attitudes about the role of law and urged that law schools change to reflect the new demands society would make on it. The rest of those in 1931–1935—all three of them—who even noted the changes taking place were quite noncommittal about what they meant for law schools. One author noted the changes taking place and urged lawyers to judge them on their merits. Another, noting the nation's economic distress, urged that preparing future lawyers to assume greater responsibility in society would require law schools to offer training in ethics.

Table 5-3
Articles On Legal Education
1921–1925 and 1931–1935

	1921–1925	1931–1935
Total Articles	226	142
Interventionist	0	2
Noncommittal	0	2
Laissez-Faire	2	1
Irrelevant	224	137

The conclusion that, in their writings on law school, legal academics largely ignored the Depression and what it meant for them as teachers is reinforced by an examination of their publications on "Legal Education." As shown in Table 5-3, the pattern from 1921–1925 to 1931–1935 again is one of largely invariant indifference. Ninety-nine percent of the articles in the former period ignored the subject, as did 96 percent of those appearing during the Depression. Roscoe Pound, one who did address the point, noted with apparent approval "ambitious" plans for a new economic and social order that were emerging, and urged that legal education be broadened to help lawyers fulfill their roles in the new order. Most of his fellow authors during the Depression, however, were noncommittal, simply observing the changes taking place and noting that law schools should consider what the changes meant for legal education. Overall, there is no important difference in the distributions for the two sample periods. Practically no one writing of legal education thought the changes wrought by the Depression of particular significance for lawyer intellectuals and their roles within legal education. Of those who did, most were noninterventionist (laissez faire or noncommittal) in both periods.

If free enterprise versus regulation was not what writers on "Law Schools" and "Legal Education" had on their minds, what were they writing about? In 1921–1925, much of the writing reflected the internal changes in law schools. Major issues concerned whether college training should be required for admission to law school, what requirements should be imposed for admission to the bar, and so forth.

In 1931–1935, the emphasis shifted to the Legal Realist agenda. To the extent that Realism had a political message, it may have been interventionist: many Realists (and other academics) were personally interventionist and themselves helped create and administer the New Deal. (Legal Realism took hold most strongly at Yale Law School, whose ranks were depleted when eight of the faculty accepted offers from the Roosevelt administration to join various agencies in Washington.) But as discussed above, the principal academic agenda of Legal Realism was methodological rather than substantive. One should not make too much of the Realists' influence outside Harvard, Columbia and especially Yale at this time, either. From a national perspective, Legal Realism was "Intellectual Excitement for the Few."[42] Away from the Ivy League, the purpose of law schools and legal education was preparation for the bar examination. Indeed, the large-scale defection of Yale lawyers to the New Deal in part reflected Legal Realism's own failure to catch hold more firmly at the Yale Law School.

Government

There is apparently little correlation between the New Deal changes of the Depression and the attitudes of legal academics toward the role of law and law school. In both the 1920s and the 1930s, legal scholars were largely uninterested in questions of the proper role of government in economic affairs, insofar as that issue might affect their notions of the role of law schools in society or what they should be teaching. It is also of interest, however, to examine the attitudes of lawyer academics toward government generally. During this period when popular sentiment became more tolerant of—even enthusiastic about— government intervention in the economy, what were the attitudes of legal scholars toward government?

Table 5-4 indicates that, again, the question of government intervention generally was not of great concern to legal intellectuals. From a review of the law journal literature for the periods 1921–1925 and 1931–1935, one finds that, overall, relatively few articles under the heading "Government" addressed the issue of government intervention in private economic affairs. Only 10 of those for 1921–1925 (seven percent of the total for that period) treated the subject, though the total increased to 20 (18 percent) in 1931–1935.

Table 5-4
Articles on Government
1921–1925 and 1931–1935

	1921–1925	1931–1935
Total Articles	137	110
Interventionist	3	8
Noncommittal	2	3
Laissez-Faire	5	9
Irrelevant	127	90

More important, though, there was no significant change in the extent to which legal scholars were pro- or anti-interventionist. Of those writing in 1921–1925 who even considered the issue of government intervention, only a minority (3 of 10) were interventionists; in 1931–1935, interventionists were still in a minority (8 of 20). As before, one finds no significant difference in the distribution of interventionist sentiments during the period.

What the data do show, to the extent one can generalize from just a handful of articles, is an increasing polarization among law scholars on the question of government regulatory involvement in economic affairs. The number of strong advocates for both intervention and laissez faire increased during the time under study. Under the first heading, for example, one author advanced the prevention of economic want as a primary function of government, leading him to advocate a "new conception" of law as "an agency for planning and executing social programs." Another claimed that the fundamental changes that had occurred in the American economy appropriately meant an end to laissez faire. Opponents of these positions decried the expansion of government power over business as unconstitutional and likely to lead to communism or a fascist planned economy. The taxonomy presented in Table 5-4 is necessarily a crude portrayal of various shadings of opinion about government,[43] but does not show a sharp swing in favor of a more interventionist state.

Business

Two final sets of writings were reviewed for the evidence they provide concerning legal academics' attitudes toward private business and government intervention in economic affairs. The first set included all law review articles on corporations for 1921–1925 and 1931–1935. The second set of publications was comprised of law-journal reviews of two controversial books that criticized American business and espoused greater regulation, one written in the 1920s and the other in the 1930s.

Law Review Articles All the articles listed under the ILP heading "Corporations" for the two comparison periods were reviewed for their attitudes toward government intervention *versus* laissez faire. The results are shown in Table 5-5. One notes, first, that the number of articles on corporations for both periods is considerably larger than that for any of the prior categories, totaling over 1000 for 1931–1935. Yet, as before, only a handful even address the issue of government intervention.[44] And of these

Table 5-5
Articles on Corporations
1921–1925 and 1931–1935

	1921–1925	1931–1935
Total Articles	405	1,050
Interventionist	17	37
Non-Committal	2	17
Laissez-Faire	11	14
Irrelevant	375	982

few, the number of noninterventionists (those with noncommittal or laissez faire attitudes) is almost as great as the number of interventionists both before and during the Depression.

The terms of the debate between interventionists and noninterventionists are different in the two periods, however. The most popular specific issue to writers in 1921–1925 was whether no-par stock should be permitted, or whether government should continue to constrain the issue of stock by requiring some par value as a protection to creditors. Each side had its advocates. More general pieces also appeared addressing the desirability of government regulation of business in other contexts.

In the 1930s, the debate over no-par stock was largely over. But there was controversy in the literature over government intervention in issues that continue to be debated today: the use of preferred shares, the distribution of rights between minority and majority shareholders, and conflicts between shareholders and directors. There was discussion of the desirability of greater corporate disclosure and of the new federal securities legislation in particular. Most of the debates were focused on relatively narrow legal issues, though questions of corporations' social purposes and responsibilities were raised, and the desirability of government intervention generally was very occasionally discussed.

In short, the business literature from lawyers in the 1930s follows much the same pattern as the earlier literatures. Very little of the total literature was devoted to the question of the New Deal, despite the changes in business affairs taking place.

There is a slight shift in the percentage of those addressing the question, however, in favor of government intervention in corporate affairs. The context in which intervention is advocated, however, is ordinarily quite restricted. Even interventionists, in other words, were cautious reformers.

Reviews of Ripley and Berle-Means The appearance of two books critical of American business, one in the 1920s and the other in the 1930s, affords a final experiment for appraising any change over time in American legal intellectuals' attitudes toward regulation of business. William Ripley's *Main Street and Wall Street* appeared in 1927,[45] following presentation of the bulk of its message in three articles for the *Atlantic Monthly*. Adolf Berle and Gardiner Means' *The Modern Corporation and Private Property*,[46] published in 1932, is better remembered today, though its message in many ways derives from Ripley's earlier work.

The "underlying philosophy" of Ripley's work is that "the large-scale business corporation possesses enormous power," and that "those in control often act in ways contrary to the best interest of the community."[47] As American enterprise increasingly organized itself into large corporations rather than sole proprietorships or partnerships, there was "steady encroachment of management upon the traditional rights of shareholders."[48] "[T]he important point to note is that the wider the diffusion of ownership the more readily does effective control run to the intermediaries."[49] To remedy resulting ills, legal solutions like restraints on holding companies and mandatory cumulative voting were proposed. More important to Ripley, however, was the need for federal legislation mandating greater disclosure by corporations.[50]

Ripley's message may strike today's reader as tame, if only because so many of the legal changes he advocated in fact occurred. At the time, though, his work was "the sensation of Wall Street"[51] and "cause[d] the author to be denounced as a dangerous radical, and threats of retaliation to be made against the institution with which he [was] connected."[52] Today he is hardly read.

Much better remembered is Berle and Means' *The Modern Corporation and Private Property*. Berle and Means' study focused on the 200 largest non-banking corporations as of January 1930. With profuse data and a more scholarly tone, Berle and Means' message was nevertheless similar to Ripley's in many respects, as the authors acknowledged.[53] Most of the nation's industrial wealth had gone "from individual ownership to ownership by the large, publicly financed corporations;"[54] the 200 corporations studied owned almost half the corporate wealth in America. Public companies' dispersal of equity among many small shareholders led to the "separation of ownership from control," because of which "a large body of security holders... exercise virtually no control over the wealth which they or their predecessors in interest have contributed to the enterprise."[55] By the same token, those controlling the wealth "and therefore in a position to secure industrial efficiency and produce profits, are no longer, as owners, entitled to the bulk of such profits."[56] This relegated the role of owner initiative to "relative insignificance," while creating "economic empires" in managements "capable of perpetuating [their] own position."[57]

Berle and Means are less explicitly normative and reformative than Ripley. The need for legal changes is only implicit in their claim that the "traditional logic" of property and profits in the theory of the firm cannot explain the corporate entity. The book concludes by noting provocatively that the modern corporation has become so powerful that it can "compete on equal terms" with the state that is supposed to be regulating it,[58] but unlike Ripley it proposes few specific legal reforms. Still, Berle and Means were understood as reformers. Reviewers noted that the Berle-Means volume was "fundamentally a further, more detailed and up-to-date study, based upon collected data, of [the] same problem [discussed by Ripley]."[59] Indeed, the Berle-Means volume was described at the time as "the law, the logic and the philosophy of the New Deal."[60]

But if their cautionary messages about American business were similar, the popular and political receptions of *The Modern Corporation and Private Property* were rather different. Whereas Ripley was pilloried, Berle joined the Roosevelt "Brain Trust" in Washington and became one of Roosevelt's closest economic advisors. While Ripley is forgotten today, the work of Berle and

Means remains the subject of study and commentary.[61] Berle and Means' influence is traced in the popular works of John Kenneth Galbraith and the political proposals of Ralph Nader and Tom Hayden.

The differing popular and political receptions that *Main Street and Wall Street* and *The Modern Corporation and Private Property* received are interesting, and hardly surprising given the fundamental shift in popular and political attitudes toward business from the 1920s to the 1930s. But our inquiry concerns legal intellectuals. Did their reviews of these rather similar books appearing at different times evidence any shift in intellectual attitudes? To answer this question I read all the reviews of both books that appeared in the law journals, categorizing them as favorable, critical or mixed reactions to the book.

A summary of the reviews appears in Table 5-6. It is seen that Berle and Means were reviewed more frequently than was Ripley; three different reviews of *The Modern Corporation and Private Property* appeared in the *Yale Law Journal* alone.[62] The reviews of both were largely favorable, though often not especially enthusiastic. Only one review of Ripley's book voiced objections, though it also praised parts of the book. All the other reviews were favorable, though as one especially prescient review noted, Ripley's reforming message was not likely to be heard "when all are basking in the sunlight of prosperity."

When, five years after Ripley's work, *The Modern Corporation and Private Property* appeared, there was less "sunlight of prosperity" to bask in. Yet, as Table 5-6 shows, at the same time that increased intervention was the political agenda in Washington, Berle and Means were actually reviewed less favorably in the law journals than Ripley had been. Most of the favorable reviews were, again, far from extravagant. With the exception of a lengthy acclamation from Jerome Frank, the favorable reviews averaged less than two pages each, typically concluding with only a rather measured recommendation.

More interesting, only 63 percent of the reviews were favorable, compared to the 80 percent of Ripley's reviews that were favorable. Those that were not favorable were more carefully considered reviews, averaging close to four pages each, more

Table 5-6
Law Journal Reviews of Ripley's *Main Street And Wall Street* and
Berle-Means' *The Modern Corporation And Private Property*

	Ripley	Berle-Means
Total Reviews	5	16
Favorable	4	10
Mixed	1	3
Unfavorable	0	3

than twice the length of the favorable reviews. Three reviews
were mixed, praising parts of the book but expressing doubts or
criticism about other parts. Merrick Dodd of Harvard, for example, thought the work "largely successful," but disagreed
with portions of it and complained of "a certain confusion of
thought." Another found the book "exceptional," but criticized
its call for more detailed blue-sky laws and bureaucratic control
of corporations, rather than reliance on common-law controls
over corporate behavior. Yet another concluded that the Berle-
Means volume left "a feeling of disappointment."

What particularly distinguished the reception accorded
Berle and Means' work from that given to Ripley's, however,
was the substantial percentage of reviews that were critical
overall. One reviewer, noting that the separation of ownership
and control that lies at the heart of the Berle-Means critique of
corporate law had been discussed by Ripley and others before,
disagreed that it was an inherent vice or that resolving any
problems associated with it required radical restructuring of
the law. Another review had only criticism for Berle and Means'
work overall, and disagreed with several specific points. Focusing on their claim that corporate wealth was increasingly
concentrated in the hands of the largest corporations, for example, the reviewer noted that of the 200 large corporations
studied in the book, at least 18 were in receivership by the time
of the review and more apparently were headed that way. The
most scathing criticism came from Maurice Wormser of
Fordham University, who complained that "the book's analysis
showed the hand either of an amateur or a sensationalist." The
review concluded:

Much of this volume is suggestive and provocative of thought, but it is marred throughout by its sweeping condemnations as well as its general trend, emphasized by the bold statement on the flap, that the authors are engaged in 'A study of the break-up of Private Property.' The reviewer wishes Professor Berle and Dr. Means a long and happy life, and assures them that neither they nor their children, nor their grandchildren, will see in this country the 'break-up of private property.'[63]

In general, then, the reviews of Berle and Means were considerably harsher than those of Ripley. As opposed to the earlier comparisons, which showed either no appreciable shift in law scholars' intellectual attitudes about the role of government between the 1920s and 1930s (Tables 5-2, 5-3 and 5-4) or a slight shift in favor of government intervention (Table 5-5) the different reactions to the Ripley and Berle-Means books indicates an intellectual shift *away* from criticism of large corporations and government intervention in corporate affairs.

CONCLUSION

The New Deal was "a distinct break from the past" in establishing a pervasive government presence in almost all phases of business activity. Yet the writings of legal academics evince no particular enthusiasm for the changes. There is little evidence from their publications that legal scholars constituted a pro-regulation pressure group. Indeed, the reverse appears more correct. Their writings show legal academics to be largely uninterested and non-partisan. There is no reason to think that they had any influence in the important regulatory changes taking place as the Depression succeeded the prosperous tranquility of the 1920s. The movement took place without them, maybe even despite them.

What accounts for this anomalous indifference? One might resort to relatively *ad hoc* theories of ideology. It is often claimed that law, with its emphasis on precedent and *stare decisis*, is fundamentally a conservative discipline. It is likewise claimed that, all other things equal, the law prefers private solutions over governmental interference, except where one's actions harm another. In this respect, one recalls that it was the federal judiciary—lawyers—that consistently thwarted much of the early New Deal legislation.

A more systematic theoretical and empirical rationale is attempted here. In principle, there is little reason to expect intellectuals to have much influence in changing law and regulation. And in practice, the data on legal academics in the Depression show, they apparently did not. The writings of academic lawyers show little interest in the New Deal, and are quite ambiguous as to whether academics applauded or abhorred the changes.

Acknowledgment

An earlier version of this paper was presented at a conference on "Intellectual Freedom and Government Sponsorship of Higher Education" sponsored by the Professors World Peace Academy, whose support is gratefully acknowledged; and at the law and Economics Workshop at Emory University. The assistance of James Hickey, Deborah Mann and Jane Tuttle in compiling bibliographies of the literature of the 1921–25 and 1931–35 periods is gratefully acknowledged. Discussions with Roger Meiners and Richard Stewart, and particularly with William Carney and David Haddock, have been very helpful in the conceptualization of this paper. Its writing would have been impossible without the research assistance of John Paul Davis, University of Chicago Law School, Class of 1988.

NOTES

1. The roots of the 1921 recession may have extended back to the first World War. It has been called an "inventory recession," as it was supposedly caused by too rapid wartime accumulation of inventories that then could not be sold at current prices. See Douglass C. North, *Growth and Welfare in the American Past* (Englewood Cliffs, New Jersey: Prentice Hall, 1966), p. 166.
2. Milton Friedman and Anna J. Schwartz, *A Monetary History of the United States, 1867–1960* (Princeton: Princeton University Press, 1963), p. 296.
3. John K. Galbraith, *The Great Crash 1929* (Boston: Houghton Mifflin, 1955), p. 30.
4. Studs Terkel, *Hard Times* (New York: Pantheon Books, 1970), p. 4.
5. North, *op. cit.*, p. 167; for the figures, see "The Industrials: From 300 in 1928...to 2000 in 1987," *Wall Street Journal*, January 9, 1987, p. 21.
6. Robert L. Rabin, "Federal Regulation in Historical Perspective," *Stanford Law Review* 38, 1986, pp. 1189, 1251.
7. Kenneth S. David, *FDR: The New Deal Years, 1933–1937* (New York: Random House, 1985).
8. See *supra* note 6, p. 1192.
9. *Ibid.*, p. 1242.
10. George Stigler, for example, claims that he is automatically an intellectual because he is a professor. This is apparently a necessary but not sufficient condition, however. Stigler also claims automatic intellectual status because he buys more books than golf clubs. George J. Stigler, "The Intellectual and the Marketplace," *The Intellectual and the Marketplace* (Cambridge, Massachusetts: Harvard University Press, 1984), p. 143.
11. Paul Johnson, "The Heartless Lovers of Humankind," *Wall Street Journal*, January 5, 1987, p. 12.
12. Albert Venn Dicey, *Lectures on the Relation Between Law and Public Opinion in England During the Nineteenth Century*, 2nd edition, (London: Macmillan and Co., Ltd., 1914), p. 1.
13. *Ibid.*, pp. 9–10.
14. John M. Keynes, *The General Theory of Employment, Interest, and Money* (New York: Harcourt, Brace and World, 1964), p. 383.
15. Milton Friedman and Rose Friedman, *Free to Choose* (New York: Harcourt Brace Jovanovich, 1980), p. 285.
16. Belief in intellectuals' influence has not been unanimous. Dicey's contemporary, Arthur Bentley, reduced all legislation to a struggle

among special-interest groups. Arthur F. Bentley, *The Process of Government* (Chicago: The University of Chicago Press, 1949). No particular individual—intellectual or other—had any role to play in the process. Bentley, pp. 211, 215. For a discussion of Arthur Bentley's work and its considerable influence, see Mancur Olson, *The Logic of Collective Action: Public Goods and the Theory of Groups* (Cambridge, Massachusetts: Harvard University Press, 1965), pp. 118–125 (Bentley's book is "one of the most influential in American social science"); Gary S. Becker, "A Theory of Competition Among Pressure Groups for Political Influence," *Quarterly Journal of Economics* 98, 1983, pp. 371–372 (describing Arthur Bentley's work as "pioneering").

The question of intellectuals' influence in regulatory affairs has most recently divided two of the University of Chicago's Nobel Prize winners in economics, along lines reminiscent of Albert V. Dicey and Arthur F. Bentley. In discussing aspects of the history of regulation in the United States, George Stigler criticizes Milton Friedman's position (see text accompanying note 15, *supra*), while elaborating a "deep skepticism of the role of opinion, and leaders of opinion, in bringing about basic changes in the direction of a society." George J. Stigler, *The Regularities of Regulation* (Edinburgh, Scotland: David Hume Institute, 1986), p. 9. Like Arthur Bentley, George J. Stigler finds that important changes in the law can be explained instead by changing configurations among self-interested groups who stand to gain or lose from government regulation. See, e.g., the essays collected in George J. Stigler, *The Citizen and the State: Essays on Regulation* (Chicago: University of Chicago Press, 1975).

17. Indeed, some have read Dicey as not necessarily suggesting there is any causality at all. "Dicey, in his day, saw a 'close and demonstrable connection during the nineteenth century between the development of English law and certain known currents of opinion.' Whether he thought this connection to be causal in character is not clear." Morris Ginsberg, "Preface," in Morris Ginsberg, ed., *Law and Opinion in England* (Berkeley: University of California Press, 1959), vii.

18. Particular attention has focused on the economist's meeting with the president in 1934. In his biography of John Maynard Keynes, Roy Harrod writes:

> I have been at special pains to find out whether it is true that the President was profoundly influenced by this interview and guided his policy thereafter to some extent in light of Keynes' theories. The evidence is conflicting. The preponderating opinion among those in a good position to know is that the influence of Keynes was not great.... It has been suggested

that Keynes gave [Roosevelt] the courage to conduct his operations on a great scale. Keynes would certainly have urged that; yet it may be thought that the President's own instincts would lead him in the same direction, and that Keynes' advice was not the actuating factor. (p. 519)

Roy F. Harrod, *The Life of John Maynard Keynes* (New York: Norton, 1971), p. 532.

19. Gordon Tullock, "The General Irrelevance of the General Theory?" in James Buchanan and Charles Rowley, eds., *Deficits* (New York: Basil Blackwell, Inc., 1987).

20. "This [public interest] theory holds that regulation is supplied in response to the demand of the public for the correction of inefficient or inequitable market practices," Richard A. Posner, "Theories of Economic Regulation," *Bell Journal of Economics* 5, 1974, p. 335.

21. E.g., Herbert Butterfield, *The Origins of Modern Science* (New York: Free Press, 1957), pp. 89–107; Milton Friedman, "The Positive Methodology of Economics," in *Essays in Positive Economics* (Chicago: University of Chicago Press, 1953). Cf. Fred S. McChesney, "Assumptions, Empirical Evidence and Social Science Method," *Yale Law Journal* 96, 1986, p. 339.

22. In economics, this subject has gained considerable interest in the past few years. Donald McCloskey notes, for example, that "[e]conomists do not follow the law of enquiry their methodologies lay down." Donald N. McCloskey, "The Rhetoric of Economics" *Journal of Economic Literature* 21, 1983, pp. 481, 482. Coase provides several examples corroborating this claim. Ronald H. Coase, *How Should Economists Choose?* (Washington, D.C.: American Enterprise Institute for Public Policy Research, 1982). See also George J. Stigler, "The Politics of Political Economists," *Essays in the History of Economics* (Chicago: University of Chicago Press, 1965), vol. LV, p. 1; and "The Economist and the State," *The American Economic Review*, 1965, p. 552 (discussing how economists reach their policy positions).

23. See *supra* note 10. The exception would seem to be economists, whose professional instincts run in more conservative directions. Stigler, "The Politics of Political Economists," *op. cit.*, p. 52 ("study of economics makes one politically conservative"). See also Bruno S. Frey, *Economists Favor the Price System—Who Else Does?*", Kyklos 39, 1986, p. 537.

24. "Case study...replaced content with method." William Johnson, *Schooled Lawyers: A Study in the Clash of Professional Cultures* (New York: New York University Press, 1978), p. 104. As Johnson explains,

Unlike the early nineteenth-century conception of law, which ultimately judged the lawyer "scientific" in terms of how much law he knew and how systematically he knew that law, the case method placed emphasis on a method of legal study and investigation.... [T]eachers who propounded the virtues of case study were not forced to argue that their students possessed vast amounts of legal knowledge. On the contrary, their students often did not possess as much information as those trained exclusively by the lecture and textbook method, a fact that case teachers themselves often admitted. However, that lack now was turned into a virtue. Students trained in case study, the argument went, acquired a method of analysis by which they could eventually gain as much knowledge as they needed....

See also Robert B. Stevens, *Law School: Legal Education in America from the 1950s to the 1980s* (Chapel Hill, North Carolina: University of North Carolina Press, 1983), p. 270 (case method is "far more a vehicle for teaching methodology or process than for imparting knowledge of the substantive law").

25. See generally Laura Kalman, *Legal Realism at Yale, 1927–60* (Chapel Hill, North Carolina: University of North Carolina Press, 1986).

26. Quoted in Stevens, *op. cit.*, p. 273. Stevens notes:

The major contribution of the Realist movement was to kill the Langdellian notion of law as an exact science, based on the objectivity of black-letter rules. When it became acceptable to write about the law as it actually operated, legal rules could no longer be assumed to be value-free. This change inevitably caused the predictive value of doctrine to be seriously questioned. The vantage point of American legal scholarship was finally established as being process rather than substance. (p. 156)

27. See generally Butterfield, *op. cit.*; Thomas Kuhn, *The Structure of Scientific Revolutions* (Chicago: University of Chicago Press, 1962). For a discussion of the evolution of ideas in economics, see William Breit and Roger Spencer, eds., *Lives of the Laureates* (Cambridge: MIT Press, 1986); Robert D. Tollison, "Economists as the Subject of Economic Inquiry," *Southern Economic Journal* 52, 1986, p. 909; George J. Stigler, "The Nature and Role of Originality in Scientific Progress," in *Essays in the History of Economics* (Chicago: The University of Chicago Press, 1965).

28. Stevens, *op. cit.*, pp. 214, 227 footnote 77.

29. Henry M. Hart and Albert Sacks, *The Legal Process: Basic Problems in the Making and Application of Law* (Cambridge: Harvard Law School, 1958), v.

30. See Harold D. Lasswell and Myres S. McDougal, "Legal Education and Public Policy: Professional Training in the Public Interest," *Yale Law Journal* 52, 1943, p. 203.

31. "Some scholars have been influenced by the 'policy-science' approach, but, for all practical purposes, law schools have not." Stevens, *op. cit.*, p. 266 (footnote omitted). Stevens notes that policy-science had several failings, from its overuse of jargon to an assumption that, as social engineers, lawyers had the power and competence to do practically anything.

32. Indeed, Lawrence Friedman claims that Langdell's case method is responsible for the very organization of the legal services industry itself.

> Why was this [case method] idea so attractive in the long run? Basically, it suited the needs of the legal profession. It exalted the prestige of law and legal learning; at the same time it affirmed that legal science stood apart, as an independent entity, distinct from politics, legislation, and the man on the street. In this period, interest and occupational groups fought for a place in the sun. Langdell provided a firm basis of theory for certain important claims of the legal profession. Law, he insisted, was a branch of learning that genuinely demanded rigorous formal training. There was justification, then, for the lawyers' monopoly of practice. The bar association movement began at exactly that point in time which coincided with Langdell's rise to power. The two movements went hand in glove.

Lawrence Friedman, *A History of American Law* (New York: Simon and Schuster, 1973), p. 536.

33. Recognition that regulation is principally explained by special-interest pressure, rather than public-interest correction of market failure, cuts across academic disciplines. In political science, see e.g., Peter Aranson and Peter Ordeshook, "Public Interest, Private Interest, and the Democratic Party," in Roger Benjamin and Stephen Elkin, eds., *The Democratic State* (Lawrence, Kansas: University Press of Kansas, 1985). In economics, see e.g., Robert McCormick, "The Strategic Use of Regulation: A Review of the Literature," *The Political Economy of Regulation: Private Interests in the Regulatory Process* (Washington, D.C.: FTC, 1984). In law, see Richard A. Posner, "Economics, Politics, and the Reading of the Constitution," *University of Chicago Law Review* 49, 1982, p. 263; Richard A. Epstein, "Taxation, Regulation and Confiscation," *Osgoode Hall Law Journal* 20, 1982, p. 433.

34. For example, regulation might be sought in order to erect barriers to new entry, which would increase the returns of incumbent academics. Yet one does not observe intellectuals seeking to be regulated. As Coase has noted, intellectuals have generally favored

not being regulated, the reverse of what the interest-group model seemingly would predict. Ronald H. Coase, "The Market for Goods and the Market for Ideas," *American Economic Review* 64, Papers & Proceedings, 1974, p. 384. And in those instances when they actually do benefit, one discovers that intellectuals had no particular enthusiasm for regulatory change. As George J. Stigler notes, "the Sherman Act would put more into economists' purses than perhaps any other law ever passed," yet there was no particular fervor among economists for its passage. George J. Stigler, "The Economists and the Problem of Monopoly," in *The Economist as Preacher and Other Essays* (Chicago: University of Chicago Press, 1982), p. 38. For further discussion, see Fred S. McChesney, "A Positive Regulatory Theory of the First Amendment," *Connecticut Law Review* 20, 1988, p. 355.

35. B. Peter Pashigian, "The Market for Lawyers: The Determinants of the Demand for and Supply of Lawyers," *Journal of Law and Economics* 20, 1977, pp. 53, 81.

36. Of course, the New Deal meant that certain courses (administrative law) became of greater interest to students. But these courses by and large focused on procedure rather than political substance. In his history of American administrative law, for example, William Chase argues that "American legal scholarship has been heavily influenced by the configuration of its institutional home, the law school," where the case method has dominated, and that "legal scholarship in turn has influenced American government." William C. Chase, *The American Law School and the Rise of Administrative Government* (Madison: University of Wisconsin Press, 1982), ix.

37. Stevens, *op. cit.*, p. 268, notes that, given law schools' trade orientation, the case method also has great financial benefits.

> [D]uring the previous century, the inherent conflicts in the purposes of legal education [have] been seriously aggravated by its remarkable underfunding. Even the leading law schools had always had faculty-student ratios that would have been unheard of in any marginally acceptable college and unthinkable in any other graduate or other professional school. This underfunding of legal education was almost certainly attributable to the Langdellian model, for the case method seemed to work as well with two hundred students as it did with twenty.... It is possible that Langdell's greatest contribution to legal education was the highly dubious one of convincing all and sundry that legal education was inexpensive.... An ability to survive with limited funds by continuing large-class case-method instruction was one of several historical realities that

faced Lasswell and McDougal, as it had faced those who came before and those who followed them.

To this should be added the relatively low costs that the case method imposes on law professors themselves. When method dominates over substance in the classroom, teachers' staying current on case-law developments becomes less important. Nor is it necessary to tailor courses to the substantive law of a particular jurisdiction; students need only be acquainted with the basic concepts and the methodological tools for learning the local substantive rules themselves.

The relative absence of truly intellectual programs in law schools thus becomes easier to understand. Law itself is a trade, and most of those attending law school seek admission into the trade. Even if students wanted a more intellectual formation, self-regulation means that law school programs are largely controlled by what the practicing bar is expected to put on the bar exams. For both reasons, demand for intellectual rather than vocational education is limited. And the costs of providing it are considerably higher than those of case-method instruction. A new product with higher costs of production and lower consumer demand is unlikely to dislodge the original.

38. The number of academic law journals during this period is much less than exist today. Although there were almost 200 law schools during the relevant period, most did not have law reviews. The number of reviews in 1937, for example, was only 50. Stevens, *op. cit.*, p. 164 footnote 13. By the same token, law review articles, comments and notes, all of which were written by attorneys, were considerably shorter than those found in law journals today.

39. On the educational attainments required of law students in the late 1920s, see Alfred Zantzinger Reed, *Present-Day Law Schools in the United States and Canada* (Boston: The Merrymount Press, 1928), pp. 129–137. In 1927–1928, there were 166 three-year law schools, only four of which (Harvard, Pennsylvania, Northwestern, and Pittsburgh) required a college degree.

40. In addition, the category included 17 foreign articles in 1921–1925 and 4 foreign articles in 1931–1935. These were not read. Nor were the article in 1921–1925 and 3 articles in 1931–1935 from non-academic sources (typically unavailable state or local bar publications). In all subsequent tables, foreign and unavailable publications were excluded as well.

41. For a detailed list of the numerous articles referred to in the following discussion, see my lengthier paper on this topic: Fred S. McChesney, "Intellectual Attitudes and Regulatory Change," *Journal of Legal Education* 38, 1988, p. 211.

42. Stevens, *op. cit.*, p. 155.

43. One topic that was of interest to those writing about government at this time was the appropriate division of power between the state and federal governments. Exit from onerous state regulation is easier than exit from a national regulatory system; avoidance of centralized power has long been thought a principal advantage of a federal system. *The Federalist* Nos. 41–46. Advocacy of a federal system thus might be thought a "conservative" position. See generally Richard A. Posner, *Economic Analysis of Law*, 3rd edition (Boston: Little, Brown and Co., 1986), pp. 599–614. Nevertheless, articles on the distribution of government power were classified as irrelevant for purposes of Table 4, as they take the exercise of interventionist government power as given and discuss only at which level power should be exercised. Advocacy that any regulatory power remain at the state level hardly constitutes a laissez faire position, given the propensity of state governments at the time to intervene in economic affairs. E.G., *Nebbia v. New York*, p. 291 US 502 (1934), (upholding state milk board establishment of minimum prices); *Home Building and Loan Association v. Blaisdell*, p. 290 US 398 (1934), (upholding Minnesota statute preventing foreclosure on and sale of real estate).

44. A large portion of the irrelevant articles registered in Table 6 were case notes, which at this time were ordinarily written by academic (and sometimes practicing) lawyers rather than law students. These are simple reports of cases, and so are irrelevant to the purposes here. There were 297 case notes in 1921–1925, and 655 in 1931–1935. Also treated as irrelevant here was the much smaller number of articles (2 in 1921–1925, 49 in 1931–1935) concerning corporate reorganization and bankruptcy, as bankruptcy can be viewed either as interventionist interference with contract or as a standard-form contract to solve a common-pool problem among creditors. See Douglas G. Baird, "The Uneasy Case for Corporate Reorganization," *Journal of Legal Studies* 15, 1986, p. 127.

As with the other counts, there are some foreign and otherwise unavailable articles that are not counted in Table 6. The number of foreign articles in 1931-1935 was 202, a much larger number than the foreign publications under the earlier categories.

45. William Z. Ripley, *Main Street and Wall Street* (Boston: Little, Brown and Co., 1927).

46. Adolf A. Berle, Jr. and Gardiner C. Means, *The Modern Corporation and Private Property* (New York: Macmillan Company, 1932).

47. Maurice Moonitz, "Foreword to the Reissue," of William Z. Ripley, *Main Street and Wall Street* (Boston: Little, Brown and Co., 1972).

48. *Ibid.*, p. 19.

49. *Ibid.*, p. 37.

50. *Ibid.*, pp. 55, 86, 100-101, 104-106, chapters VI and VII, pp. 217-220, and 227.
51. W. Lewis Roberts, "Review of Ripley," *Kentucky Law Journal* 16, 1928, p. 379.
52. Joseph M. Cormack, "Review of Ripley," *Illinois Law Review* 23, 1929, pp. 520, 524. Ripley was a professor at Harvard University.
53. Berle and Means, *op. cit.*, ix (acknowledging that Ripley "pioneered this area"). This is not to say that Ripley was the first to discuss separate specialization in ownership and management. See, e.g., Thorstein Veblen, *Absentee Ownership and Business Enterprise* (New York: A.M. Kelley, bookseller, 1923); Thorstein Veblen, *The Engineers and the Price System* (New York: B.W. Huebsch, Inc., 1921).
54. Berle and Means, *op. cit.*, vii.
55. *Ibid.*, p. 7.
56. *Ibid.*, p. 9.
57. *Ibid.*, pp. 124-125.
58. *Ibid.*, p. 357.
59. Robert S. Stevens, "Review of Berle and Means," *Cornell Law Quarterly* 18, 1933, p. 634. See also Paul L. Sayre, "Review of Berle-Means," *Iowa Law Review* 18, 1932-1933, pp. 581, 584. ("It carries on the work of Professor Ripley.")
60. Joseph V. Kline, "Review of Berle and Means," *Columbia Law Review* 33, 1933, p. 557.
61. See, for example, the papers presented at a conference, "Corporations and Private Property," sponsored by the Hoover Institution to mark the 50th anniversary of the publication of *The Modern Corporation and Private Property*, collected in the June 1983 special issue of the *Journal of Law and Economics*.
62. For a detailed list of the numerous articles referred to in the following discussion, see Fred McChesney *supra* note 41.
63. I. Maurice Wormser, "Review of Berle-Means," *American Bar Association Journal* 19, 1933, p. 114.

SIX

THE POLITICAL IDEOLOGY OF THE PROFESSORIAT

THE EFFECTS OF GOVERNMENT FUNDING ON POLITICAL SCIENCE AND OTHER DISCIPLINES

Peter H. Aranson

My assignment in this essay is to discern the effects, if any, of government sponsorship of higher education on intellectual freedom, with special emphasis on the discipline of political science. The word "effects" seems immediately too broad to be useful, and of course the term "intellectual freedom," like the more general term "freedom," suffers under the same disability. Hence, some initial reflections on meanings seem in order.

First, government sponsorship of higher education, with all of its attendant rules and regulations, can take several forms. The most obvious is general subsidy, through scholarships, construction grants, and other aid to colleges and universities that is relatively *fungible* across disciplines. These forms of subsidy, for two reasons, will not concern me here: (1) they are so general as not to create disciplinary divisions within the academy, except as they promote competing claims for funds within particular universities; and (2) as I argue momentarily, in the United States government subsidy of any particular industry correlates at best only sporadically and unevenly with the recipients' political actions and preferences. But other varieties of aid, such as discipline-specific research grants, do vary across disciplines, and these, at least initially, will be my principal concern.

Second, the word "effects" is more difficult to define. To understand adequately what we mean by an effect, we would have to construct a theoretical model or perform a natural experiment, in which we compare the kinds of preferences prevalent or activities undertaken in a discipline without such aid with an identical discipline, but one that receives some level of government grants. Even here, however, the matter seems far from settled. In the parlance of economics, the focusing of aid on various forms of research and related activities would have "income effects" and "substitution effects" of a peculiar sort (I use these terms here metaphorically and, especially concerning "income effects," not precisely as economists define them technically). On the one hand, with respect to income effects on political preferences, as government funding increases faculty incomes, we can expect those faculty members affected to become relatively less interested in government redistribution in their favor.[1] But at the same time, a greater dependence on such funding may tend to place the affected faculty members within a larger coalition in support of an expansive state. We consider this problem of changing professorial preferences in the next section.

DOES GOVERNMENT FUNDING INTERFERE WITH RESEARCH RESULTS OR AGENDAS?

Third, we cannot discern exactly what the substitution effects of government grants on research choices would be unless we have a fairly clear idea of what we mean by intellectual freedom. The most obvious sort of claim would assert that scholars change their conclusions away from what they have discovered to please their government funding agencies or that they have concentrated their research agendas in areas that would tend to support those agencies' interests. In either case, either implicitly or explicitly, one might assert that the agency has interfered with the scholar's intellectual freedom.

But even here the matter is far from clear, and I reject this implicit model of interference ("effects") on several grounds. In the case of misrepresented results, if the scholar misreports or manipulates his findings to please a funding agency (and obtain future grants), then it is not apparent why we should hold the agency fully to blame as the culpable entity. The agency has not lied, although it has supported an academic who seems willing to do so.[2] More important, such misrepresentations are easily corrigible. Either the research results are replicable or they are not. If they are not, then the academic who reports them (and indirectly, the funding agency), along with the results themselves, remain subject to condemnation.

If the results are in a form subject to replication, then the researcher (and the funding agency) will have paid the capital cost of set up, which will only invite detection and reporting of fraud by other researchers. This form of replication ordinarily costs far less than does the original research. For example, the funding agency might pay the researcher to set up the original experiment and collect the data, which then are available to all other researchers, following the traditional practice of replication. An experiment that costs millions of dollars to run, then, produces traceable results that other researchers can check at very low cost, relative to the original costs of setup. The relative prices are much lower with respect to theoretical work, of course, and lower still with respect to empirical work that rests on an incorrect or misrepresented theoretical structure.[3] Only in the case of misreported data might there prevail a parity of origination and replication costs.

Nor is the claim of interference with academic freedom more robust in the case of government funding to redirect (or restrain) individual research agendas. There surely are many examples of this phenomenon. Present regulations constrain the nature of testing of new chemical entities, and especially those developed by recombinant DNA research. It seems unlikely, and I believe justifiably so, that the federal government would seriously consider supporting research in racial intelligence differences. And for some years the National Science Foundation, reflecting political sensibilities, tended not to fund research involving the direct interviewing of congressmen. More often, the funding agencies themselves, ordinarily through their advisory committees, decide what areas of research they should fund and what areas they should let go unfunded.

Like problems of misreporting results, such agenda restrictions and tendencies, in my view, do not imply a serious invasion of intellectual freedom. First, there is a case, though a limited one, for government funding of research.[4] Whatever budget the legislative process creates, the requirement remains for choices of areas and specific projects to fund. To the extent that the legislative and bureaucratic processes accurately reflect citizens' preferences in these matters (and I entertain very serious doubts about their accuracy)[5] the choices of areas and projects simply reflect the operation of a kind of consumer (citizen) sovereignty. In other words, without a fuller development of a model of public choice, we cannot lay a claim for agency interference by the public sector without simultaneously laying the same claim with respect to university and private institutional funding decisions.

Second, the sources of funding of academic research in the United States emerge from a remarkably pluralistic universe. Within the federal government itself, diverse and sometimes competing sources of funds and unresolved policy conflicts do not permit the "rationalization" of government research-dollar allocations. Beyond government (including state) sources, a plethora of funding institutions—private foundations and industry sources—provide support for every imaginable form of research agendas. Hence, even if the federal government underwrites a large proportion of academic research, it seems unlikely that its agencies could prevail in controlling the agendas of all, or even most, scholars.

Third, the same process of replication affects the government's ability to restructure and control research agendas as affects its ability to control conclusions. The appearance of a federal agenda structure in some particular discipline is just too easy a target for those academics whom it does not favor. And because the eventual monetary and nonpecuniary remuneration of university researchers rests in the hands of colleagues, not in those of the funding agencies, a claim of federal control of agendas through funding lacks serious credibility.[6]

Fourth, the model of an aggrandizing leviathan government that seeks its own interests seriously misinterprets the nature of American politics. The institutions of American government, including the science and education bureaus and their congressional oversight committees, are constructed to be highly responsive to the demands of organized groups in the population. In scientific research, for example, these groups included communities of researchers themselves and collections of firms and households (for example, those with members suffering from relatively rare diseases) that directly or indirectly would purchase research results. Public choice scholars characterize this process as one of "rent-seeking."[7] In this view neither the government nor its agencies dominate the political process. Instead, organized interests enjoy fairly clear paths to the public treasury, and they seek ways to supply themselves with government support at collective cost. Two recent works, one by me[8] and the other by Cohen and Noll,[9] have studied this phenomenon with respect to science policy. As Price wrote over 20 years ago, in rejecting a "leviathan" government model for one of interest-group, pluralist politics,

> [T]he general effect of this new system [of non-ideological expansion of the state] is clear: the fusion of economic and political power has been accompanied by a considerable *diffusion* of central authority. This has destroyed the notion that the future growth in the functions and expenditures of government, which seems to be made inevitable by the increase in the technological complexity of our civilization, would necessarily take the form of a vast bureaucracy, organized on Max Weber's hierarchical principles, and using the processes of science as Julian Huxley predicted to answer policy questions. Where scientists have shaped this development, its

political and administrative patterns have reflected the way scientists actually behave rather than the way science fiction or Marxist theory would have them behave; they have introduced into stodgy and responsible channels of bureaucracy the amiable disorder of a university faculty meeting.[10]

Academic interest groups do affect research agendas, and occasionally they may create direct or indirect incentives for researchers to alter their results. But for reasons that I discuss earlier, I doubt seriously that this problem is substantial with respect to intellectual freedom. Of course, it does carry very serious adverse consequences for the efficiency of spending for research, but that is another matter. Early government funding for the Jarvik-7 artificial heart, for example, was a response to demands in the relevant medical community for that kind of support. At least initially, the political process failed to reflect some very predictable and *predicted* problems with the technology.[11]

Finally, freedom in general, and intellectual freedom in particular, has many components, and an even greater number of meanings. In this diversity lies a trap that threatens to undermine the coherence of claims linking a loss of intellectual freedom to government sponsorship of research. The two principal views of freedom predominating in the Western world for at least the last two centuries concern the contrast between negative, or liberal, freedom, on the one hand, and positive freedom, on the other. Negative freedom is the freedom to be left alone. It is, in Leoni's words, "the absence of constraint exercised by other people, including the authorities, over the private life and business of each individual."[12] Positive freedom, by contrast, entails "freedom" from want, "freedom" to have food, clothing, and shelter, and "freedom" to have research support.

Negative freedom is essentially a (lower case) libertarian concept, while positive freedom is essentially a socialist concept. But those who would claim aggrandizement by the state through the selective use or derivative influence of research funding, and therefore see in such funding a problem of restricted intellectual freedom, need to take care lest they make a case for more expansive funding, to even out the relative deprivations of academics not presently favored by government's goals. For if they follow this line of reasoning, they will be making a claim on the public treasury on the basis of positive freedom, the very concept that underlies government "aggrandizement" in the first place. A case based on negative freedom, then, can only assert the desirability of *no* government sponsorship of research, not even for such areas as national defense and pure basic research, where there may be no apparent residual claimants to make the effort profitable. (Among other reasons for this conclusion, we note that in the absence of unanimous consent, any government funding of research restricts the taxpayer's negative freedom).

I do not believe that we can find easy answers to the resulting conundrum. For example, my own previously reported preference for some government sponsorship, but only for pure basic research,[13] leads me into the same set of problems, except that I do not believe, as an empirical matter, that such sponsorship poses the threat to intellectual freedom that some find in practice.

I have aimed the preceding remarks at the claim that government support inhibits intellectual freedom by getting academics to change their results or to adjust their research agendas to satisfy the funding agency. But I have not yet resolved the problem of defining intellectual freedom in any relevant sense. Nor need we do so, if we believe that government spending, at present, poses no threat to intellectual freedom.

But we must resolve the larger problem of defining freedom itself. I shall do so here with the least amount of difficulty, by referring to operational constructs. In general, I use "freedom" here to mean the absence of state control of private persons and institutions, either by taxation or regulation. The dimensions of freedom, then, become operationalized measures of economic and social-policy preferences.[14] Hence, those who object to such a definition of freedom merely can substitute a title such as "Does Government Support of Higher Education Increase the Public Sector's Control of Economic or Social Life?" for the one that I have proffered here.

My own view, for reasons that I have outlined with respect to control of research results and agendas, and will now outline with respect to the general problem of government support affecting academic political preferences, is that government support of higher education in general, and of political science in particular, has little effect on the research agendas, research conclusions, or the political attitudes of academics.

DOES GOVERNMENT SUPPORT UNDERMINE GENERAL ACADEMIC PREFERENCES FOR FREEDOM?

A more difficult hypothesis to sustain, as we note earlier, is that as "wards" of the state the members of the academy make up a part of the state's supporting coalition, and they bend their efforts (in their research, in their classrooms, and elsewhere) to reinforce an ideology of leviathan government. Of course, we would have to subject this hypothesis to the same test mentioned earlier, namely that we must compare a subsidized discipline with the same discipline without subsidies. And we shall do so, though very indirectly. But even this claim seems too broad, for reasons that I explore here.

Conventional wisdom holds that on most issues the American professoriat is to the left of the median voter. And indeed, the evidence for this belief seems substantial enough. Suppose, for example, that we take Democratic percentage of the vote in presidential elections as a surrogate measure of (the opposite of) negative freedom, in either the economic or social dimension.[15] Ladd and Lipset have collected data on the reported votes of various groupings in the population, which I include in Table 6-1.[16]

The table shows fairly conclusively, that American faculty members tend to vote more Democratic than do members of the general population and far more Democratic than do members of the groups with which academics are most closely associated: those with a college education and those with professional or managerial jobs. An examination of political self-assignment appears to confirm the same tendencies. As Table 6-2 shows, in 1969 faculty members classified themselves

Table 6-1
Democratic Percentage of Presidential Vote, 1948-1972*

	Professors	College Educated	Professional/ Managerial	Entire Population
1944	57%	39	39	54
1948	61	32	31	52
1952	56	34	36	44
1956	62	31	32	42
1964	78	52	54	61
1968	61	37	34	43
1972	57	37	31	39

*Source: Everett Carll Ladd, Jr., and Seymour Martin Lipset, *The Divided Academy: Professors and Politics* (New York: McGraw Hill, 1975), pp. 29-31.

as more "liberal" and less conservative than did other members of the American public in 1970.[17]

Is there more to academic policy preferences than simple political tastes? Some believe so, and one can find any number of right-wing, conservative, or neoconservative academics who seem to enjoy hanging their institutions' "dirty laundry" out to dry.[18] That the sheets are soiled no one can doubt. One finds in academe an astonishing variety of foolishness sufficient to embarrass even the most ardent defenders of academic freedom. This richness of sublime academic indifference to reality is precisely what one would expect, of course, in a system whose members and firms remain largely unaccountable to the traditional forces of productivity, civility, and just plain manners.[19]

But it is not apparent, at least to me, that academics act peculiarly because they are left-of-center. It may be that peculiar kinds of people tend to be left-of-center (or right-of-center, for that matter). As Orwell wrote in *The Road to Wigan Pier*, "One sometimes gets the impression that the mere words 'socialism' and 'communism' draw towards them with magnetic force every fruit-juice drinker, nudist, sandal-wearer, sex-maniac, Quaker, 'Nature Cure' quack, pacifist, and feminist in England."[20]

Do academics prefer the left because of government grants? I do not believe so, because the hypothesis has no theoretical credentials and experience tends to disconfirm it. Within the

Table 6-2
Political Ideology of Academics and General Public in the U.S.*

Political Ideology	Faculty (1969)	U.S. Public (1970)
Left	5%	4
Liberal	41	16
Middle of the Road	27	38
Moderately Conservative	25	32
Strongly Conservative	3	10

*Source: Everett Carll Ladd, Jr., and Seymour Martin Lipset, *Academics, Politics, and the 1972 Election* (Washington, D.C.: American Enterprise Institute, 1973), p. 16.

academy itself physicists and others engaged in the "hard" sciences are the recipients of the greatest proportion of federal funding, while social scientists receive very little of such support. In fiscal year 1985, for example, National Science Foundation direct disciplinary spending for physics (excluding engineering, astronomical, atmospheric, earth, and ocean sciences) amounted to $115.8 million, for computer research, $39.12 million, and for chemistry, $87.56 million. But social and economic sciences received only $28.75 million.[21]

Compared with the social sciences, though, physicists and others in the natural sciences (as we report later in this section) are politically more conservative. This pattern mirrors the more general political trend of left voting being related inversely to income, not to government support itself. This pattern should occasion little surprise, considering our earlier brief discussion of rent-seeking. Many industries receive federal aid and contracts. But defense contractors, hard liners on national defense, usually are hostile to more stringent economic regulation and higher personal and corporate tax rates. And farmers, who have received substantial federal support since the turn of the century, at least until recently have provided no hotbed of revolution. So-called "agrarian revolutions," even in Latin American countries, remain largely an urban phenomenon. Indeed, in the United States, farmers' political preferences tend to be radicalized (toward both ends of the political spectrum) in proportion to the *reduction* in federal support that they receive. Doctors, lawyers, accountants, and other professionals, all of whom receive indirect government aid in the form of entry restrictions, traditionally have been among the most Republican members of the population. Academics, then, like most other economic agents, tend to prefer socialism for themselves and capitalism for everyone else.

But we can attack the question more directly by examining differences in political preferences among academics, as a function of the proportion of academics in each discipline receiving government grants. The evidence concerning differences in political preferences among different disciplines seems fairly striking. In their 1975 study, Ladd and Lipset surveyed 471 faculty members and collected information about their personal and professional characteristics, political preferences, and responses to several public-policy questions. In *The Divided Academy*,[22] they report by discipline several percentage responses to these questions. While these data form extremely imprecise measures for answering the questions that we might like to ask, I use them here to explore certain characteristics of the academy, through the use of OLS regressions.[23]

The first question we wish to ask is: do government grants lead to a greater liberal or left political self-identification? To answer this question, we regress three variables—the percentage in each discipline assigning themselves as "left" [LEFT], "liberal" [LIB], and "left plus liberal" [LAL]—against the percentage within each discipline receiving federal research grants (last 12 months) [GRANT]. The results are thus (t-statistics are in parentheses):

$$\text{LEFT} = 9.80 - 12.41\text{GRANT} \qquad \text{adj. R-square} = .1552$$
$$(0.06) \qquad (2.36) \qquad\qquad n = 26$$

$$\text{LIB} = 49.83 - 0.16\text{GRANT} \qquad \text{adj. R-square} = .0053$$
$$(9.90) \qquad (1.06) \qquad\qquad n = 26$$

$$\text{LAL} = 59.63 - 0.03\text{GRANT} \qquad \text{adj. R-square} = .0432$$
$$(9.16) \qquad (1.46) \qquad\qquad n = 26$$

These results do not support a claim that federal grants lead to a disproportionate academic disregard for negative freedom. Only one of these regressions, predicting LEFT self-assignment, has a statistically significant coefficient on GRANT, and all three coefficients are negative. If these results could support any claim, it is that the awarding of federal grants is associated with a greater academic regard for negative freedom.

But perhaps there are differences within broad groupings of academic disciplines, which, when we control for them, will indicate that the awarding of government grants does correlate with a preference for positive freedom. To test this proposition, I assigned each of the 26 disciplines to categories, using dummy variables. These include "social science" [SOC], "trade" [TRA], "humanity" [HUM], and "natural biological science" [NAT]. (A discipline receives a "1" or "0," depending on whether or not it belongs to one of these categories. A discipline with four zeros is a natural, academic—non-trade—non-biological science, such as physics.) The results of the previous three regressions with these dummy variables included are thus:

$$LEFT = 4.10 + 0.01GRANT + 6.91SOC - 2.11TRA + 5.14HUM - 1.44NAT$$
$$(1.70) \quad (0.13) \quad\quad (4.46) \quad (1.38) \quad\quad (1.96) \quad\quad (0.70)$$
adj. R-square = .5816 n = 26

$$LIB = 35.16 + 0.16GRANT + 21.23SOC - 6.55TRA + 10.38HUM - 3.26NAT$$
$$(5.35) \quad (0.96) \quad\quad (5.03) \quad\quad (1.57) \quad\quad (1.45) \quad\quad (0.58)$$
adj. R-square = .5591 n = 26

$$LAL = 39.25 + 0.17GRANT + 28.14SOC - 8.66TRA + 15.53HUM - 4.69NAT$$
$$(4.89) \quad (0.83) \quad\quad (5.46) \quad\quad (1.70) \quad\quad (1.78) \quad\quad (0.69)$$
adj. R-square = .6214 n = 26

Controlling for discipline groupings has changed the sign on GRANT in all three equations from negative to positive. But this relationship is extremely weak. In all three cases the coefficients are not statistically significant, and in all three cases they are relatively very small. Nearly all of the substantial increases in the adjusted r-squares reflect differences among discipline groupings. As expected, the social sciences (SOC) and humanities (HUM) are markedly more liberal and left than are the trades (TRA), the natural biological sciences (NAT), and the natural non-biological sciences. In sum, these results suggest that we can reject the hypothesis that additional government grants lead to more liberal or left-leaning preferences on the part of academics.[24]

POLITICAL SCIENCE AND ECONOMICS COMPARED

Tables 6-1 and 6-2 report a general left-of-center tendency among American academics, but one that we cannot explain on the basis of government funding of research grants. What is true of academics in general appears to apply to political scientists as well: the median political scientist falls to the left of the median member of the electorate. Roettger and Winebrenner, for example, report the results of general population surveys and those of members of the American Political Science Association (APSA), for the years 1959, 1970, 1976, 1980, and 1984. Table 6-3, which repeats their Table 6-1, shows the noticeable difference in self-reported party identification.[25] What is more, they report that 17 percent of the political scientists in 1984 classify themselves as "very liberal," 35 percent as "liberal," 22 percent as "moderate: closer to liberal," six percent as "moderate: strictly moderate," nine percent as "moderate: closer to conservative," three percent as "conservative," none as "very conservative," and seven percent as "other."

Table 6-3
Party Identification of APSA Members and General Electorate*

	APSA				NATIONAL		
	Dem.	Rep.	Ind.	n=	Dem.	Rep.	Ind.
1959	74%	16	8	213	47%	29	19
1970	73	12	13	304	44	24	31
1976	61	6	24	210	43	25	31
1980	61	14	17	221	41	25	34
1984	68	8	21	294	39	35	26

*Source: Walter B. Roettger and Hugh Winebrenner, "Politics and Political Scientists," *Public Opinion* 9 (September/October 1986), p. 41.

But the data reported in the last section also suggest that academics are not of one mind when it comes to their politics. The differences seem especially revealing when we compare political scientists with economists, and in that difference I believe that we can find part of the explanation for many political scientists' left-of-center preferences. Economists tend to give greater deference to market forces than do political scientists. And political scientists find it difficult to imagine a world with less government.

We can explore the degree of this difference by using the same data set that we have previously employed. We create a dummy variable for political science [POL] and one for economics [ECON]. We then redefine the social science dummy variable [SOC] to include only all other social sciences [SOCO]. The three resulting regressions of LEFT, LIB, and LAL on discipline dummy variables are thus:

$$LEFT = 4.50 + 8.50POL + 3.50ECON + 7.02SOCO - 2.32TRA + 4.75HUM - 1.41NAT$$
$$(2.99) \quad (2.32) \quad\quad (0.95) \quad\quad (4.52) \quad\quad (1.47) \quad\quad (2.19) \quad\quad (0.83)$$
$$\text{adj. R-square} = .5863 \quad n = 26$$

$$LIB = 40.80 + 18.20POL + 15.20ECON + 20.74SOCO - 7.90TRA + 5.51HUM - 0.65NAT$$
$$(9.52) \quad (1.74) \quad\quad (1.45) \quad\quad (4.69) \quad\quad (1.75) \quad\quad (0.89) \quad (0.13)$$
$$\text{adj. R-square} = .5219 \quad n = 26$$

$$LAL = 45.30 + 26.70POL + 18.70ECON + 27.76SOCO - 10.29TRA + 10.26HUM - 2.06NAT$$
$$(8.75) \quad (2.11) \quad\quad (1.48) \quad\quad (5.19) \quad\quad (1.88) \quad\quad (1.38) \quad\quad (0.25)$$

None of the coefficients on ECON is statistically significant. But in all cases both economists and political scientists appear to be more left and (20th-century) liberal than are academics from trades and natural sciences. Economists are less likely to declare themselves as "left" than are scholars from the humanities and from other social sciences, while political scientists are more so. Both political scientists and economists seem less "liberal" than do other social scientists but more so than do academics from humanities-based disciplines. Combining liberal and left categories shows economists to be much less and political scientists only a little less likely to fall into one of these two categories than are other social scientists, while both are more likely to do so than are academics in the humanities. Many of these observations, as the regression equations report, rest on less than statistically significant results. And, my impression is that economists have become less liberal and left, and political scientists somewhat more so, since 1972, when Ladd and Lipset collected the underlying data.

This difference in political preferences between political scientists and economists probably grows out of epistemological differences between the two disciplines. To explain these differences, we first return to the physical sciences. These scholars, especially chemists and physicists, have boiled any notion of teleology out of their theories, at least relative to other sciences. For example, no longer does the course of heavenly bodies mirror a divine purpose. True, elementary particles have charges, and other forces are believed to glue together the known universe into coherent matter. But chemists and physicists attribute no apparent intention to these forces.[26]

Social science differs because people, whose actions form the objects of social scientists' analysis, enjoy the (constrained) opportunity to choose their institutions and environments, as well as the allocations that they make within those institutions and environments. Hence, it is not surprising that social scientists often interpret institutions and allocations according to the purposes that they can discern in them, where those purposes are given by the goals that they postulate for the actors relevant to the institution or allocation. Social scientists also interpret the essential fitness of an institution or allocation according to how well it serves the purpose that they discern. Any model of human action that attributes purpose to human beings will accord with this characteristic. Sometimes the purpose suggested is implicit, as in functionalist models of the political process. Elsewhere and more conventionally, it takes an explicit form, as in economic models of market and non-market processes, wherein people are assumed to maximize utility or wealth.

Not surprisingly, therefore, economists tend to applaud the market because of its superior allocative consequences, merely because their theories make economists aware of these consequences. But political scientists tend to applaud the legislature because it appears to be the only, or at least the most efficient, institution for reaching distributive consequences that those who wish to have those consequences would prefer.

The information contained in the institutions, and therefore in an explicit or implicit model of political and economic processes, tends to affect the scientist's judgment of the institution itself. Political scientists, just as legislators, have no way to collect information about the allocative consequences of the institutions that they study. Stated differently, political scientists, just as politicians and voters, suffer from rational ignorance[27] and fiscal illusion,[28] two characteristics of political systems that the literature on rent-seeking has clearly identified.[29] Stated differently, political scientists, unlike economists, have no theory that would enable them to identify the allocative consequences of various public-policy proposals. So their information becomes identical to that of the legislator, who gains electoral plurality by satisfying the members of cohesive, organized interest groups, at the expense of the larger, unorganized, rationally ignorant group of taxpayers. Some political scientists even raise this identity with politicians to a methodology, an art form, which they call *verstehen*.

When political scientists step back from their explanatory mode and enter a normative one, to concentrate on how well political (or economic) institutions and those who occupy them succeed (or fail) in reallocating resources, they judge those institutions, their inhabitants, and the resulting choices according to the only distributional standards that come to mind, namely the equalization of status and material benefits. On this view, at least in theory, politics succeed where the market fails—at least in establishing equal misery.

I suspect that these tendencies among political scientists become self-reinforcing and cumulative. Once the discipline's members establish the central focus of distributive consequences, the normative justification follows. And once that justification is in place, those students attracted to the discipline will tend to reflect their own preconceived preferences for redistribution. I do not know whether this process has reached an equilibrium, though I believe that it has a bit farther to go.

Economic models (and many economists), by contrast, fix on the allocative consequences of institutions, because their theories (but not the information that the objects of their studies enjoy— they only "know" relative prices) allow them to do so. Many economists thus tend to applaud markets and criticize legislative and bureaucratic decision-making.

One thus finds among economists the opposite pattern of preferences and judgments that one finds among political scientists. For example, in their poll of economists, reported in 1979, Kearl, Pope, Whiting, and Wimmer discover a surprising agreement among their respondents on *microeconomic* public-policy issues (but not on *macroeconomic* ones or on answers to certain normative questions).[30] Only three percent of their respondents, for instance, generally disagreed that "tariffs and import quotas reduce general economic activity"; only ten percent, that "a minimum wage increases unemployment among young and unskilled workers"; only two percent, that "a ceiling on rents reduces the quantity and quality of housing available"; and only six percent, that "the ceiling on interest paid on time deposits should be removed."[31] While many economists did favor a greater equality of income distribution, more vigorous anti-trust-law enforcement, and the like, I suspect that such beliefs, too, reflect (especially with respect to antitrust) allocative judgments, though they may be misinformed.

WILL POLITICAL SCIENTISTS ATTEND TO ALLOCATIVE CONSEQUENCES?

The social sciences in recent years have tended to become more like "open economies" and less like "closed" ones. (The simile comparing disciplines with economies seems apt, because governments in open economies face a reduced prospect of imposing entry barriers against better or cheaper goods and services.) Many economists, cognizant of the untoward allocative consequences of existing and proposed public policies, have reflected at length on why the institutions of government have not achieved some fairly obvious, and even welfare-regarding, results. Their curiosity has led them into the traditional reserves of political scientists. Indeed, the same phenomenon has occurred in law, with respect to the law-and-economics movement.[32]

Thus, in an important sense it really does not matter whether political scientists begin to pay attention to the allocative, and not just the distributive, consequences of public policies and institutional arrangements. Economists will do it for them, to the extent that they fail to do it themselves. But today, with respect to both political science and law, scholars in both disciplines, at the margins if not on average, have yielded to the more general theoretical structure of economics. Even though the leftward drift may not have ended in either discipline, what many political scientists and some law professors once regarded as the superior distributional achievements of the political system they now regard as its allocative failures. Examples include the minimum wage, rent control, agency regulation of various markets, much antitrust policy, and a host of explicitly redistributional policies based on in-kind grants.

To close the circle, we note that the National Science Foundation has played some part in this process. By funding work by public-choice scholars in both economics and political science, it has supported research whose conclusions about the political process seem far less sanguine than did those that prevailed in earlier times. Hence, any claim that this form of government funding erodes (or represents an attempt to erode) freedom in general, or intellectual freedom in particular, must attribute the government's putative failure to error, which claim, while eminently reasonable, remains unfalsifiable.

NOTES

1. One of the most persistent regularities found in public opinion polling is that American voters tend to become more Republican and less Democratic in self-assigned party identification as income increases. Gallup reported in June, 1976, for example, that 61 percent of respondents with annual incomes under $3,000 classified themselves as Democrats, but only 16 percent classified themselves as Republicans. Yet, 35 percent with incomes over $20,000 classified themselves as Democrats, while 31 percent of that group classified themselves as Republicans. For a report on these data, see Peter H. Aranson, *American Government: Strategy and Choice* (Boston: Little, Brown, and Co., 1981), p. 193. As we note later, academics deviate from this pattern, at least to the extent that they vote more Democratic than their income levels would predict, although the relationship among academics between income and Democratic party identification may be in the same direction as for the general population. For example, natural scientists are both better paid than are academics in the social sciences and humanities and, as we report later, are more likely to vote Republican than are those in the social sciences and humanities. The underlying assumption of this footnote, of course, is that Democratic party identification tends to correlate with economic redistribution, which we later associate operationally with preferences for positive freedom and against negative, liberal, freedom.

2. Two essays in this volume plainly document the biased nature of government funding of research. E.C. Pasour, Jr., "Source of Funding and Freedom of Inquiry in Agricultural Economics," details the manner in which the Department of Agriculture, as well as parallel state agencies, tend to fund programs that support the interests of farm groups already receiving monies and protection from these agencies. Donald A. Erickson, "Government Funding of the Study of Education," describes a similar, and perhaps more damaging process with respect to education. I do not argue here that government never tries to subvert intellectual integrity or that academics never respond favorably to these attempts. Instead, I simply point out that in both fields the availability of alternative funding sources, not to mention the courage of those academics who maintain their integrity, make it a simple matter to correct these untoward attacks on academic freedom. Pasour and Erickson, then, themselves provide distinguished examples of the appropriate correctives.

3. I recall in this connection a lawsuit in which I participated as an expert witness. The defendant had hired an expert to prepare two reports, based largely on an implicit theoretical structure but with a large set of data and many statistical manipulations. Depositions taken of this expert revealed that he had received approximately $100,000 for his work. The plaintiff retained me to examine these reports, and that examination revealed fatal theoretical flaws in the reports' implicit models, which I described to the court during my testimony. On the basis of that testimony, the judge rejected the other expert's conclusions. I received about $7,500 for my time, and the relative costs in this instance, at least as anecdote, suggest the absence of parity between original research costs and "replication" or "evaluation" costs.

4. I review this case in Peter H. Aranson, *The Political Economy of Science and Technology Policy*, unpublished monograph, 1986. See also Kenneth J. Arrow, *Essays in the Theory of Risk-Bearing* (Chicago: Markham, 1971); and Harvey A. Averch, *A Strategic Analysis of Science and Technology Policy* (Baltimore: Johns Hopkins University Press, 1985).

5. See Peter H. Aranson, *The Political Economy, op. cit.* For reasons that I describe momentarily, the distortions and failures that occur in political attempts to reflect citizens' preferences in public policy do not grow out of a "leviathan" model of an aggrandizing government. Instead, they grow out of attempts by interest groups to secure government funding and favorable regulations at collective cost. In *The Political Economy of Science and Technology Policy*, I argue that government support of research of the sort that a welfare model would contemplate remains at best an epiphenomenon of the political process.

6. Again, as we point out in footnote two, there are two sides to the exchange between government agencies seeking to alter research findings and agendas and academics willing to bend their efforts for the funds placed before them. Hence, research distortions are as much a problem of the academic disciplines—perhaps more so—than they are a problem of a corrupting government influence.

7. See generally Peter H. Aranson and Peter C. Ordeshook, "Public Interest, Private Interest, and the Democratic Polity," in Roger Benjamin and Stephen L. Elkin, eds., *The Democratic State* (Lawrence, Kansas: University Press of Kansas, 1985), chapter 4; and James M. Buchanan, Robert D. Tollison, and Gordon Tullock, eds., *The Theory of the Rent-Seeking Society* (College Station, Texas: Texas A&M University Press, 1980).

8. Peter H. Aranson, *The Political Economy, op. cit.*

9. Linda R. Cohen and Roger G. Noll, "Government R&D Programs

for Commercializing Space," *American Economic Review: Papers and Proceedings* 76, May, 1986, pp. 269-273.

10. Don K. Price, *The Scientific Estate* (Cambridge, Massachusetts: Harvard University Press, 1965), p. 75.

11. The reader should not confuse these observations with later considerations by regulatory agencies to stop experiments using the Jarvik-7. These experiments were privately funded by Humana Corporation, and therefore I find no reason for the government to get involved in these research decisions.

12. Bruno Leoni, *Freedom and the Law* (Los Angeles: Nash Publishers, 1972), p. 90. See also Friedrich A. Hayek, *The Constitution of Liberty* (Chicago: Regnery, 1972). The distinction between positive and negative freedom has not gone unchallenged, especially by neoclassical economists who have not begun to grasp the nature of the calculation problem under conditions of change and unanticipated developments, or who have willfully ignored it. See, e.g., George J. Stigler, "Wealth, and Possibly Liberty," *Journal of Legal Studies* 7, June, 1978, pp. 213-217. I take up these issues in Peter H. Aranson, "Bruno Leoni in Retrospect," *Harvard Journal of Law and Public Policy* 11, Summer, 1988, pp. 662–711.

13. See *supra* note 4.

14. I have not included in this operationalization any measures of preferences for national defense spending. Conservatives may prefer more of it and libertarians, less. The connection between defense spending and freedom, while clear to some, is not patent to me.

15. There seems to be little problem with using such a measure as a surrogate for political expansion in economic areas, as the Democratic party, at least since the years of Franklin D. Roosevelt, consistently has pressed for more regulation of the economy, higher taxes, and higher levels of government spending than has the Republican party. The principal difficulty with this surrogate is in the area of social control. A greater percentage of Democrats than Republicans would restrict negative liberty with respect to such issues as racial quotas, the exercise of gender preferences in hiring, and in related matters. But with the rise of religious fundamentalism in this decade, we find an increasing proportion of Republicans preferring to restrict personal choice in literature, arts, personal consumption, and sexual practices. Nevertheless, the data reported here only go through the 1972 presidential election. The one policy about this issue-confusion that seems problematic is that of preferences concerning legalizing marijuana. In a survey whose details I report in the text momentarily, data were collected and aggregated for 26 academic disciplines. I regressed discipline-by-discipline preferences for legalizing marijuana [MAJ] against the same aggregated

votes for Hubert H. Humphrey in the 1968 presidential election [HHH] and against self-assignment to the categories of liberal and left [LAL]. The results are thus:

$$MAJ = -19.56 + 0.98HHH$$
$$(2.87) \quad (9.07)$$
adj. R-square = .7646 n = 26
$$MAJ = -6.70 + 0.91LAL$$
$$(92.11) \quad (15.69)$$
adj. R-square = .9075 n = 26

Therefore, it appears that at least in the late 1960s and early 1970s, members of the relative left in academe were more favorably disposed toward personal freedom in social matters than were members of the relative right. I am not certain that this tendency persists today, inasmuch as the members of the relative left seem more intent on banning smoking and sexist language than are members of the relative right.

16. Everett Carll Ladd and Seymour Martin Lipset, *The Divided Academy: Professors and Politics* (New York: McGraw-Hill, 1975), pp. 29-31.
17. Everett Carll Ladd and Seymour Martin Lipset, *Academics, Politics, and the 1972 Election* (Washington, D.C.: American Enterprise Institute, 1973), p. 16.
18. See, for example, Joseph Epstein, "A Case of Academic Freedom," *Commentary* 82, September, 1986, pp. 37-47.
19. Henry G. Manne, "The Political Economy of Modern Universities," in Henry G. Manne, ed., *The Economics of Legal Relationships: Readings in the Theory of Property Rights* (St. Paul, Minnesota: West, 1975), pp. 614-630.
20. As quoted in Kenneth Adelman, "The Road to Animal Farm," *Wall Street Journal*, December 30, 1986, p. 14.
21. National Science Foundation, *Annual Report 1985* (Washington, D.C.: GPO, 1985), p. 49.
22. The data are reported in Everett Carll Ladd and Seymour Martin Lipset, *The Divided Academy, op. cit.*, pp. 342-369.
23. The disciplines reported are: anthropology, economics, political science, clinical psychology, experimental psychology, social psychology, sociology, law, English, history, philosophy, fine arts, education, mathematics, chemistry, physics, bacteriology, biochemistry, botany and zoology, physiology, medicine, civil engineering, electrical engineering, mechanical engineering, business, and agriculture.

The division of larger disciplines into smaller parts (psychology and biology, for example) may not seem appropriate. But it helps to overcome the larger problems of small sample size (26) and aggregation leading to the possibility of ecological fallacy. Based on my own knowledge of the academy, on the results that I have obtained with these data, and on my own intuition, I do not believe that using aggregated data seriously undermines the essential conclusions that it allows me to reach, though it doubtless raises the adjusted r-squares in each equation.

24. We are left with the problem of explaining the small and insignificant positive sign on GRANT in these three equations. I have no ready explanation, but Ladd and Lipset, in *The Divided Academy*, do discern a tendency for "elite" schools, which do receive a disproportionate amount of federally-funded research support (See John W. Sommer, "Distributional Character and Consequences of the Public Funding of Science," this volume), to have more left-of-center preferences among their faculties. The small positive coefficients, then, might be an artifact of this association.

25. Walter B. Roettger and Hugh Winebrenner, "Politics and Political Scientists," *Public Opinion* 9, September/October 1986, p. 41.

26. Don K. Price, *op. cit.*

27. See Anthony Downs, *An Economic Theory of Democracy* (New York: Harper, 1957).

28. See Charles J. Goetz, "Fiscal Illusion in State-Local Finance," in Thomas E. Borcherding, ed., *Budgets and Bureaucrats: The Sources of Government Growth* (Durham, North Carolina: Duke University Press, 1977), pp. 176-187; and Richard E. Wagner, "Revenue Structure, Fiscal Illusion, and Budgetary Choice," *Public Choice* 25, Spring, 1976, pp. 45-61.

29. Peter H. Aranson and Peter C. Ordeshook, "Public Interest," *op.cit.*

30. J.R. Kearl, Clayne L. Pope, Gordon C. Whiting, and Larry T. Wimmer, "A Confusion of Economists," *American Economic Review: Papers and Proceedings* 69, May, 1979, pp. 28-37.

31. *Ibid.*, p. 30.

32. Peter H. Aranson, "Economic Explorers on Continents without Property Rights: Economics in Political Science and Law," Paper prepared for the annual meeting of the American Economic Association (Association for Social Economics Section Meeting), New York, New York, December, 1985.

SEVEN

DISTRIBUTIONAL CHARACTER AND CONSEQUENCES OF THE PUBLIC FUNDING OF SCIENCE

John W. Sommer

During the second Reagan Administration science policy reemerged on the agenda of national debate with a force that seems to erupt every 20 years. As a new president takes office Congress will continue to engage in discussion about the health of science, its contribution to the well-being of Americans, and the role of the federal government in its support. It will conduct this discussion in "national" terms but the Members will be attentive to the consequences for their districts. In the late 1940s and again in the mid-1960s Americans experienced other probing discussions which resulted in significant increases in the involvement of the federal government in the support and the conduct of science. The 1940s debate led to the creation of the National Science Foundation (NSF), a new federal agency charged specifically with minding the business of science to insure its health. The 1960s review resulted in stipulation by Congress that science must be more attentive to the application of scientific research to "national needs." In the 1980s the theme is science in support of American competitiveness in international markets. In each of these debates issues relating to the equitable distribution of funds for science were important.

During the 99th Congress the House Committee on Science and Technology raised a number of difficult questions and sought advice through the hearings process to help the Committee craft a science and technology policy responsive to the current conditions. The House Committee on Science and Technology study document "An Agenda for a Study of Government Science Policy" should be read to gain insight into the scope and quality of questions asked by the Congress of the United States.[1] In raising so many questions of a specific nature it is inevitable that some meta-questions would emerge. Prominent among these questions are: What is the federal government doing in the science and technology business? In what direction does this involvement appear to lead? What are the distributional consequences of these actions? More provocatively, what does this mean for intellectual freedom in our institutions of higher education? Some remarks by central actors in the science policy process during 1984–1988 help set the context for the chief focus of this paper, the distributional characteristics and consequences of federal funding of science. We are well reminded by the contribution of Liggio and Meiners to this volume that these questions have historical roots which extend to the early days of the Republic.

THE CONTEMPORARY POLITICAL CONTEXT

On March 14, 1985, Dr. Lewis Branscomb, then an IBM executive, soon to become head of Harvard's Science and Technology Program, testified before Congress that "a national science and technology policy must be grounded on economic policy that provides the climate within which science can serve the public effectively."[2] Dr. Branscomb then proceeded to call for "greater coordination" of university and private sector research through federal science policy.

A week later Dr. Roland Schmitt, chairman of the National Science Board, the governing body of the National Science Foundation, charged a committee of its members to review science policy because "the National Science Board must have a vision of the future of US science and engineering—of the challenges before it, and of the means for meeting them."[3] Coordination was again emphasized.

A week after that, on April 4, Mr. Erich Bloch, director of the National Science Foundation, remarked to a gathering of the American Association for the Advancement of Science (AAAS) that in order to meet the challenge of foreign competitors and to keep our economy strong, "industry, state and local governments and the universities themselves must cooperate with each other and with the federal government to increase support for research, modernize the infrastructure and help set new directions and priorities."[4]

In the April 6, 1984 issue of *Science* the following remarks by Dr. George Keyworth III, then science advisor to the President and director of the Office of Science and Technology Policy appeared: "From its early days, the [Reagan] Administration had repeatedly stated its intention to develop and implement a new science and technology policy, one developed not so much in response to the needs of the science community as in response to the broader needs of the nation."[5] This policy was declared to be a renewed, and strengthened commitment of federal support for basic research, "Not only [because] basic research [is] an essential investment in the nation's long-term welfare, but it is largely a federal responsibility because its benefits are so broadly distributed..." and because "basic research is a vital underpinning for our national well-being."[6]

These sentiments were echoed and amplified two years later in the May 2, 1986, lead article in *Science*, in which Mr. Bloch specifically urged that federal science policy should be aimed at "putting mechanisms in place to serve the goal of economic competitiveness."[7] He proposed this be done by "cooperation" rather than coordination, but the distinction between these terms is unclear from the text. There is no question that centripetal enthusiasm prevails.

By contrast, in the April 24, 1985, issue of the *Chronicle of Higher Education* it was reported that "the Government of China [People's Republic] has approved major reforms in the country's research-and-development system to make scientific institutions more market-oriented."[8] Quoting Song Jian, who heads the Chinese Academy of Sciences: "the goals of the policy will be to enable research institutes to become well off without any government subsidy."[9] This to be done by reducing or removing outright central coordination. Could there be wisdom in the East?

In this, the bicentennial of the drafting of Article I, Section 8 of the US Constitution, which states that "The Congress shall have Power...to promote the Progress of Science and the useful Arts, by securing for limited Times to Authors and Inventors the exclusive Right to their respective Writings and Discoveries," it is time to call into question the unified pronouncements of the White House, the Science funding bureaucracy, the scientists' lobbying organizations, and many in Congress concerning the need for greater government involvement in, and coordination of, science. Is massive federal support of science, on the order of a $6 billion supercollider, or the creation of a cabinet-level Department of Science and Technology warranted? To what ends are such reorganization and allocation aimed, and what bearing do these have for welfare improvement? Does not being Number One in World Science, the commonly uttered justification for increases, raise more questions than it answers? Is there any evidence that this federal infusion will promote the "progress of science," or is the concept of "progress," or "health," and its assorted "measures," merely a convenient vehicle chosen for purposes of public policy? Even members of Congress who are truly concerned with abstract ideas of scientific "progress" for national well-being must also be concerned with tangible local investment of general science funds. How can science, with its putative public goods characteristics, be promoted in some places rather than others such that we are assured that net welfare gains, as distinct from regional transfer payments, will occur? What are the distributional characteristics and consequences of federal funding of scientific research? This paper cannot address all of these questions, but it does present information and ideas to augment our ability to frame answers. This paper, read as an ensemble with the excellent contribution of Aranson to this book, takes on added meaning and improves our comprehension of the interaction between scientists and the state.

If there is any evidence to confute the reasons to fund science and technology with public resources it has surely been disregarded by the high priests of the American science establishment, as were Milton Friedman's remarks to the same effect in 1980.[10] Since 1985, the House Committee chambers have rung with testimony to increase funding for science, to give generous support for research, to encourage the "production" of scientists and engineers to meet future unspecified, but "dead certain" manpower needs, to coordinate scientific activity, and to guide science out of its chaotic state for its own good, and for the good of the country.

Nothing short of a national commitment has been touted as necessary to ward off foreign devils and to sustain American leadership in some kind of ill-defined, and, in the view of a large proportion of practicing scientists, probably spurious, international scientific competition to be Number One.[11] "Partnership," public "leveraging" of private funds for Big Science, such as the superconducting super collider, federally sponsored cooperative arrangements between universities and industries, and targeted, high-impact projects like the federally-bankrolled space station all have the effect of increasing the government role in the progressive shaping of knowledge. These initiatives also, not incidentally, provide the mechanisms for regional redistribution (congressional district or state), a function organic to a territorial democracy.

The direction of policy is toward control. The conduct of science, to quote Lewis Thomas is fundamentally "wild."[12] The means of control may be different in a territorial democracy, such as the United States, than it is in other countries, but public expenditure demands accountability through the political system. Science and technology (S&T), while uttered almost as one word, "essentee," are differentially sensitive to policy, and the implications of this difference are profound. Basic scientific research is funded on the premise that the market will under-supply it despite Article I, Section 8 cited previously, and much of this funding is directed at institutions of higher education. But what is really desired by the chief actors in the political process is tangible technology, which is partially dependent upon scientific advance and usually developed in the laboratories and ateliers of private firms where public funding is not as easily justified. This divergence of ends and means promotes stress in the relationship between scientists and the federal establishment. The amount and direction of funding is telling and is described in detail later.

SCIENCE AND POLICY: THE ENDLESS TENSION

There exists an "endless tension" between science and policy and this tension is fundamental and unavoidable. It produces a conundrum not yet resolved. Science is a self-correcting method of apprehending the world around us, which has, at the heart of its practice the humble admission that what has been discovered is only tentative and subject to revision upon adduction of better evidence. Furthermore, it is the scientist's responsibility to be forthright about the weakest part of his or her analysis so that successive scientists do not have to waste time overcoming a muddle. Science, in this sense, expands our ability to ask *questions*, and to provide provisional description of the world *ex post* investigation.

The *art* of politics, and the artisanal construction of policy ill comport with science because a premium in this domain of thought is placed on *answers*, therefore the scientific ethic of conditionality is anathema to policy. No one gets elected on the promises of more and better questions in the future, nor on the premise of continuing uncertainty!

Increasingly, those who have tried to justify the public funding for science in a cost-benefit framework *ex ante* have run up against the canonical inability of the scientist to promise a certain result of research not yet conducted. Unfortunately, in the situation where politicians must be prepared to answer to constituents on what they have done with public resources they are pressed to show local benefits, and, by extension, to seek guarantees of results for the money given. This is obviously true with applied or mission research and development, as Piel has noted, but it is also the case with basic research.[13] Guarantees of predetermined results are contrary to the conduct of scientific inquiry. Funding agencies such as NSF and the National Institute of Health (NIH) must also be responsive both to congressional concerns and to an increasingly dependent group of universities. This awareness by the agencies is an incubator for the multiplication of justification for the value of science and for the germination of bureaucratic control of scientific research. The university-based scientific research cadre is more and more linked to federal monies, to the point that some regard their support as an entitlement, and others, whose positions are predicated on federal "soft money" are responsive to the "needs" of the funding bureaucracy.

This dependency promotes pathological fear of loss of funding that effects the conduct of inquiry, such as premature release of results, and sometimes publication of pure fiction. These are not consequences unique to publicly funded research, neither can they be disassociated. That so many scientists perjure themselves by submitting proposals to do research they have already completed only serves to illustrate the perversity of the relationship of science and policy. But this practice may be regarded as convenient by officers of public granting agencies who do not lust after surprises and who do not want the responsibility of drawing negative criticism from Congress, such as Senator Proxmire's "Golden Fleece Award," for an ill-fated project they have supported.

Congress avoids the science/policy conundrum by ignoring "science" in the sense of a process for apprehending the world, in favor of "Science" as an existent, that is, an establishment of groups and physical facilities, which, it is supposed, if properly maintained, will deliver valued products. Some raise the definition of science to that of an "enterprise," spelling it with a capital "S" implying an organism composed of systemic sets of interdependencies working toward a common end. Structure is substituted for substance. The attractive feature of this conception of science for the Member of Congress is that even if the process does not yield "reportable" results in terms of discovery, "success" is guaranteed by virtue of having brought tangible resources such as buildings and equipment into one's district. Beyond these inputs what the political side wants is technology—which is only a partial product of science; innovation and entrepreneurship are what animate the technological arts to transform scientific discoveries into items for consumption.

From the science bureaucrat's point of view this definition of "Science" is also attractive because it involves "quantities" (of inputs) which provide more visible benchmarks of administrative action than do qualitative assessments of outputs. Failure to understand this fundamental epistemic difference dooms the conduct of scientific inquiry to poor policy prescriptions and comprehension of the science policy process to permanent occlusion.

DISTRIBUTORS AND DISTRIBUTIONS

To place this analysis into perspective the main distributors and distributions must be identified. There is only one big distributor of federal funds for research and development and that is the Department of Defense (DOD). The DOD share of the total budget for research and development (R&D) has steadily risen until in fiscal year 1987 it represented three-fourths of the total requested, up from half in fiscal year 1977.[14] As this figure has mounted however, DOD has lagged in its support for basic research, such that it allocated less than one billion of 45 billion to that purpose in 1987. This, however, represents 11 percent of all federal funds to be spent on basic research.

Basic research in the 1987 budget accounts for $8.6 billion out of a federal "science budget" of $61.5 billion.[15] The rest is spent on applied research or development. The relative proportions of the three budget items have changed little over time. In 1972, 11.3 percent of the total R&D budget was allocated to non-defense related basic research and 14 percent in 1984.[16] Development funds have increased slightly and funds for applied research have decreased slightly. That said, there has been an increasing demand for specific and accountable results for the investment of public funds, even for basic research, traditionally the least controlled sector of scientific inquiry. The Hon. Don Fuqua, departing chairman of the Committee on Science and Technology of the House of Representatives, remarked in his final report to Congress:

> The most basic purpose of scientific research is to solve the unanswered question about ourselves and our universe, always to add to the existing body of knowledge. However, the Federal Government's role in supporting a major portion of the nation's basic research is in the belief that over time this research will serve as a well-spring for diverse application to advance the nation's technological innovation and thus improve our ability to compete in world trade and to stimulate our economic growth.[17]

and,

> Because their research efforts are vital to the national interest universities need not be obsequious in their gratitude for federal support. On the other hand, it needs more recognition that federal support of university activities is neither a God-given nor a constitutional right. A university doing federally-supported research is not granting a unilateral favor to the government. No megauniversity would be anything like it is if it were not for federal support.[18]

These remarks are suggestive of the sentiment of Congress concerning support for universities, where two-thirds of the federal basic research budget is spent. If federally-funded research and development centers are excluded, most of which are administered by universities, the proportion is closer to one half. One-quarter of the basic research budget supports federal laboratories, and the remainder, less than a 10th, goes to private industry.

These federal imbursements represent about two-thirds of the universities' basic research budget, one fourth comes from the university budgets, and the remaining one-tenth divided between industry and foundations. The point is that there is a strong interdependency between the federal government and the universities relative to basic research. That basic research is only a small part of the total federal expenditure for research and development does not diminish its importance for universities nor its potential to affect the conduct of inquiry and the course of science education.

To close the circle, of the remaining roughly 30 percent federal R&D funds not in the DOD budget, the Department of Energy, National Institutes of Health, NASA, US Department of Agriculture (USDA), and the National Science Foundation account for the bulk of the distribution. NSF, for example, accounts for only about 2 percent of federal R&D expenditures but nearly 20 percent of the budget for basic research at universities. NIH provides nearly half of all funds for basic research, and DOD, DOE and the USDA account for the rest. Finally, it is notable that R&D represents a little over 6 percent of the total United States budget, and basic research less than 1 percent.

CONGRESS AND "UNDUE CONCENTRATION"

Congress has been attentive to the distributional outcomes of science funding, indeed, the debates which preceded the establishment of the National Science Foundation were vigorous on this issue.[19] Early versions of some of the legislation drafted to create the National Science Foundation included formulas for determining the appropriate geographic distribution. Some bills allowed from one-half to three-quarters of the agency's funds to be distributed on merit and the rest by geographical formula. Subsequent congressional debates about science funding have focused on geographical distribution sufficient to describe this as a perennial issue for the NSF.[20]

At the root of this issue were different visions of federal funding of science. One vision, typified by Senator Kilgore in 1945, was the cultivation of research capability across the United States by distributing funds widely.[21] A competing vision was advanced by Senator Smith of New Jersey, who sought concentration of funding among excellent research scientists and at recognized research centers. Vannevar Bush, architect of the National Science Foundation, saw the issue in Smith's terms and sought to deflect the arguments of land grant and state university presidents who were urging wealth spreading by formula funding.[22] On one side are those who urge the increase in access by all Americans to science, on the premise that everyone should have a "fair" opportunity to participate; and on the other are those who see science as a national enterprise whose output should be maximized by concentrating resources on the best people, in the best research settings, as determined by peer review of basic research proposals. This difference in goals remains a source of tension today. Remarks by Senator Russell Long of Louisiana during an Appropriations Committee hearing June 26, 1986, as reported in *Science* are an echo of earlier congressional doubts about the allocation process for science:

> At this point [in the hearing], Senator Russell Long (D-LA) appeared puzzled. "I am sort of in the dark in this matter," he said. "When did we agree that the peers would cut the melon or decide who would get the money?" When Danforth pointed out that Congress included language in the 1984 Deficit Reduction Act to the effect that government grants should be awarded competitively and that peer review constitutes an appropriate procedure for basic research, Long said, "Am I to understand that...Congress said we are not going to have any say about who gets this money: are we going to have some peers decide who gets this money?" He seemed incredulous.[23]

In the 1960s Congress made its concerns clear when Rep. George Miller of California introduced legislation in 1966 to create a national program of institutional grants, one-third of which would be distributed among states proportional to the number of high school graduates in the preceding year relative to the total number of high school graduates in the United States.[24] It did not pass. In 1975 Sen. Stuart Symington demanded a science sub-committee insert strong language emphasizing the need for wider geographical distribution and avoidance of undue concentration, but, according to Hechler, NSF did little to respond to the intent of Congress.[25] In 1977 Congressman Flowers is reported to have said: "This is the annual exercise in futility that I go through with NSF.... It will be easier to defend these grants if maybe one or two of them went to your district."[26] The essence of Flower's remarks is the perfume of politics.

The National Science Foundation Act of 1950 mandates that,

> In exercising the authority and discharging the function [of the Foundation] it shall be an objective of the Foundation to strengthen research and education in the sciences, including independent research by individuals, throughout the United States, and to avoid undue concentration of such research and education.[27]

The phrase "undue concentration," current during the debates at the inception of NSF, is not statutorily defined, making it particularly subject to politically motivated interpretation. In late 1986 the General Accounting Office circulated a draft of a report on patterns of distribution of federal research funds to universities and colleges requested by Sen. Mark O. Hatfield, in which a variety of measures were employed.[28] "Concentration" depends greatly upon the variables chosen to measure it, some of which are: the level of federal support of academic science and engineering in states, regions, congressional districts, or universities, measured in terms of total federal R&D funds, NSF academic award, number of awards, or other such variables. They can be viewed in terms of shares for the territorial unit, related to population, level of economic activity, or by proxies for research capacity. Different analytical objectives result in different deployment of measures. For the following section of this paper on the distributors of federal funds for academic science, and the distributees, or recipients, the techniques chosen are simple and descriptive; the data are largely those collected by the National Science Foundation.

DISTRIBUTEE AND DEPENDENCY

Distributees come in many forms as has been noted: states, congressional districts, universities, and disciplines to identify four. Each form of distributee touches political sensitivities differently. Disciplinary distributees evoke the least overt political concern because the impact of changes in funding level is diffuse relative to almost any jurisdictional or institutional entity. There exist obvious notable exceptions which occur from time to time; for example, groupings of related fields such as "space science" may gain significant attention following an event like the Challenger catastrophe. Effective pressure groups emerge, such as Council of Social Science Associations (COSSA), which seeks to advance the interests of a consortium of social science disciplines. Universities, by contrast, are entities with locational attributes and vocal adherents; they also have various lobbying organizations to help them make their case in the political arena. In fact, differentiation within the academic community has produced conflicting lobbying among more specialized interests such as liberal arts colleges *versus* major research universities.[29]

States and congressional districts embody explicit constituencies and the subject of "geographical distribution," so elemental to "pork barrel" public works projects, is manifest in the public funding of science as well. This concern often surfaces in questions of support for specific universities but it is generalized from time to time to considerations of states and regions.[30] Rarely does the public debate turn on the specific congressional district as a distributee, which is not to say that this unit is without consideration; it just requires interpretation of the terms of congresspersons' arguments!

University Distributees:

Patterns of distribution of research funds from federal sources to universities have remained highly stable over the past two decades. The early establishment of strong support in the better universities in the United States evidently has confirmed their place as major research universities. In this sense the strategy of Sen. Smith seems to have won out: since 1967 the "top 100" universities, that is, the list of those 100 universities which receive the most federal funding, has been relatively stable. Only 19 new institutions have replaced universities that were on the list in 1967. Former Congressman Don Fuqua has characterized this stability as a university system that has reached "maturity," from which one should expect little change.[31] Figure 7-1 displays the rank order of research universities in terms of federal R&D funding for 1985. Figure 7-2 shows the "mobility" of NSF-funded universities within the top 100 since 1969, and the obvious decline of new entries over time seems to bear out Fuqua's observation.

Figure 7-1
Federal Obligations to the 100 Universities and Colleges Receiving
The Largest Amounts: FY 1987[1] (Dollars in Thousands)

Institution	Total All Activities	Research & Dev.	R&D Rank
Total, All Institutions	13,466,552	7,240,090	
Johns Hopkins University	528,442	374,656	1
Stanford University	225,369	201,049	2
Mass. Inst. of Technology	209,520	187,623	3
University of Washington	202,073	164,891	4
Univ. of Cal., Los Angeles	174,488	147,795	6
Cornell University	169,259	128,695	11
Univ. of Cal., San Diego	167,637	151,768	5
Howard University	166,784	9,173	—
University of Michigan	162,625	134,977	7
University of Minnesota	160,994	119,746	14
Total 1st 10 Institutions	2,167,191	1,620,373	
Univ. of Wis., Madison	160,121	134,021	8
Columbia Univ., Main Div.	157,970	130,724	10
Yale University	152,379	132,909	9
Harvard University	152,077	123,301	13
Univ. of Cal., San Francisco	144,658	124,811	12
Univ. of Ill., Urbana	138,686	96,761	17
Pennsylvania State Univ.	132,135	94,615	19
Univ. of Pennsylvania	130,570	109,338	15
Univ. of Cal., Berkeley	122,112	96,748	18
Univ. of Southern Cal	120,928	104,395	16
Total 1st 20 Institutions	3,578,827	2,768,046	
University of Colorado	109,561	87,623	21
Washington University	102,795	89,055	20
Duke University	98,594	84,622	23
University of Rochester	96,567	85,674	22
Ohio State University	95,453	64,573	31
University of Chicago	95,144	82,769	24
Univ. of N.C., Chapel Hill	92,141	81,473	25
New York University	91,528	75,966	27
University of Pittsburgh	89,070	72,236	28
University of Arizona	87,546	64,491	32
Total 1st 30 Institutions	4,537,226	3,556,528	

Figure 7-1 (continued)
Federal Obligations To The 100 Universities And Colleges Receiving
The Largest Amounts: FY 1987[1] (Dollars In Thousands)

Institution	Total All Activities	Research & Dev.	R&D Rank
Univ. of Texas at Austin	81,014	76,495	26
Inter. Am. Univ. PR, San German	80,102	58	—
University of Iowa	79,871	63,479	33
University of Massachusetts	77,837	57,913	35
Michigan State University	76,270	48,897	47
Carnegie-Mellon Univ.	75,967	69,454	29
Indiana University	75,887	50,005	45
University of Florida	75,850	52,888	43
Univ. of Ala., Birmingham	75,304	62,240	34
University of Utah	71,609	56,590	38
Total 1st 40 Institutions	**5,306,937**	**4,094,547**	
Yeshiva University	71,603	65,028	30
Purdue University	71,346	46,332	50
Georgia Institute of Tech	68,747	45,187	52
Boston University	67,030	53,331	41
Case Western Reserve Univ.	65,418	56,774	37
University of Miami	65,227	49,547	46
Northwestern University	64,774	53,061	42
Louisiana State Univ.	63,203	36,581	61
Texas A & M University	62,408	38,642	58
Univ. of Md., College Park	62,327	48,728	48
Total 1st 50 Institutions	**5,969,020**	**4,587,758**	
Vanderbilt University	62,124	54,653	40
Univ. of Cal., Davis	61,667	50,289	44
California Inst. of Technology	60,845	57,122	36
Baylor College of Medicine	59,609	56,255	39
University of Virginia	55,644	44,732	53
Gallaudet College	55,184	1,050	—
University of Cincinnati	53,938	34,488	65
Oregon State University	53,775	40,059	55
Emory University	53,698	47,294	49
U P R - Regional Col. Admin.	53,687	0	—
Total 1st 60 Institutions	**6,539,191**	**4,973,700**	

Figure 7-1 (continued)
Federal Obligations to the 100 Universities and Colleges Receiving
The Largest Amounts: FY 1987[1] (Dollars in Thousands)

Institution	Total All Activities	Research & Dev.	R&D Rank
University of Oregon Main	52,123	16,560	—
Univ. Tex., Hlth. Sci. Ctr. Dallas	51,827	45,994	51
Princeton University	51,224	44,286	54
University of Kentucky	49,237	23,906	85
University of Georgia	49,184	33,489	66
University of Connecticut	49,089	38,806	57
Univ. of California, Irvine	48,863	39,384	56
N.C. State Univ., Raleigh	48,129	30,195	70
Iowa St. U. of Science & Tech.	46,046	17,459	—
Univ. of Ill., Chicago	45,772	32,490	67
Total 1st 70 Institutions	**7,030,685**	**5,296,269**	
New Mexico State University	45,567	25,072	83
Colorado State University	44,153	31,492	68
Univ. of South Carolina	44,118	11,741	—
Rutgers, the St. Univ. of NJ	43, 597	25,730	79
University of New Mexico	43,426	25,158	82
Tufts University	43,122	36,241	62
SUNY at Stony Brook	42,514	38,014	59
Univ. of Missouri, Columbia	41,993	22,035	89
Virginia Commonwealth Univ.	41,172	31,477	69
Univ. of Hawaii, Manoa	39,899	29,154	71
Total 1st 80 Institutions	**7,460,246**	**5,572,383**	
Rochester Inst. Technology	39,567	2,485	—
Brown University	39,327	27,710	74
Rockefeller University	38,888	37,051	60
CUNY Mt. Sinai Sch. of Med.	38,437	34,851	63
Puerto Rico Jr. Col.	38,182	0	—
Utah State University	37,849	25,170	81
VA Polytech. Inst. & St. Univ.	37,204	23,588	87
Univ. Tenn., Knoxville	37,019	18,517	98
Temple University	36,762	21,361	91
SUNY at Buffalo	36,235	27,255	76
Total 1st 90 Institutions	**7,839,716**	**5,790,371**	

Figure 7-1 (continued)
Federal Obligations to the 100 Universities and Colleges Receiving
The Largest Amounts: FY 1987[1] (Dollars in Thousands)

Institution	Total All Activities	Research & Dev.	R&D Rank
Woods Hole Ocngrphic Inst.	35,620	34,711	64
University of Kansas	35,200	22,988	88
Univ. of Cal., Santa Barbara	34,253	27,322	75
Georgetown University	33,939	20,046	—
Univ. of MD, Balt. Prof. Sch.	33,575	28,278	72
Univ of VT & St Agric Col.	33,229	23,922	84
Oklahoma State University	33,188	11,383	—
Arizona State University	33,164	14,201	—
Florida State University	32,902	25,680	—
University of Nebraska-Lincoln	31,901	15,126	—
Total List 100 Institutions	**8,176,687**	**6,014,028**	

Source: National Science Foundation, NSF 88-330.
1. Detailed explanation of this table may be found in "Technical Notes, Scope of Survey" in the Source.

Adding to the importance of institutional concentration is the actual magnitude of the distribution of the "top 100" no matter which institutions are on the list. More than four-fifths of all federal obligations for research and development at universities and colleges are received by this benighted set of institutions. Figure 7-1 shows rank of institution and amount received, cumulative by decile for fiscal year 1987; note that the top 50 institutions account for two-thirds of all such funds. The NSF sometimes cites the stability of the distributional outcome over time as an example of the inexorable working out of its mission to support excellence based on intrinsic merit of proposals. Such an argument lacks plausibility in the face of the similarity of the composite distribution of funds by all other federal agencies which do not state that excellence is an overriding goal. Alternatively, what value is the concept of excellence if it accounts for the overwhelming part of the distribution? Common sense suggests that "excellence" is a convenient label for maintaining a set of client universities, most of which, given unduly concentrated funding over the years, are more likely to

Figure 7-2
Mobility Among NSF R&D Funding Recipients

	1969 OUT	1973 IN	1973 OUT	1977 IN
Top 5	Cornell	MIT	Berkeley	Cornell
	U Chicago	Columbia		
Top 10	U Wis-Madison	U Washington	Harvard U	Michigan
	U Pittsburgh	U Ill-Urbana	U Chicago	U Wis.-Madison
Top 20	NYU	UCLA	Colorado St	Indiana U
	U Southern Cal	Woods Hole	U Miami	U Md-College Park
	Yale	Colorado State	Princeton	Oregon State
	U Arizona	Purdue		
	U Pittsburgh	U Miami		
Top 50	U Georgia	SUNY-	U Florida	U Rhode Island
	U Cal-Santa	Stony Brook	U Pittsburgh	U Virginia
	Barbara	U Mass-Amherst	U Rochester	Florida State
	U Notre Dame	U Cal-Davis		
	U Virginia	Carnegie Mellon		
Top 100	Polytech Inst.	Utah State	Ill Inst Tech	U Nebraska
	of Brooklyn	Brandeis	U Missouri-Rolla	U Cal-Riverside
	Kansas State	Va Polytech	Dartmouth	Arizona State
	U California-	Georgia Tech	Drexel U	U South Carolina
	Santa Cruz	U Mo-Rolla	Desert Res Inst	Wayne State
	U Nebraska-	U Illinois-	U Wyoming	CUNY-City College
	Lincoln	Chicago Circle	Stevens Inst	U Maine-Orone
	Arizona State	U Wyoming	Tech	U Cal-Santa Cruz
	Tulane	U Houston	NM Institute	U Kentucky
	U Cal-Riverside	U Delaware	Mining	U New Hampshire
	U S. Carolina	Desert Res Inst	U New Mexico	
	Clarkson Col	U Wyoming	Northeastern	
	Tech	U Oklahoma	Yeshiva U	
	Catholic U	Stevens Inst Tech		
	Wayne State	NM Institute		
	Georgetown U	Mining		
	U Kentucky	Northeastern U		
	SD School	U Texas-Dallas		
	of Mines	Boston U		
	U Wisconsin-	U California-		
	Central System	San Francisco		

harbor high quality research facilities and researchers, and to have schooled an influential alumni. The price paid for their installation as an academic elite is the development of a high

Figure 7-2 (continued)
Mobility Among NSF R&D Funding Recipients

1977 OUT	1980 IN	1980 OUT	1983 IN	
Columbia	U Ill-Urbana	Stanford	Columbia	*Top 5*
U Michigan	Woods Hole			*Top 10*
U Maryland- College Park	U Minnesota Yale	Yale Purdue	Michigan State Princeton	*Top 20*

Florida State
Case Western
U Virginia
Washington U
Duke
U Alaska-
  all Insts
	U Alaska-
	  Fairbanks
	U Cal-Santa
	  Barbara
	U Utah
	U Rochester
	U Pittsburgh
	U Florida
		U Cal-Davis
		NYU
		U Alaska-
		  Fairbanks
			Duke
			Case Western
			U Georgia
				Top 50

Utah State
U Oklahoma
U Texas-Dallas
U Denver
U Kentucky
U Alaska-
  all Insts
Oklahoma State
	U Alaska-
	  Fairbanks
	Dartmouth
	Northeastern
	U Wisc0nsin-
	  Milwaukee
	U Cincinnati
	Kansas State
	U New Mexico
		U Missouri-
		  Columbia
		U Wisconsin-
		  Milwaukee
		U California-
		  San Francisco
		Northeastern
		U New Hampshire
			U Wyoming
			Utah State
			U Oklahoma
			Montana State
			U Kentucky
				Top 100

Source: Derived from National Science Foundation series on "Federal Support to Universities, Colleges and Selected Nonprofit Institutions, prepared by the Division of Science Resource Studies.

degree of dependency on federal agencies, which, in turn provides leverage for the agencies on the course of research at the universities.

Disciplinary Distributees

Pre-WWII support for agricultural sciences was transformed in the postwar period to support for more fields of inquiry. Figure 7-3 shows the percent of federal R&D going to academic institutions by generalized field of science in fiscal year 1987.

Figure 7-3
Percent of Federal R&D to Institutions by Field of Science
Fiscal Year 1987

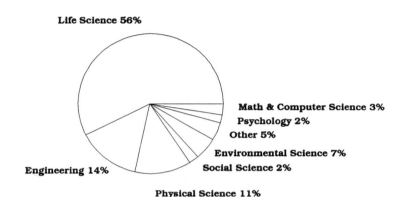

Life Science 56%

Math & Computer Science 3%
Psychology 2%
Other 5%

Environmental Science 7%
Social Science 2%

Engineering 14%

Physical Science 11%

Source: National Science Foundation. NSF 88-330.

This distribution, like the institutional distribution, has been relatively stable among the major categories.[32] Concentration on the life sciences reflects both the strong endorsement for research on health and the wide distribution of medical schools in all parts of the United States. The National Institutes of Health are the chief distributors of these funds. DOD has an important role in support for engineering and physical sciences. The National Science Foundation's specific role as a distributor to certain disciplines at academic institutions is identified in Figure 7-4, which compares NSF funding to all federal funding for research at colleges and universities such that its potential influence might be gauged. Clearly, there are sources of support other than federal for any discipline, including the unrecorded and incalculable expenditures of individuals who work on their own time without the benefit or the burden of formal research funding. However, given the relative weight of federal funding in the calculus of all specifically identified sources of funds for basic research, the potential for government influence on the direction of knowledge creation is great.

Even when considered more broadly, in Fiscal Year 1987, the overwhelming role of some federal science funding agencies in fields such as anthropology (NSF 55 percent), economics (USDA 50 percent), physics (DOE 64 percent) or mathematics and computer sciences (DOD 52 percent) places the responsibility for the direction of research in the hands of a very few individuals who are subject to pressures endemic to bureaucracies, prominent among which is "never to do anything for the first time." In a very real sense it is important for the program officer in an agency which is organized by recognized disciplines, to adhere to the central tenets of these disciplines, not venture beyond their boundaries. What this means for the continuous transformation of science as new ideas emerge is an enormously important question unable to be addressed satisfactorily in this paper, however, one might be alert to the affliction, "hardening of the categories."[33] Moreover, disciplinary distributions also have geographical consequences which must be treated at another time.

Suffice to remark that public funding of disciplines is something like intellectual zoning, in which some regions of thought are protected and encouraged by the State while others are left to fend for themselves, or worse, to protect themselves from the depredations of those which have been endowed. Supersaturation of research funds for some fields can have the effect of drawing scientists from related fields of inquiry, thereby depleting the research potential in the abandoned field. In some instances the average quality of research in the well-funded field is reduced. An example of this phenomenon is the huge endowment of cancer research and its impact on other fields of medicine.[34] Another example has been the struggle of the social sciences to gain support within NSF where an agency mandate of support already exists. The impact on the career trajectory of university scientists is well known: grants generally lead to publication and promotion, and ultimately to positions of judgment about who else would be promoted. Such a system can have a depressing impact on creative scientists.

Figure 7-4
Federal Obligations to Universities and Colleges for Research:
NSF Share of Federal Support to Fields of Science
in Fiscal Year 1987

Field of Science	NSF $ Oblig (thous)	All Fed & Oblig (thous)	NSF Percent of Fed
Total	1,096,246	6,348,281	17.2
Anthropology	6,584	8,415	81.5
Civil Engineering	31,476	61,654	51.1
Oceanography	111,463	160,477	69.5
Political Science	2,854	3,678	77.6
Geological Sciences	52,165	111,982	45.7
Atmospheric Sciences	53,372	114,762	46.5
Environmental Biology	52,881	96,905	54.6
Mathematics	55,784	111,538	50.0
Chemical Engineering	32,548	54,597	59.6
Astronomy	27,569	71,710	38.4
Chemistry	107,080	281,119	38.1
Computer Sciences	52,464	111,039	47.2
Physics	135,637	403,838	33.6
Mechanical Engineering	25,283	76,282	33.1
Electrical Engineering	42,236	143,214	29.5
Metal & Materials, Eng.	21,136	107,790	19.6
Social Sciences, Nec.	9,715	44,150	22.0
Economics	9,891	39,278	25.2
Biological Psychology	5,376	55,571	9.7
Other Sciences, Nec	46,185	133,264	34.5
Engineering, Nec	15,495	95,788	16.2
Sociology	3,009	33,651	9.0
Social Psychology	2,502	54,219	4.6
Biological (excl Environ)	140,836	2,107,345	6.7
Physical Sciences, Nec	50,287	65,840	76.9
Environ. Sciences, Nec	44	13,129	—
Life Sciences, Nec	3,651	141,086	2.6
Aeronautical Engineering	184	66,900	—
Agricultural Science	—	116,887	—
Psych Sciences, Nec	84	76,841	—
Astronautical Engineering	—	14,084	—
Medical Sciences, Total	—	1,361,849	—
Math & Computer Science	4	65,953	—

Source: National Science Foundation SRS Report on Federal Funds for R&D,
*Federal Obligations for Research to Universities & Colleges by Agency & Detailed
Field of Science,* FY 87-89, pp. 110–121.

State Distributees

Distribution of federal science funds to states corresponds to the population of the state, the number of scientists and engineers and the number of Ph.D.s granted in the state, but it corresponds poorly to the magnitude of the state's own contribution to scientific research and development.[35] The GAO study, and others have sought to explain the relative stability of funding to states in terms that do not offend those from states wherein federal funds are not unduly concentrated. This issue afflicts NSF, whose distribution of funds, ranked by state for the years 1976–1987, is shown in Figure 7-5. Special programs have been developed periodically to increase the number of proposals and to improve the success ratio of the proposals from low ranked states. Success has been limited in the sense of improving the ranking of a state, although South Carolina, a special recipient of funds under one program is sometimes cited for its ascent. It is obvious that in a closed system of 50 recipients the changing of ranks will anger some congresspersons and please others.

More broadly, we can consider the role of the federal government in the funding of academic science by state relative to other sources of funding by inspecting Figure 7-6. Here, federal research and development dollars distributed to academic institutions are shown as a percentage of total academic research and development for three years: 1977, 1981, and 1985. In 1985, 35 states relied on federal dollars for more than half of the funding of academic science in the state; in 1977 and 1981 there were 40. Whether this is an explicit outcome of the Reagan administration concerns about reducing the federal role or not, the magnitude of dependency is large. States such as Maryland, Rhode Island, California, and Massachusetts have been dependent for three-quarters to four-fifths of their academic science research budget from federal sources. These can be compared to South Dakota where less than one-quarter of such funds are from federal agencies. States that experienced major changes in rank between 1977 and 1985, e.g. Nevada, Idaho, and Alaska, had very small science budgets and were probably affected by relatively small amounts of federal funding.

If state government funding is added to federal funding, the

Figure 7-5
Rank of NSF R&D Obligations by State and Year

State	1976	1977	1978	1979	1980	1981	1982	1983	1987
California	1	1	1	1	1	1	1	1	1
New York	2	2	2	2	2	2	2	2	3
Massachusetts	3	3	3	3	3	3	3	3	4
Illinois	4	4	4	4	4	4	4	4	5
Pennsylvania	5	5	5	5	5	5	5	5	7
Wash. D. C.	6	7	7	8	9	13	16	25	2
Indiana	7	8	9	9	8	9	6	8	12
Michigan	8	6	6	6	6	7	7	6	10
Colorado	9	10	13	14	15	8	14	14	6
Texas	10	9	8	7	7	10	8	7	11
Washington	11	11	14	11	12	12	9	9	13
New Jersey	12	14	15	13	13	6	11	10	8
Maryland	13	12	10	13	14	15	13	12	14
Florida	14	16	16	16	16	17	18	15	17
Ohio	15	13	13	15	11	14	12	13	18
Wisconsin	16	15	11	10	10	11	10	11	16
Connecticut	17	18	19	19	18	16	17	19	23
Virginia	18	20	20	21	23	22	23	23	19
No. Carolina	19	17	18	17	17	20	20	16	15
Oregon	20	19	21	20	19	19	22	20	20
Rhode Is.	21	21	24	18	22	18	15	18	25
Missouri	22	22	25	25	25	26	26	26	26
Minnesota	23	25	22	22	20	23	19	21	21
Utah	24	26	26	26	26	25	25	24	27
Georgia	25	24	17	24	24	21	24	22	24
Arizona	26	23	23	23	21	24	21	17	9

role of government in science is heightened. Figure 7-7 displays combined government support. In 1985 only four states derived more than half of their funding for academic scientific research from private sources. Oklahoma's academic scientists were the least tied to government agencies; they received slightly more than one-third of their research money from public

Figure 7-5 (continued)
Rank of NSF R&D Obligations by State and Year

State	1976	1971	1978	1979	1980	1981	1982	1983	1987
Oklahoma	31	34	35	39	38	37	36	37	36
Louisiana	32	35	34	34	40	38	39	33	38
Kansas	33	32	31	37	30	32	21	31	39
Nebraska	34	31	38	32	36	33	38	39	37
New Mexico	35	36	37	27	35	36	37	32	33
N. Hamp.	36	39	41	41	33	35	33	34	34
Wyoming	36	46	44	45	42	41	41	42	40
Alabama	37	37	40	35	41	43	44	40	41
Nevada	39	43	42	46	49	46	46	48	45
Maine	40	38	39	40	34	39	34	35	42
Delaware	41	41	36	33	39	34	33	38	32
Kentucky	42	33	32	38	37	40	40	41	44
Mississippi	43	42	43	42	45	45	45	46	48
Montana	44	45	49	43	46	44	42	43	43
So. Dakota	45	47	47	50	48	48	49	49	50
So. Carolina	46	40	33	36	32	31	28	29	35
No. Dakota	47	49	45	49	51	51	50	51	47
W. Virginia	48	50	46	47	43	47	47	45	22
Arkansas	49	44	50	44	44	42	43	44	46
Idaho	50	48	48	51	50	50	51	50	51
Vermont	51	51	51	48	47	49	48	47	49
Tennessee	27	30	28	28	27	30	32	27	28
Iowa	28	27	30	29	29	29	29	28	31
Alaska	29	27	31	31	31	28	30	36	30
Hawaii	30	28	29	30	28	27	27	30	29

Source: National Science Foundation. NSF 89-304. p. 156.

sources. Hawaii, on the other end of the distribution, derived nearly 95 percent from public treasuries, largely on the basis of a huge state effort in the late 1970s. Maryland is 90 percent dependent on public sources of funds. The interplay between federal and state funding should be examined more closely to see what role federal agencies have in "crowding out," or serving as a replacement for state investment in science.

Figure 7-6
Federal R&D to Academic Institutions
as Percent of Total Academic R&D

	1977 %	1977 Rank	1981 %	1985 %	1985 Rank	Change (% Pt)	Change (Rank)
Alaska	70.1	16	51.8	44.1	44	-26.0	-28
Alabama	66.0	22	66.7	59.5	24	-6.5	-2
Arkansas	46.5	44	31.1	40.4	47	-6.1	-3
Arizona	55.0	35	55.8	47.8	39	-7.2	-4
California	78.9	2	73.7	71.1	6	-7.8	-4
Colorado	74.7	8	74.4	71.0	7	3.7	1
Connecticut	74.3	9	77.9	70.1	8	-4.1	1
Dist. Columbia	74.0	10	73.5	75.9	3	1.9	7
Delaware	55.9	33	54.7	45.0	43	-10.8	-10
Florida	53.2	38	56.4	51.1	35	-2.1	3
Georgia	51.5	41	52.3	53.0	33	1.5	8
Guam	53.0	39	41.5	49.8	37	-3.3	2
Hawaii	62.1	26	58.5	64.6	17	2.5	9
Iowa	51.5	40	52.7	48.5	38	-3.0	2
Idaho	43.1	46	45.7	66.9	14	23.8	32
Illinois	73.0	12	69.7	60.4	23	-12.6	-11
Indiana	67.9	20	66.0	61.1	21	-6.8	-1
Kansas	51.4	42	53.2	43.0	45	-8.4	-3
Kentucky	42.8	48	43.4	37.2	50	-5.6	-2
Louisiana	43.0	47	40.6	35.3	52	-7.7	-5
Massachusetts	78.8	3	79.2	75.6	4	-3.1	-1
Maryland	76.5	6	89.7	84.2	1	7.7	5
Maine	42.0	51	43.3	51.7	34	9.7	17
Michigan	57.5	32	57.8	58.2	27	0.7	5
Minnesota	58.5	31	58.5	50.6	36	-7.9	-5
Missouri	64.0	24	62.7	57.1	30	-6.9	-6
Mississippi	42.1	50	39.2	38.9	48	-3.2	2

The geographic distribution of dependency by state for 1985 is captured in Figure 7-8, which maps the degree of dependency by a state on federal funds. The darkest shaded states have the greatest dependency and the lightest, least. In effect, the map shows which states have their eggs in one basket and which have a more diversified portfolio upon which to draw. In practical terms the maps might suggest to state houses where their risks are if federal R&D funds are subjected to budget balancing

Figure 7-6 (continued)
Federal R&D to Academic Institutions
as Percent of Total Academic R&D

	1977 %	1977 Rank	1981 %	1985 %	1985 Rank	Change (% Pt)	Change (Rank)
Montana	53.6	37	54.8	37.7	49	-15.9	-12
North Carolina	69.7	17	68.7	63.4	18	-6.3	-1
North Dakota	42.3	49	38.8	37.1	51	-5.2	-2
Nebraska	38.6	53	35.8	40.7	46	2.1	7
N. Hampshire	69.7	18	70.1	68.9	11	-0.8	7
New Jersey	59.0	30	61.8	53.7	32	-5.3	-2
New Mexico	78.1	4	74.0	65.8	16	-12.3	-12
Nevada	38.5	54	68.2	69.8	10	31.3	44
New York	71.1	14	69.9	67.4	13	-3.7	1
Ohio	60.3	29	65.6	61.5	20	1.1	9
Oklahoma	54.9	36	33.1	31.4	53	-23.5	-17
Oregon	63.8	25	61.6	59.5	25	-4.3	0
Pennsylvania	66.5	21	71.5	65.8	15	-0.6	6
Puerto Rico	45.0	45	47.7	46.1	41	1.1	4
Rhode Island	89.9	1	88.5	76.4	2	-13.5	-1
South Carolina	50.8	43	52.4	45.3	42	-5.5	1
South Dakota	39.3	52	39.4	24.9	54	-14.5	-2
Tennessee	72.9	13	68.5	62.0	19	-10.9	-6
Texas	61.6	27	61.2	57.7	29	-3.9	-2
Utah	70.8	15	70.9	70.0	9	-0.8	6
Virginia	68.0	19	70.3	59.5	26	-8.5	-7
Virgin Islands	76.7	5	85.5	56.6	31	-20.1	-26
Vermont	74.8	7	71.5	67.8	12	-7.0	-5
Washington	73.4	11	73.3	74.4	5	1.0	6
Wisconsin	61.2	28	62.8	57.9	28	-3.3	0

formulations. What the map cannot show is that in over half of the states a single agency provides more than 40 percent of their federal funds, thus heightening their dependency and making them vulnerable to an action like the Mansfield amendment of 1970, which reduced the DOD role in explicitly non-military basic research, thereby dislocating research programs at many institutions dependent on that agency.

Although this is only a snapshot, we know that a majority of states are increasing their dependency on a single agency, but there is also an increasing number of states which have "spread

Figure 7-7
Government R&D to Academic Institutions
as Percent of Total Academic R&D

	1977 %	1977 Rank	1981 %	1985 %	1985 Rank	Change (% Pt)	Change (Rank)
Alaska	72.5	40	50.0	40.7	51	-22.8	-11
Alabama	84.3	14	82.2	73.9	18	-10.4	-4
Arkansas	85.1	13	68.4	65.5	34	-19.6	-21
Arizona	79.5	25	73.7	53.4	49	-26.1	-24
California	80.2	23	75.9	72.5	21	-7.8	2
Colorado	81.5	18	80.5	74.9	14	-6.6	4
Connecticut	76.4	31	80.3	72.0	23	-4.4	8
Dist. Columbia	74.2	35	74.8	76.8	9	2.7	26
Delaware	59.7	48	57.6	48.3	52	-11.4	-4
Florida	58.5	49	60.3	54.8	47	-3.7	2
Georgia	54.2	51	55.0	54.6	48	0.4	3
Guam	60.2	47	55.8	65.3	36	5.1	11
Hawaii	64.3	46	91.9	94.7	1	30.5	45
Iowa	70.5	41	66.7	58.6	43	-11.8	-2
Idaho	83.9	15	51.6	76.0	11	-7.9	4
Illinois	76.9	30	73.7	66.0	33	-10.9	-3
Indiana	77.5	29	74.2	68.6	30	-8.9	-1
Kansas	75.8	33	81.0	78.0	7	2.2	26
Kentucky	73.4	38	62.2	57.7	44	-15.7	-6
Louisiana	45.6	53	70.3	59.6	42	14.0	11
Massachusetts	80.9	20	80.7	76.5	10	-4.5	10
Maryland	85.5	10	93.1	89.7	2	4.2	8
Maine	50.2	52	60.3	57.7	45	7.5	7
Michigan	65.6	45	64.7	66.1	32	0.5	13
Minnesota	75.1	34	68.4	61.9	40	-13.2	-6
Missouri	72.7	39	71.1	63.8	38	-8.9	1
Mississippi	74.0	36	69.6	69.1	28	-4.8	8

out" their risk: in 1978 only Delaware, Georgia, and Indiana were in the most diversified category. In 1982 Hawaii, New Jersey, Nevada and South Carolina joined the group while Georgia dropped out. By 1984 Georgia reentered, Nebraska and Oregon joined, and New Jersey dropped out.

Looked at in another way, by identifying states that were at least 40 percent dependent upon a single agency for their basic scientific research budget, we find the number of dependent

Figure 7-7 (continued)
Government R&D to Academic Institutions
as Percent of Total Academic R&D

	1977 %	Rank	1981 %	1985 %	Rank	Change (% Pt)	Change (Rank)
Montana	87.2	7	84.2	65.3	35	-21.9	-28
North Carolina	87.7	6	87.9	70.2	27	-17.4	-21
North Dakota	81.2	19	84.8	85.0	4	3.9	15
Nebraska	77.6	28	38.2	44.3	53	-33.3	-25
N. Hampshire	73.8	37	74.6	75.9	12	2.0	25
New Jersey	69.8	42	70.0	63.1	39	-6.8	3
New Mexico	88.3	5	80.7	79.4	6	-8.9	-1
Nevada	79.0	27	72.3	72.1	22	-6.8	5
New York	76.2	32	74.3	72.0	24	-4.2	8
Ohio	68.5	44	73.1	67.2	31	-1.3	13
Oklahoma	85.5	11	38.9	34.4	54	-51.2	-43
Oregon	80.7	21	78.4	74.4	16	-6.3	5
Pennsylvania	69.4	43	73.1	68.8	29	-0.5	14
Puerto Rico	80.4	22	71.5	70.8	25	-9.6	-3
Rhode Island	91.8	1	94.9	77.8	8	-14.0	-7
South Carolina	55.2	50	76.6	60.9	41	5.8	9
South Dakota	44.4	54	43.4	85.8	3	41.4	51
Tennessee	81.8	16	83.1	74.3	17	-7.5	-1
Texas	80.0	24	73.4	70.3	26	-9.8	-2
Utah	85.1	12	82.4	79.6	5	-5.5	7
Virginia	85.7	9	83.1	73.6	19	-12.1	-10
Virgin Islands	86.1	8	98.6	56.6	46	-29.6	-38
Vermont	81.6	17	77.7	73.4	20	-8.2	-3
Washington	90.4	2	88.7	75.7	13	-14.7	-11
Wisconsin	79.1	26	79.6	74.7	15	-4.4	11
West Virginia	89.5	3	89.9	63.9	37	-25.6	-34
Wyoming	89.1	4	53.6	51.7	50	-37.4	-46

states increased from 32 in 1982 to 36 in 1984. During the three years, 1978, 1982, and 1984 the same proportion of clients by agency remained about the same: NIH dominated with roughly 29 states; USDA followed with 9; DOD had 2 each year; NSF averaged 1 and DOE had 1 during the entire period. Obviously, the number of observations and the time period is too compressed to do more than remark that dependency appears to be increasing.

Figure 7-8
Dependency on Federal Funding, 1985

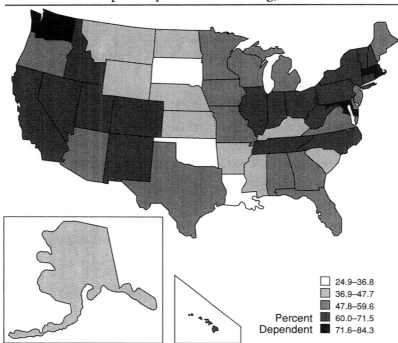

Percent Dependent

- □ 24.9–36.8
- 36.9–47.7
- 47.8–59.6
- 60.0–71.5
- ■ 71.6–84.3

These distributions to states relates both to historical accidents of funding and to rules. Historical accidents include the reasons for the initial choice of certain universities to support or fields to fund. For example, one might have anticipated Maryland's high reliance on federal sources of support for science on the basis of propinquity and by virtue of the immense role of Dr. Isaiah Bowman, the powerful president of Johns Hopkins University in the 1940s and chief supporter of Vannevar Bush in the struggle to establish NSF. Or, the fact of being an historic center such as Harvard, Yale, Chicago or Stanford with influential alumni in important institutional settings certainly guided the early selection process for what would become America's research universities.

Similarly, the choice of fields of science to fund depended much on the sociology of science at the time, and early jousting for position in the funding hierarchy has already been alluded to with respect to the "poor relative" role of the social sciences. Admission of the social sciences under the NSF umbrella was resisted by Bush and others and only grudgingly confirmed at the last. This sentiment exists at NSF today and certainly it infects the views of social scientists there about each other's disciplines! A consequence of the determination to have some fields of inquiry supported, and others not, has been to engender a resistance to interdisciplinary ideas, thereby making the introduction of new organizations of thought a challenge, or competition, rather than a welcome sortie on the frontier. Public support has aided the development of monopolies in the domain of ideas.

Rules may then take over to augment the directions given by accidental initial conditions. A major rule for NIH and NSF, as well as other agencies from time to time, is the use of peer review to advise program officers on the quality of proposals. The idea was grafted from the longer standing practice of judging papers for publication, but instead of judging the quality of completed work peers are asked to determine potential quality of proposed research. Greater reliance is placed on the reputation of the researcher, and, very importantly, on the reputation of the researcher's institution. As fields have developed specializations, a sanctification process occurs which permits a subgroup of researchers to become the peers for that branch of science. Each specialization reduces the size of the peer group and increases their mutual dependence. At some point, and in some cases, the distinction between a "peer" and an "old boy" becomes blurred.

Other events, conditions, and rules influence distributions: national focus on environmental issues in the late 1960s and 1970s propelled the development of the field of ecology; chairmanships, or even membership in powerful committees of Congress may help to define a distributional consequence, or the promulgation of Executive Order 12291, which requires a benefit/cost analysis on many federal projects, thereby increasing the emphasis on this kind of accountancy and inducing changes in the offerings of most economics departments at universities.[36] Distributional consequences of these and other events and conditions are legion and undoubtedly multiplicative, but what do they mean for the "health" of science?

DEPENDENCY AND THE HEALTH OF SCIENCE

The distributional characteristics of federal funding of science have been described and some of the consequences suggested, but what does this mean for the "health of science?" Earlier it was remarked that this term is essentially vacuous, like "public interest," to be filled by whomever is constructing an argument: the remarks that follow are not different in that respect, simply contentious in the face of received wisdom.

The "health of science" depends mightily on what one takes science to be. If it is a process for apprehending the world, "health" could mean the qualitative improvement in the questions we are able to ask. If it is regarded as an existent, some quantitative measures of numbers of scientists, size of facilities, or amount of equipment might be used for definition. Those who prefer the first view recognize that scientists, facilities, and equipment are required to conduct inquiry; and those who prefer the second view would accept that qualitative improvement is a desirable outcome of the interaction of people and equipment in scientific research facilities. The extremes are not worth discussion, but, the second view of science does prevail in public agencies because of the managerial designs and responsibilities of the agents of the state who must account for their actions. Coordination, and concentration of decision authority permits greater control of the tangible elements of science and is therefore preferred by those agents. Fellowships can be given to encourage scientists to enter certain disciplines; facilities, such as centers can be funded so as to create a physical presence; and, equipment can be purchased to fill the buildings. Each of these actions results in indisputable outcomes, measurable and manageable. It does not follow that qualitative improvement in science is a result, and, as has been indicated before, there may be negative consequences.

At the heart of any assessment of the health of science as a public enterprise or activity is the relationship of the individual scientist to the public agency. Dependency has been described in corporate terms (discipline, university, state) not individual terms, but one can suppose (even know from personal observation) that the effects of these relationships reach the individual and can influence the scientist's conception of relationship of self to these corporate entities.

In Bush's day the prevailing notion of the public enterprise of science was that it was investment in science as a process of inquiry which would have undetermined beneficial consequences for the United States. The result of this investment would be a larger supply of scientists to aid industry, and a reservoir of talent in case of an emergency. In general, scientists were recognized by the political/bureaucratic system actors as the valid arbiters of the "direction" of science. Some have regarded this as the foundation of a kind of "social contract" between Science (the existent) and the Nation (another existent), which ultimately binds all scientists to the State.[37]

As numbers of scientists increased and differentiated so did the pressure to increase public funding. Academic scientists reproduced themselves and organized their issue into more effective pressure groups. With this development emerged an ever-widening view of science as an organized community of claimants on the Treasury, whose central identifiable and discriminating characteristic from other claimants related more to the kinds of buildings and equipment for which they lobbied than to the habit of mind for which they trained. Furthermore, many scientists began to regard public support as a kind of "entitlement," without which the edifice would collapse. This transformation did little to dispel the notion of a social contract, and the distributors, upon whom the distributees were becoming increasingly dependent, demanded more justification for public expenditure. More "applied" research was sought and programs such as RANN, Research Applied to National Needs, at the NSF were created.

The growth of the view that science is less a form of thought than an enterprise or establishment made up of people, buildings, and lobbyists which require care and feeding, and from which useful products will emerge, had inevitably concatenated into a contractual conception in which units of public funds go in and units of science are expected to be produced. Current arguments for increased budgets for science are universally predicated on the expected useful payoffs for the investment. Contracting for outcomes can be hazardous to the conduct of scientific inquiry.

Not all scientists are comfortable with this transformation of the relationship of scientists to the State; indeed, in a recent penetrating survey of scientists conducted by Sigma Xi, The Scientific Research Society, some dramatic results contribute to evidence that the dependency described has, in fact, contributed to "unhealthiness" in the conduct of scientific inquiry.[38] The survey was administered in early 1986 to 10,000 members of this 100-year-old scientific honor society and 4000 completed responses were returned. It sought to probe the opinions of scientists about science policy issues and to learn their views of the relationship between scientists and government, and more broadly, between scientists and society. Responses to 36 questions yielded, among others, the following generalized opinions: 1) public representatives misconstrue the nature of scientific endeavor when they give money to "science" to "solve" targeted problems within specific time frames; 2) there is a tendency for funding agencies to be paradigm dominated, and to fund research on a personal basis regardless of project worthiness; 3) the democratic "give and take" at Federal funding agencies will not protect scientists against the establishment of scientific orthodoxies; 4) there should be much greater support for interdisciplinary research.

Questions in the survey were framed as strong statements to which the respondents could choose a response scaled from "emphatic agreement" to "emphatic disagreement." For the purposes of this paper the responses have been dichotomized into a simple agree/disagree framework.[39] For example, the following statements were made:

> Every funding agency empowered to award government research monies is dominated by a particular methodological paradigm by

which it judges what is and what is not acceptable science in the agency's area of specialization. The chance of any non-mainstream proposals being funded is very small.

More than two-thirds of those who offered an opinion agreed with the statement.

Much governmental funded research is "discipline specific," with different agencies funding small pools of talent working on narrow research agendas. More interdisciplinary research should be funded because many of the most significantly scientific problems cannot be accommodated within arbitrary disciplinary structures.

Three-quarters of those who offered an opinion agreed with the statement.

This [democratic] system will also be sufficient to insure that government funded research will not result in the establishment of scientific orthodoxies.

Three-quarters of those who offered an opinion disagreed.

Scientists engaged in nationally targeted research agendas are under pressure to produce results. Such pressure can, and does, lead to the release of selective experimental results that prematurely raise the public's expectations of eventual success.

More than three-quarters of those who offered an opinion agreed.

Many individuals, institutions, and interest groups compete for government research funds. I believe that research monies and research trends are tied too closely to prevailing political priorities and fashions.

More than two-thirds agreed.

Many colleges and universities do not have state-of-the-art scientific equipment. Those without such equipment are denied research funds even though the researchers are competent, their designs valid, and the research does not require state-of-the-art equipment.

Two-thirds agreed with the statement.

Any opinion poll is fraught with methodological difficulties, but because our aim is to identify what scientists think about the current state of dependency it is hard to escape the conclusion, after analysis of these and other questions of the survey, that an unhealthy malaise exists among scientists, which stands in contrast with the "growth" of tangible federal inputs to the enterprise of Science.

CONCLUSION

To recapitulate, science and policy are at odds because truth-regarding scientific inquiry *must* be independent, whereas policy constructs its own truths and requires dependence. Efforts to control science or to "coordinate" it are self-defeating. Furthermore, science by its nature is the infinite unfolding of questions which defy the construction of priorities and the possibility of funding by public agency, whose allocations are neither characterized by the test of a freely operating market nor a random process which insures "fair" redistribution. A consequence of science policy has been a tableau of non-random distributions. What other consequences flow from this distribution can be the subject of further analysis, and are likely candidates for further policy prescriptions. If science is to be subject to policy at all, and the merits of that proposition are certainly open to questions raised here, then attention should be paid as to how to intrude least. In practical terms, given the existing intertwined nature of government and scientists described in this paper, a thoughtful withdrawal strategy should be developed by those who are most acutely conscious of the potential for abuse—but it is unlikely that those individuals, either politicians or science bureaucrats will adopt this thought. It is, therefore, incumbent on others of us to devise such strategies. In another paper I shall advance a proposition aimed not at the immediate dissolution of the relationship between scientists and government, because that will not occur, but at a strategy to demonstrate that an alternative arrangement can be supportive of the important process of scientific inquiry without systematic introduction of negative outcomes, and which holds the potential for exposing a logic of why total withdrawal of public funding would improve the health of science.

The development of creative alternatives will take time and the resistance to them will be great so I conclude with a final suggestion to any who will listen. Before embarking on the coordination of science through public policy I recommend consideration of an observation by Robert Frost, who once said: "Some people worry because science doesn't know where it's going. It doesn't need to know. It's none of its business."

NOTES

1. US Congress, House Committee on Science and Technology, Task Force on Science Policy, *An Agenda for a Study of Government Science Policy*, Washington, D.C.: GPO, December, 1984.
2. Lewis Branscomb, mimeograph statement prepared for US House of Representatives, Committee on Science and Technology Hearing, March 14, 1985.
3. Roland W. Schmitt, memorandum to members of the Committee on Science Policy Review, National Science Board, NSB/C-85-10, March 21, 1985.
4. Erich Bloch, "New Directions for the National Science Foundation," mimeographed text of a speech delivered to the Tenth Annual AAAS Colloquium on R&D Policy, Washington, D.C., April 4, 1985.
5. G.A. Keyworth III, "Four Years of Reagan Science Policy: Notable Shifts in Priorities," *Science*, Vol. 224, April 6, 1984, p. 9.
6. *Ibid.*
7. Erich Bloch, "Basic Research and Economic Health: The Coming Challenge," *Science*, Vol. 232, May 2, 1986, pp. 595–599.
8. Malcolm G. Scully, "China to Stress Market-Oriented Science," *Chronicle of Higher Education*, April 24, 1985.
9. *Ibid.*
10. Milton Friedman, "Why Government Should Not Fund Science," *Science*, Vol. 210, October 3, 1980, p. 33.
11. C. Ian Jackson, *A New Agenda for Science: Preliminary Report* (New Haven, Connecticut: Sigma Xi, The Scientific Research Society, 1986), p. 19.
12. Lewis Thomas, "National Science," *Science*, Vol. 179, March 39, 1973, reprinted from *The New England Journal of Medicine*, Vol. 288, No. 307, 1973.
13. Gerard Piel, "Natural Philosophy in the Constitution," *Science*, Vol. 233, September 5, 1986, pp. 1056–1060.
14. National Science Foundation, Science Resources Studies, "Highlights," NSF 86-312, August 22, 1986.
15. *Ibid.*
16. National Science Foundation, *Science Indicators: The 1985 Report* (Washington, D.C.: GPO, 1986).
17. US Congress, House Committee on Science and Technology, *American Science and Science Policy Issues*, (99th Cong., 2d Sess., 1986), p. 105.
18. *Ibid.*, p.28.
19. J. Merton England, *A Patron of Pure Science* (Washington, D.C.: NSF,

1982), p. 34.

20. Martha Newton, "Geographical Distribution: A Legislative History," National Science Foundation mimeograph report, December 19, 1979.

21. J. Merton England, *op. cit.*, pp. 54-56.

22. Vannevar Bush, *Science: The Endless Frontier* (Washington, D.C.: National Science Foundation reprint, 1980).

23. Colin Norman, "News and Comment," *Science*, Vol. 233, July 11, 1986, p. 146.

24. Ken Hechler, *Towards the Endless Frontier: History of the Committee on Science and Technology*, 1959–1979 (Washington, D.C.: GPO, 1980), p. 516.

25. *Ibid.*, p. 516.

26. *Ibid.*, p. 536.

27. National Science Foundation Act, Public Law 81–507, 81st Cong., 2d sess., May 10, 1950; 64 Stat. 149 (1950).

28. US General Accounting Office, "Patterns of Distribution of Federal Research Funds to Universities and Colleges," draft, December, 1986.

29. David Davis-Van Atta, Sam C. Carrier and Frank Frankfort, "Educating America's Scientists: The Role of the Research Colleges," report for a conference on "The Future of Science at Liberal Arts Colleges," Oberlin, Ohio, June 9–10, 1985.

30. Hon. Michael A. Andrews, Texas 25th District, press release, dated June 18, 1985. Remarks protest NSF's "top twenty" funding for 1985, which did not include a southern or southwestern university.

31. US Congress, *American Science, op cit.*, pp. 11–23.

32. National Science Foundation, *Science Indicators, op. cit.*, appendix table 2–14, p.229.

33. Jack Sommer, "Grass Roots Versus Bird's Eye," *American Scientist*, Vol. 75, March-April, 1987, p. 224.

34. Stan Carpenter, personal conversations, anatomist, Dartmouth College Medical School Faculty.

35. US General Accounting Office, *op. cit.*, table 7.

36. 46 Fed. Reg. 13193–13198 (1981).

37. Gerard Peil, *op. cit.*

38. C. Ian Jackson, *op. cit.*

39. During 1987 the author wrote a series of columns for the *American Scientist* which discuss the Sigma Xi Survey of Scientists in detail. The March/April issue column, "Grass Roots Versus Bird's Eye," is concerned with the issue of interdisciplinary science.

EIGHT

SCIENCE, GOVERNMENT AND THE EXPLORATION OF CORAL REEFS

Michael T. Ghiselin

For hundreds of years governments have been sending expeditions to distant portions of the globe, and scientists have been traditional participants. Because ships are notoriously expensive to build and operate, such expeditions provide a good example of big science. Because the activities of naturalists such as geologists and zoologists are often carried out upon a much more modest scale, their experience makes a good contrast. This essay is restricted to a few expeditions that have been important for the study of coral reefs. The topic has interested me both as a zoologist and as a historian of science.

In studying such matters I have found it useful to treat scientific investigation in broadly economic terms.[1] As I see it, scientists aim at optimizing discovery: at finding out as much as they can and getting maximum credit for doing so with the minimum amount of effort. Scientists do not maximize certitude, except insofar as it helps maximize discovery. They take risks in the face of great uncertainty. Discoveries, be these of facts, theories, or whatever, are a sort of capital good, used to make more discoveries. The scientific community rewards scientists for producing such goods on the basis of how useful the goods are in producing more discoveries. Of course, there are also applied science benefits that bring in pecuniary rewards as well. These tend to complicate the foregoing picture, which of course applies only to pure science. Applied science does not generally aim to produce the sort of intellectual capital good that is used for making discoveries, but only makes use of it. Governments may invest in science as infrastructure, though they tend to emphasize the applied aspects. They may also seek to maximize things like revenue and managerial participation. Sometimes the interests of science coincide with those of government, but obviously that is not always the case.

Given this background, let us consider the reasons why voyages of exploration have been undertaken. Such reasons should not be confused with the "justification" though the two might be the same.[2] Somebody who wants to undertake a scientific expedition ordinarily has to justify the expenditure. Generally the only persons who have been exempt from such requirements have been reigning monarchs. Prince Rainier I of Monaco is a good example. He wanted to put his skill at sailing to philanthropic use. More modestly, someone with independent means or unrestricted funds such as a MacArthur Fellowship can undertake scientific travel without having to justify it in a grant proposal.

In many cases voyages of exploration have been undertaken in order to extend colonial empires and propagate religion. The latter may have been the justification for much of the former. Sometimes expeditions have been carried out for the sake of national glory, to establish territorial rights, or for espionage. When this happens the interests of science are often invoked in justification. A good example at present is research in Antarctica, which helps to establish the "presence" of various national states. A lot of research has been justified for its military applications. The navy has wanted to know all sorts of things that are useful in submarine warfare. Among graduate students at

Scripps Institution of Oceanography there is a well known saying: "We all work for the CIA." The ulterior motives obviously affect how scientists' resources are allocated. If the only consideration is keeping a presence, say, in Antarctica, the government may not care very much what gets done. In that case those who do the research will have intellectual freedom as well as opportunity. Good scientists will volunteer to do the research that needs to be done. So will the bad ones who cannot get funded otherwise. When the government wants to do cosmetic research on coral reefs it may or may not attempt to control what the scientists do. But because a lot of us enjoy diving in warm water, we are eager to participate.

Marine exploration probably has been motivated more by commercial than by political interests. Transportation benefits from investment in infrastructure—especially by the charting of coastlines and the development of navigational aids. Safer navigation means effectively lower cost of carriage. Coral reefs were particularly treacherous because they were often hard to see.

Voyages whose main purpose has been the improvement of navigation have often involved scientists whose responsibility it was to report on the natural history of the places visited. This practice makes a great deal of economic sense. Once the fixed costs of the expedition have been paid, a handful of scientists as supernumeraries is a minor expense. The cost can further be lowered through the combination of labor. Darwin's close friends and supporters, the zoologist Thomas Henry Huxley and the botanist Joseph Dalton Hooker, both served as medical personnel on scientific expeditions.

Early voyages that provided important information on coral reefs include those of the Englishman Cook, the Frenchman Bouganville, and the Russian von Kotzebue. The last of these had on board Adelbert von Chamisso, who later became distinguished as a popular writer and poet. But the most important research ever done on coral reefs was that of Charles Darwin, who circumnavigated the globe on board H.M.S. *Beagle* from 1832 to 1836.[3] Darwin was not the official naturalist on this voyage. Rather, he was there to provide gentlemanly companionship to Captain FitzRoy, who suffered from bouts of depression. FitzRoy was an outstanding navigator and explorer. His main assignment was to chart the coasts of South America and carry out a series of chronometric observations around the world. He went out of the way to help Darwin achieve his specific goals, which changed during the voyage as opportunities presented themselves. He began mostly studying marine biology, but shifted to biogeography and geology in order to follow up his most important discoveries. Darwin was young and inexperienced, but not to the degree that legend has it. Actually he was as knowledgeable as the best modern graduate student beginning work on research for a doctoral dissertation.

Darwin invented his theory of coral reefs before he had seen any. While in South America he found evidence that vast tracts of land had been elevated, and considered the global consequence of subsidence. Corals grow only in shallow water, but if the land on which they were growing should sink, the corals would keep growing in shallow water and build up a thick layer of limestone. Coral growing on a volcanic island would form a "fringing reef" next to the shore. If that island then sank, the coral would grow upward at the edge of the reef, leaving a shallow lagoon between the island and the reef itself. With further subsidence and growth, the summit of the island would disappear, leaving just a ring of coral with a central lagoon—an "atoll."

This, in very simple outline, was Darwin's hypothesis. To develop a well-tested general theory he had to show how coral growth related to the global pattern of rise and fall of the land. In his book on coral reefs he documented his case with immense erudition, mainly gained from the literature.[4] His personal observations were limited to a few days at Tahiti and Mauritius and a little more than a week at Cocos Keeling atoll in the Indian Ocean. However, he had excellent cooperation from FitzRoy, and made the best of his time. The coral reef theory established Darwin's reputation as an outstanding scientist, and his semi-popular account of the voyage brought him general recognition as a man of letters.[5]

With Darwin and FitzRoy we have an excellent formula for success. An outstanding captain at the helm cooperating with a genius of the first rank who was free to do more or less as he pleased. Furthermore, Darwin was rich enough by far that he never had to work for a living, and he was highly motivated to produce work of unsurpassed quality.

The US Exploring Expedition of 1838–1842 was the largest ever carried out by any nation up to that time.[6] It explored vast areas of the Pacific, and was justified partly by the needs of America's whaling industry and similar navigational considerations. Although Commander Charles Wilkes had a rather difficult personality, he was very able, and had serious scientific interests of his own. There were several scientists on board the vessels. Of these the most outstanding was James Dwight Dana, ultimately a professor at Yale.[7] Like Darwin he was a geologist as well as a zoologist of diverse accomplishment. To Dana goes the credit for extending and corroborating Darwin's coral reef theory. Dana had much more opportunity than Darwin did for observing the details of reef structure firsthand. His most important theoretical contribution was to show that the shape of islands that have sunk correlates with the presence of barrier reefs around them.

The US Exploring Expedition was surrounded by a great deal of petty bickering among military and governmental officials. Wilkes himself behaved like a martinet, and was court-martialled. There was much quarrelling about the disposition of specimens and publication of the results was held up for years. Early enthusiasm coupled with lavish expenditure was followed up by indifference and neglect with respect to following through with the project. Perhaps the worst example is the manner in which the publications were handled. Only a hundred copies of the volumes based on the expedition were published, and these were mainly given to foreign governments. The reason was not to save money. Rather the Library Committee of Congress felt that making the publications scarce would increase their value! Such problems are by no means unusual.

Darwin's coral reef theory, supported by Dana, remained unchallenged until the 1870s. Resistance to it may have had something to do with the controversies surrounding Darwin's evolutionary views. His critics were mainly zoologists, not geologists, and some of them were Lamarckian. At least this is true of Karl Semper, who spent some time studying the reefs and fauna of Palau in the West Caroline Islands.[8] Skepticism and alternative hypotheses were abundant. It was thought that one island or another was hard to interpret in the light of Darwin's theory. Could coral islands build up from sediments deposited at great depths? Or could the lagoons within atolls be formed by solution of the limestone rock?

One of Darwin's opponents, John Murray, was on board the *Challenger*, which circumnavigated the globe exploring the great depths of the oceans.[9] The expedition was well funded, thanks to the generosity of the British Government, well planned, thanks to the active participation of the Royal Society of London, and well led by Charles Wyville Thompson. Among the motives for the expedition was the practical matter of deep-sea telegraph cables. Life in the deep sea was virtually unknown at the time, and a large body of other material was gathered as the expedition progressed. When the *Challenger* returned it had a vast number of specimens, and a fight ensued over who would get them. It was wisely seen to that the specimens would be studied by the very best scientists, irrespective of nationality. A series of massive volumes reported the results. But the British Government dragged its feet with respect to providing support. Thompson's health broke down as a result of the political struggle, and he died.

Another of Darwin's opponents was Alexander Agassiz. He was a good zoologist.[10] He succeeded his father, Louis Agassiz, as the Director of the Museum of Comparative Zoology at Harvard. Most important, he was rich, having earned a fortune supervising a copper mine. Unlike his father he was not an anti-evolutionist, but he was something of a dissident. One symptom of this often-misplaced dissidence was an ill-fated program to show that there are no fishes in the open waters of the deep sea. He carried out extensive survey work on various aspects of marine biology and oceanography. He also directed a great deal of research for the US government, research that was mainly concerned with cataloging marine resources.

Agassiz had no particular theory of his own, but held that all sorts of data could not be explained by Darwin's theory. Being a wealthy administrator he had no trouble publishing his results. They fill page after tedious page of in-house journals.

Shortly before Darwin died, he wrote to Agassiz suggesting how the controversies might be resolved: "I wish that some doubly rich millionaire would take it into his head to have borings made in some of the Pacific and Indian atolls, and bring home cores for slicing from a depth of 500 or 600 feet...."[11] Agassiz began to do some drilling in Fiji, but gave up at 85 feet when he got equivocal results.[12] The Royal Society attempted the same task at Funafuti around this time, but that effort did not give decisive results either. Shallow borings were hard to interpret and cost increased greatly with depth.

For some years marine exploration was largely funded by the great foundations. Gradually support shifted to government, especially in the late 1930s and during and after World War II. The Carnegie Foundation supported a marine laboratory in the Dry Tortugas near Florida where a great deal of reef biology was carried on. But that was hardly big science. The major advances in the first half of the present century were mainly theoretical, and the data used to support them were mostly individual field work and synthesis from the literature. Reginald Daly developed a "glacial control" theory.[13] He suggested that the rise and fall of sea level has led to periods of erosion and deposition. It is now agreed that this accounts for many details of reef structure.

William M. Davis was a professor of geology at Harvard. He was a profound student of methodology, and contributed a great deal to the study of land forms. At the time of his retirement in 1912 he rediscovered Dana's theoretical contribution to the study of coral reefs, which had been forgotten. This led him to devote may years to rethinking the issues. His book, *The Coral Reef Problem*, is a classic and still widely read.[14] It supports Darwin's views. As part of his research he travelled extensively, visiting coral islands and observing their structure at first hand. He had the modest financial support that was necessary through grants from professional societies.

During World War II oceanography became strongly allied with the military. Especially at Scripps Institution of Oceanography, marine biologists and oceanographers supported the war effort through research, especially in acoustics.[15] A great deal of information accumulated about the topography of the oceans. This contributed to the global picture of geology, of which coral reefs are an interesting aspect. Among other things evidence turned up for numerous flat-topped mountains (guyots), often at considerable depths. These must have been planed off at sea level.

The connection between marine science and the military continued after the war. Scientists continued to cooperate with support from such governmental organizations as the Office of Naval Research (ONR), which encouraged pure, as well as applied, science. This post-war support by the ONR makes sense if it is looked upon as a kind of retainer. A group of experts were more or less on call should they be needed. It also helped as a mechanism for keeping the Navy in communication with the scientific community and in maintaining good relationships.

After the war the United States found itself in possession of a vast Pacific empire. Information was needed about the people and resources in order to plan for economic and political development. In addition, the Northern Marshalls were selected as sites for the testing of nuclear weapons. This included the study of biological, as well as physical effects of the bombs and radiation. Extensive biological surveys were carried out at both Bikini and Enewetak, both before and after the nuclear tests. Of this we will have more to say later.

At both Bikini and Enewetak drilling was carried to considerable depths, and the borings were supplemented by geophysical studies.[16] The drills passed through thousands of feet of reef limestone containing the remains of shallow-water plants and animals. The deepest limestones were of Eocene age at 4,154 feet, at which point igneous rock—basalt—was recovered. Enewetak was obviously a "thick cap of limestone resting on the summit of a volcano that rises 2 miles above the floor of the ocean."[17] Darwin's theory was at last established beyond a reasonable doubt. Subsequently the theory has been integrated into the modern science of plate tectonics. The ocean floor moves and sinks in places, but sometimes it rises and such complications created the appearances that seemed to conflict with Darwin's theory.[18]

A marine laboratory was established at Enewetak in 1954.[19] The laboratory was supported by the US Department of Energy, and to some extent from NOAA, the Department of Commerce, and the Department of Defense. There were excellent facilities, and the laboratory was visited by over a thousand scientists, producing hundreds of publications. Enewetak soon became the most extensively studied atoll in the world. Operations, however, stopped on September 22, 1983. This decision was made as a matter of high-level policy. According to one of my informants, the Department of Energy wanted the National Science Foundation to take over, but the National Science Foundation insisted that the laboratory was the responsibility of the Department of Energy. Perhaps this was simply a matter of political expediency. The radioactive materials had largely been cleaned up and buried, and it was no longer expedient to give the appearance of having concern for the environment. Indeed, having scientists present would only serve to attract attention to the kind of problem that the government would prefer to have ignored. Be this as it may, the pattern is typical insofar as ongoing programs are often cancelled, incidentally destroying institutions that have been built up with great difficulty over a period of years. The laboratory's collection of specimens was transferred to the Bernice P. Bishop Museum in Honolulu but that institution has had to put up with its own financial crisis. Museums are repositories for scientific information, but because their role in the intellectual economy is infrastructural, they are apt to be neglected.

Opportunities such as the ones at Enewetak are apt to be unusual, or downright unique, and cooperation of government can be most valuable for science. One of my informants, a geochemist, was delighted at having the opportunity to use the radioactive fallout as a tracer of materials in the reefs. Ordinarily there is no way to set up a contrived experiment along those lines. Sometimes the appropriate person to take advantage of such an opportunity is hard to find. Another of my informants works on freshwater snails. There are no freshwater snails at Enewetak, but he accepted an invitation to go there, and worked on marine slugs instead.

As to the academic freedom issues, the relationship of individual scientists to government is very subtle. So long as scientists are willing to do what the government wants, the government is apt to make the resources available. But government can determine what topics will be studied, where and how they will be studied, and to some extent what will be done with the results. Work on systematic biology at Enewetak led to a greatly improved catalog of fishes and other organisms. But that sort of work is quite innocuous. For environmental research in general a major motive is to appear concerned and give the impression that something is being done. If nothing else, this allows government to put off making a decision. By carefully selecting the questions that are asked and the people who will ask them it is easy to justify policy on the basis of what purports to be well-informed expert opinion. In consequence scientists who are willing to go along with such procedures find it easier to get funded. Not only are resources diverted from meritorious projects, but scientists are rewarded for compromising their integrity.

In general, important scientific discoveries are the unintended consequences of projects directed toward some other purpose. The modern theory of coral reefs and the modern theory of evolution are equally good examples. When good scientists encounter such opportunities, they make the best of them. They also seek out what look like the most promising areas for investigation. Administrators and funding agencies are apt to direct resources elsewhere, toward desired results rather than toward opportunities for productivity. Such interests may or may not coincide. For good scientists much of the problem is how to do good research in spite of what government would have them do. It is the same basic problem however, with other institutions, such as universities. How can one get an education in spite of school? Darwin coped by doing what was minimally necessary in the training of a clergyman and gaining his scientific education on a strictly extracurricular basis. Academic freedom has to be created. It is not simply bestowed upon one.

As may be seen from other chapters in this book, there is considerable disagreement about how much, if any, of its resources the federal government ought to be investing in science, either pure or applied. The arguments are often of a rather abstract character, and some of them rest upon questionable premises. Arguments in favor of the government supporting pure science generally invoke the notion that science is a kind of infrastructure, or a public good, comparable to highways. Arguments to the contrary tend to stress the greater efficiency of individual enterprise in a free market intellectual economy. At an extreme it may be suggested that the government might perhaps have to engage in applied research, especially military research, but everything else should be left to private philanthropy and industry.

Economic theory in general makes simplifying assumptions that facilitate calculation at the expense of realism. Among these assumptions have been the equilibrium state, perfect markets, and the absence of frictional forces resisting change. A rapidly-changing intellectual economy is precisely the sort under which such assumptions are apt to be misleading. The goal of the legislator here is to accelerate the natural movement of the economy away from its state of quasi-equilibrium. Scientists inevitably work under conditions of incertitude with very limited knowledge of what other scientists are doing. And the flow of information and skills takes a considerable amount of time, thereby limiting the rate of change. Furthermore, we must not take it for granted that the available resources or factors of production are readily substituted. Discoveries are largely contingent upon the availability of unusually talented people or extraordinary opportunities.

This essay has provided several examples of how a government may be in a particularly good position to invest in scientific research and thereby make a particularly valuable contribution relative to the expenditure. A government's need to inventory its resources may create opportunities for fruitful cooperation with those who would like to participate for their own reasons. And because the cost of such additional effort may be low once the fixed costs have been paid, such investment may be very efficient and productive in spite of any putative inefficiencies in the public sector. So really the question we ought to be asking is not whether government should participate in scientific research, but rather what form that participation should take.[20]

NOTES

1. Michael T. Ghiselin, "The Economics of Scientific Discovery," Gerard Radnitzky and Peter Bernholz. *Economic Imperialism: The Economic Approach Applied Outside the Field of Economics* (New York: Paragon House, 1986), pp. 271-282. Michael T. Ghiselin, *Intellectual Compromise: The Bottom Line* (New York, Paragon House, 1989).

2. Jacqueline Carpine-Lancre, "Les expeditions oceanographiques et la publication de leurs resultats (etude bibliographique)," *Bulletin de L'Institut Oceanographique de Monaco* Special No. 2, Part 1, 1968, pp. 651-666.

3. Michael T. Ghiselin, *The Triumph of the Darwinian Method* (Berkeley: University of California Press, 1969).

4. Charles Darwin, *The Structure and Distribution of Coral Reefs* (London: Smith Elder & Co., 1842).

5. Charles Darwin, *Journal of Researches into the Geology and Natural History of the Various Countries Visited by H.M.S. Beagle, under the Command of Captain FitzRoy, R.N. from 1832 to 1836* (London: Henry Colburn, 1839).

6. William Stanton, *The Great United States Exploring Expedition of 1838–1842* (Berkeley: University of California Press, 1975); C. Ian Jackson, "Exploration as Science: Charles Wilkes and the US Exploring Expedition, 1838-42," *American Scientist* 73, 1985, pp. 450-461.

7. Daniel C. Gilman, *The Life of James Dwight Dana: Scientific Explorer, Mineralogist, Geologist, Zoologist, Professor in Yale University*, (New York: Harper & Brothers, 1899).

8. Karl Semper, *The Natural Conditions of Existence as they Affect Animal Life* (London: Paul Kegan, 1881).

9. H.L. Burstyn, "Science and Government in the Nineteenth Century: The Challenger Expedition and its Report," *Bulletin de L'Institut Oceanographique de Monaco*, Special No. 2, 1968, pp. 603–613.

10. George R. Agassiz, *Letters and Recollections of Alexander Agassiz with a Sketch of His Life and Work* (Boston: Houghton Mifflin, 1913).

11. Donald J. Zinn, "Alexander Agassiz (1835–1910) and the Financial Support of Oceanography in the United States," M. Sears and C. Merriman, eds., *Oceanography: the Past* (New York: Springer-Verlag, 1980), pp. 83-93.

12. Alexander Agassiz, "The Islands and Coral Reefs of Fiji," *Bulletin of the Museum of Comparative Zoology* 33, 1899, pp. 1–167.

13. Reginald A. Daly, "Pleistocene Glaciation and the Coral Reef Problem," *American Journal of Science* (4) 30, 1910, pp. 297–308.

14. William M. Davis, *The Coral Reef Problem* (New York: American Geographical Society, 1928).
15. Helen Riatt and Beatrice Moulton, *Scripps Institution of Oceanography: First Fifty Years* (San Diego: Ward Ritchie Press, 1967).
16. H.S. Ladd, Earl Ingerson, R.C. Townsend, Martin Russell, and H. Kirk Stephenson, "Drilling on Enewetak Atoll, Marshall Islands," *Bulletin of the American Association of Petroleum Geologists* 37, 1953, pp. 2257–2280.
17. *Ibid.*, p. 2277.
18. G.A.J. Scott and B.M. Rotondo, "A Model for the Development of Types of Atolls and Volcanic Islands on the Pacific Lithospheric Plate," *Atoll Research Bulletin*, No. 260, 1983, pp. 1–33.
19. John T. Harrison III, "Recent Marine Studies at Enewetak Atoll, Marshall Islands," *Bulletin of Marine Science* 38, 1986, pp. 1–3.
20. My thanks to my informants and critics: Robert Buddemeier, Jack Burch, Lorrie Colin, and Leighton Taylor.

NINE

THE GROWTH OF GOVERNMENT CONTROL OF AMERICAN HIGHER EDUCATION

Leonard P. Liggio and Roger E. Meiners

The assertions that American higher education is in crisis are true and false. The claim is false in that never have more resources been devoted to higher education than are at present. So the cries for more funding are those persistent from any sector that has come to rely on the public purse. Constant lobby pressure is necessary for colleges to compete with others who grow at public expense to be assured of ever expanding support. The crisis claim is true in the sense that government domination of higher education is at an all time high and can be expected to continue. The vitality that was present under a system that relied more on private support and was free of federal control is being lost, and we are suffering institutional torpor that is always a product of central government control.

This chapter provides an overview of the development of American higher education, with a focus on sources of support. We begin with a review of the evolution of higher education from colonial times to the growth of modern universities. Attention is given to the primary sources of subsidies for colleges: churches, foundations, and governments. Remarks are then made concerning the role of the modern university and the issue of academic freedom.

SUPPORT FOR HIGHER EDUCATION IN COLONIAL TIMES

The modern college and university are the product of the civilization of western Europe. The Greeks and Romans had schools of great importance, although the Chinese have the longest tradition of higher education, and the Arabic schools were a crucial forerunner of European higher education. When the Europeans' discovery and expansion of the 15th and 16th century was undertaken, European settlement and models were not directed at Asia (or Africa) where there were established political systems, but to the New World.

In the New World in the early 16th century, the Spanish conquests of the empires of Mexico and Peru and the establishment of colonial rule were accompanied by the creation of universities in each capital—Mexico City and Lima. These universities were established in form but not substance on European universities. While European, especially Iberian, rulers were founding new universities at home at this time, their principal funding was not from government revenues. In Latin America, the European tradition of private funding of universities did not survive the ocean voyage.

When the 17th century witnessed the northern European expansion to the areas that were indifferent to the Spanish and Portuguese—the lesser islands of the Caribbean and North America (north of Florida and of Spanish Mexico)—the English made the major contribution to the foundation of higher education. The French limited themselves to purely ecclesiastical education in Quebec. The Dutch and Swedes did not pursue in the New World what they were pursuing in founding new universities at home. An important reason was that the French, Dutch, and Swedish settlements were not at religious odds with the universities in their homelands. Those who wished to study could return.

The Dutch imprinted their commercial culture on the colonies of the Hudson and Delaware River valleys. Early on New York was a city of religious and cultural diversity since commercial freedom required toleration of all religions or none. New York's role as the New World center of Jewish culture is 350 years old, dating from the Spanish-Portuguese Jewish merchants welcomed in the Dutch commercial orbit. When the Dutch (and Swedes) came under English rule, it was High Anglican—hardly likely to interfere in the religious toleration and commercial profits that were its fruits. This regime welcomed the Huguenots at the revocation of the Edict of Nantes in 1685; the Palatine Germans were welcomed in later years. At that time, the Quaker (and German pietist) settlements of West Jersey, Delaware, and Pennsylvania meant the establishment of an important tradition equal to the Dutch in commercial freedom and religious toleration. The Middle Colonies (to which Rhode Island and Providence Plantations were connected in commercial and cultural toleration) did not see fit to initiate higher education until the pre-revolutionary period saw the creation of King's College (Columbia) in New York, Queen's College (Rutgers) in New Jersey, the College of New Jersey (Princeton), Brown University and the University of Pennsylvania (see Table 9-1). These colleges initiated the major tradition in American higher education, as the Middle Colonies (later States) and their ports were the major intermediaries for migration into the American interior—even the Southern piedmont and beyond. The commercial toleration and institutions of the Middle Colonies became the basis for interior American culture, despite assaults by the Puritan and the Southern Tidewater institutions.

Higher education in the Middle Colonies was religiously-based, but not narrowly or exclusively. Princeton, Queen's (Rutgers), and Brown were founded by Presbyterians, Dutch Reformists, and Baptists, respectively. Yet like King's (Columbia)

Table 9-1
College Formation in Colonial Times

College	Colony	Religion	Charter Year
Harvard University	Massachusetts	Congregational	1636
College of William & Mary	Virginia	Anglican	1693
Yale University	Connecticut	Congregational	1701
Princeton University	New Jersey	Presbyterian	1746
Columbia University	New York	Anglican	1754
University of Pennsylvania	Pennsylvania	Anglican	1755
Brown University	Rhode Island	Baptist	1765
Rutgers University	New Jersey	Dutch Reformed	1766
Dartmouth College	New Hampshire	Congregational	1769
Washington College	Maryland	Anglican	1782
Washington & Lee Univ.	Virginia	Presbyterian	1782
Hampden-Sidney College	Virginia	Presbyterian	1783
Transylvania College	Kentucky	Presbyterian	1783
Dickinson College	Pennsylvania	Presbyterian	1783

Source: Donald G. Tweksbury, *The Founding of American Colleges and Universities Before the Civil War* (New York: Columbia University, 1932), pp. 32–34.

College and the University of Pennsylvania they shared an Enlightenment attitude (to be distinguished from the Scientific Revolution which is a century earlier and found early interest in Puritan New England). Each allowed multiple religious affiliations, including Anglican, Presbyterian, Dutch and French Reformed, Quaker, Lutheran, and Deist.

Later, independence from the English Crown and the Enlightenment attitude created a positive atmosphere of toleration out of which various religious associations could express their educational interests. Many independent colleges were established throughout the new states, establishing the trend that would dominate until the last few decades. In the first century after the Revolution most new colleges were affiliated with Protestant denominations. In the second century, the new institutions of higher learning tended to be founded by Catholic religious orders and by Jewish organizations. More recently, that tradition has been maintained by the Fundamentalist Protestant groups, mainly related to the Southern Baptist tradition and certain Calvinist churches.

The American tradition of cultural and religious diversity encouraged by independent private higher education has been challenged in the past few decades by an approach that had been a minor key in American history of higher education—government education, and in particular, federally-supported and regulated higher education. Until recent decades, government and federally-supported higher education were not a significant part of the structure of American higher education.

When the American colonies were founded in the 17th century, the Southern and Middle Colonies relied for their higher education needs on sending students to the great European universities. Oxford, Cambridge, the Inns of Court, and the four Scottish universities were more than satisfactory for the Anglican gentry and lawyers and Presbyterian merchants. Similarly, the Catholic great families of Maryland were satisfied to send their sons to Louvain, Paris, or Salamanca after education by the English Provence Jesuits of Maryland in the context of government prohibition of establishment of Catholic educational institutions. The College of William and Mary was founded late in the century by Anglicans in England fearful that Anglican traditions would be diluted in the New World wilderness.

The Puritans who settled New England wished to establish a New Zion separated from the corruption of English society and church. Although Puritans had been gaining institutional bulwarks in the Church of England, including in colleges at Cambridge, the Atlantic migration represented the belief that Old England was doomed for the adherents of True Religion. The establishment of Harvard University was the expression of the need to be completely separated from the depraved institutions of England. Although the chartering of the College by the General Court of Massachusetts Bay Colony in 1636 included a grant of £400, the College remained unorganized until the death and bequest in 1638 of Rev. John Harvard's library and £780 (Harvard, as many of the Puritans, had been at Emmanuel College, Cambridge). In addition to local contributions, gifts from England were important in the early period of Harvard.

Due to the drift in religious direction which led Harvard to become the center of Unitarianism, the Congregationalists of more conservative Connecticut wanted their own educational institution. In 1701, the General Court of Connecticut chartered Yale University. The students studied with the various ministers who were their tutors in their parsonages around the colony until Jeremiah Dummer, agent in London for the colony, contributed a thousand volumes and Elihu Yale, former governor of Madras, India, and a Boston merchant, contributed books and the money to build a college building in New Haven. Although more restrictive in religious direction initially than the later colonial colleges, these earlier colleges tended to evolve along the lines of the toleration of the Middle Colonies.

Dartmouth College, which evolved from a colonial academy, was established on the upper Connecticut River in Hanover in 1769 where it became involved in the competing claims of New Hampshire and emerging Vermont. Its development is associated with the post-Revolutionary generation. The Dartmouth College case decided by the United States Supreme Court in 1819, after the arguments for the college by Senator Daniel Webster, ensured the independence of private colleges from state interference.

American independence had given an opening for new colleges to be established. The Dartmouth College case assisted the explosion of new higher education enterprises, alongside the explosion of commercial enterprises associated with the Jacksonian Era. This spirit is revealed in the chartering of state colleges and universities in the Old Northwest, the Middle West. The Northwest Ordinance (1787) had imposed the "New England Model" of public education on the territories north of the Ohio River. But, this was in the form of allocation of government held lands for educational use. States chartered colleges as state universities either without major support, or with limited state participation through land grants (in Wisconsin the state legislature charged a fee for its management of the lands granted to the university; the University of Michigan was almost a private entity). The state governments expected major financial support for the universities to come from tuition and from private donations. The states did not hold control over the trustees, who were chosen by election in districts, or by vote of the alumni. Perhaps the desire to avoid the expense of a public university makes it appear that state support for colleges was essentially "charitable."

The state universities established in the first half of the 19th century had strong religious requirements. The state of South Carolina decreed that at its state university "...a religion 'pure and undefiled' was to be preached to the youth of the State; and from the College as from a fountain, were to go forth the waters of salvation...Christian doctrine was to be taught from the pulpit, and from the Professor's chair...." [1] Many state universities' boards of trustees were dominated by representatives from the ministries of particular religions. Even Mr. Jefferson's University of Virginia took on the character of a religious institution during the mid-1800s.[2]

THE DEVELOPMENT OF FEDERAL INVOLVEMENT IN HIGHER EDUCATION

The federal government and the states battled to determine which level of government would have control over certain activities. Presidents Washington, Adams, Jefferson, and Madison lobbied for the establishment of a national university. Congress was not as interested in that scheme, preferring to devote some federal resources to support existing colleges or to help establish state colleges. The exception to this was the creation of the US Military Academy at West Point in 1802. Congressmen made sure that admission to the institution was in their hands.

During the first half of the 19th century, Congress was pressed by various interest groups to endow agricultural schools or other institutions of higher learning in the states. There were repeated attempts to have federal lands turned over to the states to be sold for the support of various institutions.

The first great federal government intervention in education, the Morrill Act of 1862, remained in the spirit of the preceding era. Passed as legislation only due to the withdrawal of the states-rights representatives and senators in the War Between the States, Congress granted public lands to establish an agricultural and mechanical college in each state. The revenues from these lands, freed from federal control, were used to establish new state entities, or to fund agricultural and engineering schools associated with private universities. Thus, alongside the private colleges and universities which continued to expand in the century after the Morrill Act, there were state universities treated largely as private institutions and land-grant colleges.

The Morrill Act of 1862 motivated the states to spend money on higher education. The Second Morrill Act of 1890 helped induce states to spend a certain amount on their colleges by establishing the matching grant principle. Under the Act, the colleges were required to meet specific standards or be ineligible for the federal money. This move, especially with respect to land-grant colleges, was also spurred by Hatch Act subsidies for agricultural research, the Smith-Lever Act of 1914 that provided federal support for extension services, and the Smith-Hughes Act of 1917 that provided federal support for vocational education and home economics at land-grant colleges. Federal support for land-grant colleges, which especially stimulated the growth of state universities, seemed to do less with a desire to support higher education than to respond to political pressure from agricultural interests.[3] Funding for such programs reached $23 million a year by 1930. Although few politicians ever questioned the legitimacy of the federal role in higher education, President Hoover's Advisory Commission on Education assured him that there are 31 provisions in the Constitution under which the federal government can find authority to support higher education.[4]

One of the earliest examples of federal regulation of college activities that did not bear directly on the subject matter being supported occurred under the Second Morrill Act in 1890. It required that the colleges must not deny admission on the basis of race unless there were separate but equal facilities. Seventeen states were stimulated to create separate colleges for the instruction of blacks.[5]

World War I produced the first federal research contracts to universities. Massachusetts Institute of Technology (MIT) was awarded $800 in 1915 by the National Advisory Committee for Aeronautics. From 1915 to 1918 that agency supported university research totaling $12,000.[6] The National Academy of Sciences, a private organization chartered by Congress, created a National Research Council (NRC) in 1916 to help coordinate research relating to national defense. The NRC was composed of government personnel and scientists from educational institutions and industry. It initially operated on funds provided by the Rockefeller and Carnegie Foundations. By the end of World War I federal funding for research had become institutionalized, although on a trivial scale compared to more recent years.

Numerous federal programs created during the Great Depression provided direct or indirect assistance for colleges and universities. During the years 1935–1943 about 620,000 students were employed in work programs at the college or graduate level and earned a total of $93 million. The average monthly employment during this period was over 110,000. Various federal construction programs (WPA) during the Depression provided new facilities for many colleges.

All but a few hundred thousand of the millions of federal dollars allocated for research in 1940 was distributed by the Department of Agriculture. Much of the subsequent increase in research expenditures is attributed to the rapid rise in government spending on military research during World War II. By 1950, over $150 million a year was being spent by at least 14 federal agencies on research by higher education. Over two-thirds of all budgeted university research came from federal money. Approximately 90 percent of all research money for the natural sciences was dependent on federal support. Most of the funds were for defense-related projects, agriculture, and public health. As has always been true of federal support, this money was distributed mostly to the larger and more prestigious universities.[7]

The social sciences soon benefited from the explosion of federal research funds. Much of the initial funding for social science research came through the Department of Defense. The Office of Naval Research sponsored research in the fields of human relations, manpower, psychophysiology, and personnel and training. The Air Force, through the RAND Corporation and the Human Resources Research Institute, sponsored studies on group motivation and morale, role conflict, leadership, social structure in the military community, and such.[8] This research support, combined with federal support for veterans of World War II and the Korean War (the GI Bill), helped boost the higher education industry.

At its peak in 1947, over one million veterans were enrolled under the GI Bill. This support, which is like a voucher system, averaged $1,000 a year to each veteran in college, subsidized a large portion of the doubling of college enrollments from 1.3 million to 2.6 million from 1938 to 1948. To help handle the rapid increase in enrollment after World War II, numerous colleges were given land and government buildings (that often had been constructed during World War II for military purposes adjacent to a campus). Colleges and universities have been loaned billions of dollars at below-market interest rates since the Korean War under the College Housing Loan Program for the construction of dormitories and other revenue-producing facilities by colleges.[9]

The National Science Foundation (NSF) was created in 1950. Congress allocated $3.5 million to the NSF for fiscal 1951. About the same time, federal funding for hundreds of graduate fellowships was initiated from sources such as the Atomic Energy Commission, the Public Health Service, and the Reserve Officer's Training Corps. Federal support for graduate and postgraduate study has expanded to fund thousands of students each year. The Public Health Service, Veterans Administration, and other federal agencies began to underwrite the cost of operating medical schools. Such funds have turned many medical schools into research institutions, the research interests often determined by the funding source.[10]

Through the 1950s federal support of higher education was tied to defense spending. Because it accounted for the majority of direct federal expenditures, it is not surprising that federal intervention in higher education came through this avenue. The National Defense Student Loan program, initiated in 1958, spurred by the *Sputnik* scare, declares:

> The present emergency demands that additional and more adequate educational opportunities be made available.... This requires

programs that will give assurance that no student of ability will be denied an opportunity for higher education because of financial need....[11]

This loan program was designed to provide support on a need basis for students interested in science, math, and foreign languages. This was followed in the late 1960s and early 1970s with various guaranteed loan programs, which, by the mid-1980s required $7 billion federal authorizations. Other federal grant programs, such as Pell grants, which are usually income based, required another $4 billion federal support. Veterans' assistance, which had risen to over $4 billion per year in the mid-1970s, declined to about $1 billion per year in the mid-1980s.

The creation of the federal Department of Health, Education and Welfare by the Eisenhower administration in 1953 reflected the bipartisan interest in the expansion of federal involvement in education.[12] The Secretary, Mrs. O. C. Hobby, and the Under-Secretary, Nelson Rockefeller, undertook in 1953 to expand the federal role in education. However, their role was mainly to create the institutional structures on which the Kennedy and Johnson administrations were able to build the expansion of federal involvement in education, including higher education.

These developments were paralleled by huge increases in state higher education funding, for example, in New York under Governor Nelson Rockefeller and in California under Governor Pat Brown. In addition to major state university centers and colleges, the United States experienced a quick growth of "post-secondary education" institutions—junior, community and county colleges. In the face of this development, private education stopped expanding—the trend of new private college foundations ceased, and some small or newer private colleges eventually closed.

Public sector expansion culminated in the creation of the Department of Education under President Carter, and despite the campaign promise to abolish the Department of Education by Ronald Reagan, the role of the federal government in higher education continued to expand during his administration.

ACADEMIC FREEDOM
AND GOVERNMENT SUPPORT

As Table 9-2 illustrates, no matter how it is measured, college education is heavily subsidized by government. Federal subsidization of higher education has become increasingly important in the past 35 years. State governments concurrently provide the bulk of the support for higher education. This support has the effect of redistributing income in general from lower income families to higher income families. Because our political economy produces a complex redistribution of income via a series of taxation and expenditure measures, it is not particularly useful to claim that the redistribution that occurs by higher education expenditures by the various levels of government is "unfair." It is simply part of a larger redistributive scheme that cannot easily be analyzed outside that context.

Table 9-2
Government Support of Institutions of Higher Education
% Current Fund Revenue

Year	Federal	All Government
1920	6.4	37.3
1930	3.7	30.9
1940	5.4	30.0
1950	22.1	45.4
1960	18.0	44.3
1970	12.5	43.0
1980	15.2	49.3
1986	12.6	44.8

Sources: US Department of Education, *Digest of Education Statistics, 1985-1986*; (Washington, D.C.: Government Printing Office, 1986). US Department of Education, *Statistical Abstract of the United States* (Washington, D.C.: Government Printing Office, 1986).

This does not mean that we cannot or should not make efficiency evaluations about the financing and provision of higher education, but such studies are likely to have little impact.[13] There is no reason to predict a change in the system unless there is a massive shift in electoral support or a change in the composition of the electorate. Regardless of one's perception about the desirability of government support for higher education, government support of higher education necessarily poses a threat to academic freedom. Only a trivial number of colleges have divorced themselves from all government ties. The decision by Congress in 1988 to override the Supreme Court decision in the Grove City College case makes clear congressional intent to mandate more aspects of the functioning of higher education.

Private colleges are an important part of the maintenance of academic freedom. Some worry that private colleges will be unable to compete with state colleges. It is increasingly difficult for subsidized private colleges to compete with state colleges that are even more subsidized, yet the political system may be generating an odd balance in this regard. In 1983, 26.8 percent of all fulltime college students were in private institutions (32.6 percent of full-time equivalent in four-year colleges were in private institutions). Private colleges received 44 percent of the federal dollars spent on higher education. Hence, the federal subsidy per student at private colleges is greater than for students in public colleges. This result may emerge, one might speculate, because private colleges have greater incentive to lobby for federal dollars. In any event the result is for the federal government to somewhat ameliorate the competitive disadvantage faced by private colleges relative to state colleges (although the bulk of the federal funds goes to support the prestige private universities).

The fact that public universities are mostly state, rather than federal institutions is, arguably, beneficial to academic freedom. Unlike in European nations, we have no national monopoly provider of higher education. Some states provide relatively little support for higher education (for example, New Hampshire, Connecticut, and Massachusetts), while other states devote two to three times as much of state income to higher education (for example, Alaska, Arizona, Hawaii, Mississippi, New Mexico, North Carolina, and Utah). Such diversity in amount and origin of support will produce more alternatives than would exist under a federal regime of universities.

IS PRIVATE PHILANTHROPY AND FUNDING A WAY OUT?

Breneman and Finn in "An Agenda for the Eighties," add to the important contributions of the other authors on financing of higher education by examining the marketplace for higher education.[14] It is interesting to compare the roles of the federal government and of private philanthropy, especially foundation support. While federal financing of higher education is centered in particular areas and disciplines, private philanthropy is spread much more evenly across the higher education spectrum. This raises the important question of why the decisions of the use of American citizens' income are better made by the politicians and bureaucrats than they are made by the individual citizens whose income it is? The source of the answer is that some groups benefit more from the government role of contributing the citizens' income to higher education than would benefit from the citizens' own choices. Current levels of federal government funding of higher education are determined by political pull rather than free market choices as in private philanthropy.

The rationale for federal government funding of higher education shares with all other rationales for government funding—the rationale of central planning. Millions of consumers choosing among a vast variety of higher education institutions will contribute to the diffusion of knowledge, the transmission of knowledge between generations, and the encouragement of the development of new knowledge. But, the central planner has a much better idea, bolstered by desirable mechanisms, such as peer review, of how the money should be spent. The central planner is able to harness the politician and bureaucrat to support his claim to better knowledge than the millions of earners of the income to be dispersed.

Breneman and Finn describe the marketplace provided by private philanthropy as "the idiosyncratic world of private philanthropy, which in higher education is capable of fostering pedagogical excellence, of encouraging bold innovation, of underwriting outright experimentation, of succoring odd institutions, of sustaining schools with 'viewpoints' and 'values' and even theologies."[15] One can well imagine that the advocates of "rationality" would fear that their disciplines would not receive the level of funding in the marketplace which is received in the system of taxation and political allocation of funds.

A valuable study would be to compare the cumulative consequences of private philanthropy with the funding of higher education by the federal government. The private philanthropy would indicate the wide diversity of interests that actually exists among the citizenry and which can only find true expression by the free market of voluntary donations. Federal government program funding would be found in fewer institutions and for fewer purposes. If the politicians' and bureaucrats' control of this part of the citizenry's income is not challenged, at the least, the system should be limited to matching the funding of private philanthropy in order to eliminate any central planning role by the federal government. If redistribution is forced on the citizenry, the minimum acceptable bureaucratic behavior would be a rule of law approach which gives absolute control to the voluntary decisions of the citizens by private philanthropy. If citizens are to be in control, then those politicians and the bureaucrats must not be permitted to have any choices in the distribution of citizens' income other than its transfer from the citizens to the federal government for distribution according to the citizens' expressed preferences of distribution by their consumer donations in the marketplace.

Obviously, other salutary improvements in the present system of government funding of higher education have been presented. The extensively studied systems of tax credits for tuition to public or private institutions offer one way to encourage wide choice by purchasers of higher education services and competition from the seller of the services.

CREATING A FUTURES MARKET IN HIGHER EDUCATION

Secretary of Education William Bennett has achieved notoriety for being a secretary who has been something besides a shill for the public education system. He has raised substantive questions concerning the structure of higher education, its costs, and the future burden society will bear in supporting a higher education system that contains numerous recognized weaknesses. Criticism generates debate that is useful in increasing the chances that constructive change will be introduced. But unless there are structural changes, the best intended suggestions will have little impact.

One major issue under discussion is the rate of increase in college tuition. As Secretary Bennett notes, since 1980 tuition has risen faster than the consumer price index. He argues that such increases are in part due to the expansion of federal student loans and grants, and the incentive of nonprofit colleges to maximize revenue, not contain costs. That is, there is little incentive for colleges to be efficient given the current structure of property rights. There are no owners or shareholders to discipline the managers nor is there a market for control.

The concern over rising tuition is also being addressed at the state level. Many states have enacted or are considering legislation that permits parents to save now in return for a promise of a guaranteed tuition in the future. For example, Michigan allows parents to deposit $3,000 to $4,000 with the state, depending on the age of the child and the plan chosen, in return for a payment guarantee of the average tuition when the child enters college. The Michigan plan is seen as a model that is being considered in many states. Some private colleges (e.g., Hillsdale College) have adopted similar plans.

The save-now-pay-later plan represents a unique opportunity, if structured properly, to directly introduce market evaluations into higher education. This is not to suggest that current plans will do so. The save-now-pay-later plan is simply a futures contract whereby the parent is speculating that tuition will increase at a greater rate than the yield received on these same funds if invested in the market with instruments that have smaller risks. It is tempting to say that the university, or state, is speculating that the yield it will receive on parents' deposits will equal or exceed the increase in the costs of providing education. Thus, the contracts, similar to futures contracts for wheat, are simply an allocation of risk that is mutually beneficial.

The problem with the latter argument is that it avoids the problem of opportunistic behavior on the part of universities or states. There are several interpretations of the current state plans. First, save-now-pay-later plans may simply be a means for the state to avoid constitutional balance budget constraints with the result of deficit financing similar to the Social Security system. That is, similar to the argument proposed for Social Security as an insurance policy to spread the risks, the save-now-pay-later plan may result in students attending under the plan being subsidized by taxpayers or future generations of parent-students with the result of inter-generational income transfers under the guise of a fully funded and actuarially sound program just like Social Security. The problem with plans guaranteed by the state is that both legislators and universities do not have incentives to ensure the financial integrity (i.e., actuarial soundness) of the plan because they are not the residual claimants of the gain nor are they the residual bearers of the liability of a loss. Taxpayers or future parent-students may ultimately bear the loss. Because that loss is spread over a large number of people or across generations, no one has an incentive to be informed about the financial integrity of the plan. Thus legislators and university administrators have an incentive to behave opportunistically. University administrators benefit by creating a future demand thereby increasing the likelihood of survival. Legislators benefit by giving the appearance that they are addressing the issue of rising tuition costs and access to higher education. Under this scenario the save-now-pay-later plans will be under priced similar to Social Security.

On the other hand, the plans may be over priced. That is, the parents would be better off if they invested in a private annuity or zero coupon bonds with future pay-outs to correspond to the period when the child is anticipated to attend college. None of the save-now-pay-later plans guarantee the parents that their child will be admitted to college. The Michigan plan provides that in the event of the death of the child, the parent is only entitled to the principal less administrative costs. Presumably this provision would also apply to students who are denied admission or flunked out before completion of their degree. It can be argued that the absence of a guarantee of admission or successful completion is essential in maintaining the reputation of institutions offering such plans. But long term contracts that deny any return on the principal, let alone guarantee the education, over a prolonged period like 10 years can be interpreted as an unconscionable contract and are certain to raise both legal and political issues when these contracts are exercised.[16] These contracts may involve certain consumer protection issues such as misrepresentations to parents that they are purchasing access in conjunction with an annuity to fund college.

All state plans have a common characteristic in that the contract is non-transferable. If these contracts are to avoid opportunistic behavior, as discussed above, it is essential they be transferable in the same way as, say, a futures contract in wheat is transferable. That is, individuals without children should also be entitled to invest in these contracts similar to those who purchase wheat futures contracts. These purchasers have no intention of consuming the wheat in the future. There are no apparent reasons to restrict transferability other than to permit opportunistic behavior through the absence of market signals.

Assume the contracts are made transferable. Consider the first case of an under-priced contract to permit deficit financing. If the market anticipates deficit financing, then when the contracts are issued they will immediately increase in value. The market reaction will be similar to someone holding wheat futures and the government suddenly increasing the price support for wheat. Thus divergences between contract issue prices and market prices will signal deficit financing. The disparity between the contract and market price will create excess demand for the issue and an embarrassment to the state or institution. This disparity will also mean foregone current revenues to the institutions who will have no incentive to set a market price.

Note that the same adjustments would have occurred in the Social Security market if the program were voluntary and contract rights were transferable similar to annuity contracts. That is, if the Social Security system was in reality what it was represented to be, namely an insurance program, the market would have provided information of the underpricing. So it is with the save-now-pay-later programs, if contract rights are not transferable, there will be no market signals and the programs will be represented and disguised as simply prepayments of tuition when in reality they are income transfer programs.

Now consider the overpriced contract. First of all, transferability of contract rights handles a number of problems associated with state plans. For example, the death of a child, the decision of a child not to attend college, the decision of a child to attend a college other than the college for which the parent owns a contract or the inability to be admitted to the college will not result in the forfeiture of interest or any other penalty in terms of the underlying investment character of the contract provided rights are transferable. Indeed, transferability eliminates these specific risks to the parent, thereby making such contracts much more attractive. Of course, if the contracts are overpriced, there will again be a divergence between the issue price and the market price permitting parents to evaluate these contracts for what they are—namely investment instruments instead of some vague guarantees of the government. Again, for the contracts to be viable, the issue price will have to come in line with the market price to sustain a demand for the contract.

Perhaps the most important feature of transferable rights and therefore market evaluations is the effect of this information on university decision makers. Contract holders in essence would be shareholders in the university who have claims to the residual. University programs or investments that have high rates of return such as increasing the reputation of the university as perceived by the market will increase the value of the contract. Similarly, those investments that have low, zero, or negative returns will lower the value of the contract. Holders of contracts will have an incentive to influence boards of trustees. Indeed, it would be difficult for the board of trustees to ignore the market information especially in light of competing institutions' changes in contract prices. Of course, no one individual has the incentive or the ability to fully evaluate the performance of a university. But, at the margin, investors with shares (contracts) will have an incentive to be informed and will determine market prices of contracts.

Contract prices will differ across institutions for a number of reasons such as anticipated reputation, extent of private and public subsidies, demand for college graduates, etc. But the relative changes in the contract prices over time would serve to monitor the behavior of trustees and managers. That is, a futures market in contracts would create a class of residual claimants with incentives to monitor. Under the current property right structure in academe there are no residual claimants. Thus Secretary Bennett's criticisms of higher education are not likely to change anything without a change in the structure of rights. Transferable rights in contracts would be a significant structural change. Given the political viability of such plans, they represent a major opportunity to be structured in such a way as to improve the responsiveness of higher education to the purchasers of college services.

NOTES

1. Donald G. Tewksbury, *The Founding of American Colleges and Universities Before the Civil War* (New York: Columbia University, 1932), p. 179.
2. Frederick Rudolph, *The American College and University* (New York: Knopf 1962), p. 219.
3. Homer D. Babbidge, Jr. and Robert M. Rosenzwieg, *The Federal Interest in Higher Education* (New York: McGraw-Hill, 1962), p. 10.
4. *Ibid.*, p. 17.
5. Rudolph, *op. cit.*, p. 254. This does not imply that the federal regulation was not beneficial to higher education opportunities for blacks.
6. Richard G. Act, *The Federal Government and Financing Higher Education* (New York: Columbia University Press, 1952), p. 78.
7. *Ibid.*, pp. 85–94.
8. *Ibid.*, pp. 112–113.
9. *Ibid.*
10. *Ibid.*, chapter 8.
11. Title I, National Defense Education Act.
12. In 1948, when New York Governor Thomas E. Dewey was nominated for the second time for the Republican presidential nomination, he convinced Governor Earl Warren of California to be the vice-presidential candidate by the promise to give him supervision of the social policy areas of health, welfare and education.
13. George J. Stigler makes a similar point in "Economists and Public Policy," *Regulation*, May-June, 1982, p. 13.
14. David W. Breneman and Chester E. Finn, Jr., eds., *Public Policy and Private Higher Education* (Washington, D.C.: Brookings Institution, 1978).
15. *Ibid.*, pages 419–420.
16. While many unconscionable contract cases can be interpreted as shifting interest in the principal to avoid usury statutes, a zero or negative return is also likely to be viewed as unconscionable. For example, suppose Social Security benefits were suddenly required to be actuarially sound without inter-generational transfers. Those who are young and contributing to Social Security would argue it is unconscionable to receive a negative return under the rubric that it is simply an insurance program.

TEN

MARKET FAILURE, GOVERNMENT FAILURE, AND THE ECONOMICS OF HIGHER EDUCATION

Edwin G. West

According to the leading US textbook on the subject of economics of education,[1] the rationale for public support of higher education rests mainly on the market failure argument concerning externalities.

> If higher education provides social benefits to society that individual students cannot capture, then the private demand for education will be less than the social demand, and underproduction of education will result.

But however plausible, the assumption of positive marginal externalities is yet unsupported by evidence. Meanwhile well over $30 billion are granted to institutions of higher education each year in the 1980s. Tuition and fees to students account for about 20 percent of revenues, the remainder being funded from government, private sources, endowment income, and sales and services.

An economic externality is said to exist when the self-interested action of one person or group in society indirectly affects the utility of another person or group. In other words, when individual X educates himself he benefits not only himself but others in society. The content of the external benefits has not always been made clear but the following examples have been suggested: increased economic growth for the nation, a more informed electorate, greater political participation, improved and extended research, reductions in crime and other antisocial activities.

With respect to economic growth, it should be noticed that the argument reduces to the proposition that increased human capital is beneficial in causing economic expansion generally. But, as the Friedmans have argued, the same proposition could be made about physical capital such as machines and factory buildings, yet hardly anyone would conclude that, because of the consequences for growth, tax money should be used to subsidize the capital investment of General Motors or General Electric.

The main difficulty with external benefits, to repeat, is that they have still not been empirically measured. And if they are to be measured, some critics point out, the investigator should also look for negative externalities. An instance of the latter, especially in less developed countries, is the case of the social unrest among a highly educated, yet significantly unemployed, intelligentsia. But the main point remains that if there are no attempts to measure external benefits, even if only crudely, the case for subsidies to higher education remains weak.

Suppose marginally significant externalities do exist. The success of a government program for internalizing them will be measured by the increase in higher education that it accomplishes. Suppose that, typically, the authorities operate a college that provides X units of education. Previously some families were purchasing zero amounts, others something less than X while a third group were purchasing more than X. The subsidized public college would obviously attract population from the first two groups so that, to this extent, total expenditure on education would increase. Consider, however, members of the third group who normally purchase more than X education units. Economic theory predicts that some of them will settle for the lesser X units at the public college since they will be more than compensated by their escape from about 75 percent of the per capita operating costs. *Their* action will have a *downward* influence on total educational expenditure. The final outcome thus depends on the numerical size of the different populations mentioned.

After his empirical study in 1973, Sam Peltzman estimated that if public colleges were eliminated college enrollment would fall by only 25 percent while total expenditure on higher education would fall by something between zero and 25 percent.[2] This result implies fewer students in college but with each receiving, on the average, more education. On further reflection, however, Peltzman appears to have overestimated the fall in college population. The main reason is that in his calculations he omitted the fact of deadweight loss from taxation, the fact that it costs the taxpayers more than one dollar for one dollar tax revenue to be raised. This extra cost is called the deadweight loss from taxation and the latest general equilibrium estimates of it in the period of Peltzman's experiment range from 17 cents to 56 cents.[3] Intervention, therefore, involves considerable negative income effects. Conversely, the withdrawal of government will involve a decrease in both taxation and the deadweight losses. As a result there will be positive income effects. The latter will raise the demand for higher education because it is a normal good. For this reason the decline in higher education following government withdrawal would have been less than Peltzman's 25 percent.

Deadweight loss from taxation of the magnitudes mentioned is, however, only one item in the costs of raising revenue. Others include the extra welfare costs of tax collection and tax evasion. Incorporating all these considerations, Usher has estimated that in Canada it costs $2.19 to raise a dollar in revenue.[4] It is strongly arguable that in the US in 1987, 15 years after Peltzman's investigation, the marginal deadweight loss from taxation has grown significantly. This follows from the fact that

(a) the proportion of gross national product (GNP) taxed is higher, and (b) deadweight loss increases with governments' share of GNP at an exponential rate. And when we allow for the increased costs of tax collection and evasion (see above), it would appear to be a conservative conjecture that it now costs about $2 to raise $1 of extra tax revenue in the US. The final implication is that US government intervention is maintaining the quantity of education at levels not much different from what would occur without it.

This conclusion is strengthened when we take into account the change in market structure after government institutions have "crowded out" private ones. The tendency, as will be argued below, is for higher cost public monopoly establishments to replace, or squeeze out, the lower cost services of a private and competitive college system.

Having reached this position we must conclude that even if positive marginal external benefits from higher education were demonstrated by collected evidence, it is not obvious that government intervention is very capable of capturing them. Government failure seems at least as strong as market failure. Alternatively one may entertain doubts whether external benefits are relevant at the margin. Judging from Peltzman's findings (even before our own adjustments to them), most college students in the US would go to college even without subsidies and they would receive better educations.

GOVERNMENT FAILURE

There are even deeper misgivings, not only about the externality argument, but also about government educational intervention in general. Implicitly it is being argued that the preferences of an undifferentiated electorate will be respected via an electoral process and by subsequent executive, bureaucratic, and judicial actions. Yet such a scenario is inaccurate. The fact is that the electorate is not undifferentiated. Typically it is represented by special interests whose preferences dominate those of the general electorate. When citizens are brought together into a group, as for instance at their place of occupation, the political office holder has an interest in transacting with its leaders. Representation of dispersed individual citizens, in contrast, is much more costly. The office holder himself will receive more direct rewards by behaving in this way and the result is a political process that produces private benefits to interest groups at collective costs. Expressed in other terms there is no assurance that representative democracies can easily deliver optimum subsidies to internalize external benefits from education as the usual welfare-regarding models of the public sector predict. Instead the real world political process can be more confidently expected to produce particularized rather than generalized benefits. Subsets of the population (including the office holders), therefore, stand to benefit at the expense of the general public.

Such argument predicts that educational subsidies will indeed emerge but that they will be directed more to the interests of the suppliers of education than to the general public. The supply interests here will be the organized teaching profession, the members of education bureaucracies, and the politicians. The result is that we start with a proposition about externalities that has been described as an instance of market failure, and we finish with the realization that, if political action is instigated as a corrective, we soon run into at least equally serious problems of government failure.

Even if evidence of externalities of net positive marginal value does emerge, this would still not constitute an argument for the present system of government financing. Ideally government intervention has to be designed to extend educational purchases beyond what the market would achieve. If this is at all possible the most effective way to do it is to direct the subsidies to students in the form of scholarships or voucher. Because students would then have the freest of choices between universities, the resultant competition between them would keep costs down to a minimum. The fact that the supply interests have managed to persuade governments to avoid vouchers and instead to finance the universities directly is testimony to their political power.

Typical public universities have conventional bureaucracies that are interested in expanding their own budgets and enhancing the welfare of administrators and others involved on the supply side. The inefficiency of such bureaus stems largely from their monopoly position. It is true that there exist some private institutions of higher education side-by-side with the public ones. Numerically, however, the private sector is small and relatively shrinking. One must reiterate that this situation occurs largely because of the tendency of the public system to "crowd out" the private. The circumstances that make this possible include the obvious fact that tuition fees in private establishments are higher than those in public institutions where the subsidy element tends to dominate. In 1986 average tuition and other fees in private universities amounted to $5,120 whereas the public equivalent was only $1,040.[5]

The crowding out phenomenon is not new. In his *Wealth of Nations* published in 1776, Adam Smith not only observed the tendency but also offered the crucial diagnosis. Unsubsidized private education institutions in his day were a declining minority, he argued, because the salaries of the teachers in the public or subsidized establishments

> ...put the private teachers who pretend to come into competition with them, in the same state as the merchant who intends to trade without a bounty [subsidy] in competition with those who trade with a considerable one...[6]

It is not surprising therefore that the proportion of private to public higher education institutions in the US has fallen from 35.7 percent in 1963 to 22.3 percent in 1983.[7] What is more, this decline is officially predicted to continue. Thus it is estimated that by 1990 the proportion of private to public will have fallen to 20.5 percent.[8]

Insofar as bureaucracy increases the costs and reduces the efficiency of education, the freedom and encouragement of the genuine scholar is seriously impaired. His working environment is likely to become the subject of tight routing and regulation. Furthermore, the administrative hierarchy with whom he is saddled will attempt to direct his energies towards obtaining the maximum financial return from government to pay the salaries of all participants including those of the administrators and of the least efficient academics.

Some relevant evidence has recently been produced by William Orzechowski.[9] He tested the hypothesis that staff inputs in public institutions are used in greater proportion than in private firms supplying the same service. His empirical analysis covered 31 states for the year 1968. He found that, for the same relative price of labor to capital by state, the public colleges in a state employed roughly 40 percent more labor than private colleges for the same size capital stock. He concluded that such a labor bias of public colleges and universities was due to behavioral reasons associated with the difference in ownership. The public institutions were operated by administrators who were utility maximizers and the fiscal residuum generated by these organizations was used to a considerable extent for overstaffing.

In another piece of research, David Sisk has argued that, because tuition is held below the market clearing price in public universities, market evaluation of the product mix is prevented and the public authority is forced to monitor product attributes. The main one is enrollment.[10] Consequently, because the public funding is directly linked to the number of students, university managers divert resources toward enrollment and away from instruction. The result is larger classes, lower admission standards, and less preparation for the classroom by instructors.

Although this analysis would lead one to predict that there would be a fall in standards for awarding degrees, in fact Sisk discovered that the standards for the Ph.D. are maintained. The reason is that such standards are conspicuously connected with the reputations of the individual faculty. This being so, and given the incentive to maintain an expanded enrollment, the lowered chance of each student's success implies that it will take more student years per Ph.D. awarded in public universities than in private universities of equal quality. Sisk found, indeed, that it takes on average twice as long to obtain a Ph.D. in public compared with private colleges.

Sisk mentions a Californian Report that suggests that the financing, and therefore the monitoring, of the University of California be based on degrees awarded and not students enrolled. He predicted that under this system the administrators would certainly push for a greater output of degrees; but this result could only be obtained either (a) by providing students with more service or (b) by lowering the standards for the award of a degree. The second possibility is the danger that should be avoided. And it could be avoided, Sisk contends, by subsidizing the students directly and letting *them* do the monitoring. Thus an argument for the voucher system appears once more.

EXCELLENCE *VERSUS* EQUITY

A second argument to justify government intervention is that income distribution can be improved by granting educational facilities, especially to the poor. Champions of the traditional kinds of universities will complain that this will involve such an expansion of numbers as to worsen the environment for scholars and to reduce the level of excellence. Before we can enter this debate we must examine more closely the nature of equality of opportunity. A part of the argument for it consists in the claim that some families could not afford to provide a given level of education so that there would be a loss of human resources not only to the individuals concerned, but to society as a whole. Alfred Marshall's argument in favor of public support of education, for instance, was that "the economic value of one great industrial genius is sufficient to cover the expenses of the education of a whole town.... All that is spent during many years in opening the means of higher education to the masses would be well paid for if it called out one more Newton or Darwin, Shakespeare or Beethoven."[11] What is interesting in Marshall's list of personalities that have enriched the world is that they all emerged without the benefit of government subsidy via education at state universities. It should be kept in mind, however, that subsidies can be paid publicly or privately. In the case of Shakespeare, private subsidy or patronage appears to have been particularly successful.

The other aspect of the concern for equality of opportunity is related to income distribution. If additional education is required in order to obtain more income, then allowing poorer individuals to obtain higher education is one means by which future income distributions will become more equal. One must reiterate, nevertheless, that even if governments pursue this line of thought, the division of subsidies directly to universities is only one possible instrument available; an alternative is to direct the money to students so as to maximize their choice and to encourage competition between institutions.

Before we accept the case for intervention on equity grounds, however, we should probe further. It is first necessary to make a distinction between two broad types of equity in the context of educational finance. Equity (Type 1) will refer to equity within the college-ability group. Equity (Type 2) will relate to equity between the college-ability and non-college, typically lower ability, groups (or between users and non-users of the education system). The emphasis here will be upon equity Type 2.

It will be interesting to examine the position of John Rawls who has argued that any change or intervention can be allowed so long as those lowest on the income scale are not made any worse off.[12] By income scale is meant a lifetime scale. The avoidance of injury to the poorest has its corollary that the taxes they pay will be used in the most efficient manner and not to the disproportionate benefit of more fortunate classes. Now "the less fortunate class" overlaps considerably with the group in society that does not receive post-secondary education. The fact that there are millions within these groups that do not receive the benefits, together with the fact that the same individuals are obliged to contribute via taxes to the finance of the higher education of the more fortunate, brings the present system into serious question on the very criterion of equity that is supposed to justify higher educational subsidies.

The percentage of the high school class of 1980 participating in full time post-secondary education two years later was 34.46. For the lowest quartile socioeconomic status it was only 18.84 percent. It should be remembered, moreover, (a) that not all students complete high school; (b) that of those who proceed to post-secondary education less than a quarter attend universities. More important, even if we did find that all socio-economic groups were equally "represented" in post-secondary schooling, this does not deny that millions of non-users of higher education at the bottom of the income scale would be forced to pay for the post-secondary education of others whose lifetime income expectations are considerably higher than their own. Equity Type 2 would be sacrificed for Equity Type 1.

The argument that higher education should be supported because in the long run graduates will pay back the subsidy in the form of higher taxes over their lifetimes is not convincing either because the repayment strictly should consist of subsidy money *together with accumulated interest*. This brings us to the question of the efficiency of capital markets which will be examined in the next section.

EFFICIENCY

Another major explicit rationale for intervention in higher education is the attempt to remove what are called "barriers to access." The most widely quoted examples of barriers are financial ones. Higher education would, of course, occur without government intervention, but would involve the "barriers" of significant positive prices. Yet millions of other goods and services are also sold at significant positive prices. Should we speak of financial barriers here too? Obviously, the case for intervention must be linked not merely to the existence of prices, but to an argument that in higher education they are so "artificial" or arbitrary as to constitute what can truly be called *unusual* financial barriers. There seems a consensus among economists that the main reason for specially "artificial" barriers and the consequent lack of inter-student equity, is the prevalence of "excessive" interest charges facing qualified but low income students.[13]

These "excessive" prices of finance are, in turn, often construed as stemming from capital market imperfections. It is fair to say, however, that no rigorous empirical demonstration of this proposition has yet been made. A crucial issue is the distinction between the student borrowers' rate and the lenders' realized rate. When we deduct transaction costs, the lenders' realized rate may be no different from that realized on physical capital. Education loans are associated with high transaction costs. They include the costs of information, screening, collection, defaulting, and they are likely to be appreciable. With "high" prices, the allocation of capital could well be efficient; that is no "artificial financial barrier" need exist. Meanwhile the absence of evidence of abundant use of private loans for education does not necessarily mean that a capital market is imperfect or does not potentially exist.

If a government has no better methods than private agencies for reducing the special transaction costs that are associated with human capital lending, it will create a misallocation of capital, not eliminate one, if it intervenes to lower interest rates to one common level. It is arguable, however, that governments are in a position to reduce transaction costs. This is because they have access (a) to superior information, and (b) to exceptional administrative economies. Governments have already invested large resources in establishing machinery for income tax assessment and collection. The marginal costs of using this machinery for educational loans collection could be relatively small.

The result is that an argument can be made for intervention by the government on efficiency grounds, but such intervention is in terms, not directly of education, but of finance. The argument, in other words, leads at best to a case for a government loan system. Government-sponsored loans *could*, so the argument goes, involve lower interest rates, not because of subsidies from nonusers, but from "genuine" cost reductions in lending.

To pursue the basis of these possible cost reductions further, we should focus on the incentives to default. It is realistic to assume that there is a significant margin of people who have no compunction in evading repayment if they believe the chances of escape without cost are good. Because the borrower does not pledge physical collateral, he is more tempted to skip. One can predict, meanwhile, that these chances will be better if the collecting agency is a bank rather than the income tax authority. If the bank is given federal guarantees of loan repayment in case the student defaults, it will have negligible incentives to pursue the debtor. If, however, the loan is registered in the income tax files, the only way to default is to become a vagrant and forego lifetime Social Security benefits. *This* is the fundamental ("deterrent") advantage that governments have over private markets: the costs imposed on defaulters are automatic and likely to be highly effective when the income tax machinery is employed. But so far it has not been.

CRITICISMS OF THE PRESENT US EDUCATION LOAN SYSTEM

The previous argument implies that governments might efficiently help students to pay for their own education without recourse to third parties. But this would mean the availability of a loan system involving rates of interest only slightly lower than market rates. If the taxpayers are brought in at any point to subsidize or to "rescue" the loan system by substantial rate reduction then it begins to defeat its purpose.

In recent years we have witnessed unprecedented high interest levels on the capital market. Yet as late as the fall of 1981, students taking advantage of the American Graduate Student Loan Program were asked to pay only seven percent interest. In addition, there are periods of grace including the duration of college attendance. Equally important the rates of delinquency on these loans have been astonishingly high. By the late 1970s and early 1980s default rates had climbed to 16 percent! Clearly the taxpayer *is* being forced to "rescue" and subsidize the system; and because taxpayers include non-users in the poorest sections of society (they pay indirect taxes if not income taxes), the system has been grossly inequitable.

Some object that it is morally wrong to saddle young people with debt at such an early age in life. The appropriate answer was given a quarter of a century ago by Milton Friedman who argued for a *contingent* loan system. Under this arrangement, students would only be called upon to repay their loans if their human capital investment turned out to be successful, that is, if they reached a high or above average income. The successful students, meanwhile, would be obliged to pay some surcharge to cover the costs of the less successful. In this case, students as a class would cross subsidize. Third parties including the poor nonusers would not be forced, as they are now, to participate in the operation.

Despite the logic behind these arguments it is a striking fact that, a quarter of a century after Friedman wrote, the principle of a *contingent loan system* has still not been introduced by the public sector in America. Equally arresting is the continuance of a bureaucracy with its own special constituency persisting with an inefficient method of loan policing and collection. In other words, the loan system is still not operated by way of the income tax machinery, the method that Friedman originally advocated.

The largest financial intervention, meanwhile, continues to be, not the loan system, but the Basic Educational Opportunity Grant (BEOG) program. In the 1980s total outlays on BEOGs are exceeding $3 billion. Such subsidies to college students, to repeat, result in making individuals with higher expected incomes in the future even wealthier and at the expense of the less fortunate. The comment of the Friedmans in 1980 is still apposite:

> In this area those of us who are middle- and upper-income classes have conned the poor into subsidizing us on a grand scale—yet we not only have no decent shame, we boast to the treetops of our selflessness and public spiritedness.[14]

PRIVATE NON-PROFIT UNIVERSITIES

There is a temptation to think that because most private universities are legally nonprofit institutions, there is not much difference between them and public universities. Conducting a private university without any private motive, such as the pursuit of profits, might seem to produce an essentially impossible task. Yet because a firm is described at law as being a nonprofit undertaking does not mean that something like profit is not operative in reality just beneath the surface. At private institutions students pay high fees that very often cover most of the cost of their schooling. The money spent by the student is either his own or comes from a loan or a scholarship. For this reason such students have strong incentive to see that they get value for money. If they do not they can go elsewhere. Administrators, in other words, are not the only actors in the process of responding to incentives. If private students are able to shop around aggressively, which is the case if their fees cover most of the cost, administrators have to respond to their needs in the sense of producing at lowest cost as well as providing the appropriate pattern (mix) of services. Moreover, the student himself will be a more efficient learner. It has been observed, for instance, that one graduate at Dartmouth College once remarked, "When you see each lecture costing $35 and you think of the other things you can be doing with $35, you are making very sure that you are going to go to that lecture."[15]

Another illustration of the argument that private colleges usually follow market incentives to the full is the recent contention by the Friedmans that, besides teaching services, private colleges and universities also produce and sell monuments and research. Buildings, professorships, and scholarships are often financed by a benefactor who receives in return a memorial for his services. In the process students become, in effect, like shareholding employees in the joint educational process. "The combination of the selling of schooling and monuments exemplifies the much under-appreciated ingenuity of voluntary cooperation through the market in harnessing self-interest to broader social objectives."[16]

It is prudent to keep in mind, however, a whole spectrum of educational institutions from the pure public (state) university at the one polar extreme to the complete market or private enterprise university at the other. It is interesting that in his *The Wealth of Nations* we find Smith attacking, not *all* universities in the 18th century, but some kinds in contrast to others. The most grotesque deteriorations in efficiency occurred, Smith insisted, where the whole of the incomes of the university personnel came directly from private (bequests) endowments, regardless of efforts.

> In every profession, the exertion of the greater part of those who exercise it, is always in proportion to the necessity they are under of making that exertion.... The endowments of schools and colleges have necessarily diminished more or less the necessity of application in the teachers.[17]

In other universities, the administrators and professors had to rely also on the fees from their students. Smith observed that the necessity of application, though more or less diminished wherever there was any element of private endowment finance, was not in this case entirely taken away from the teacher.

> Reputation in his profession is still of some importance to him, and he still has some dependency upon the affection, gratitude, and favorable report of those who have attended upon his instructions; and these favorable sentiments he is likely to gain in no way so well as by deserving them, that is by the abilities and diligence by which he discharges every part of his duty.[18]

Smith asks us to contrast this kind of university, which was like the one at which he taught in Glasgow, with those whose teachers were prohibited from receiving any fee from pupils. In this case a teacher's endowment-financed salary constituted the whole of his revenues from office. "His interest is, in this case, set as directly in opposition to his duty as it is possible to set it."[19]

Although Smith was referring to endowments made directly to a university, the same consequences arose from the custom of tying certain scholarships to a particular college. In this case the student had no redress when finding inefficient teaching since he could not transfer the scholarship elsewhere. Adam Smith, himself, seems to have been caught in this same trap. In 1740 he was appointed as a student to one of the Snell Exhibitions at Balliol College, Oxford.[20] It would have been much more in keeping with his system of efficiency had his scholarship been transferable between universities just as in the modern proposal for the education voucher. Had such a choice been available it is very probable that Smith would have chosen one of the Scottish universities because he had a much better opinion of them than those below the border. Unlike them, most Scottish universities charged student fees that covered a considerable proportion of total costs.

PRIVATE ENDOWMENTS

In the 19th century the practice of endowing universities with bequests received further scrutiny by the political economists. John Stuart Mill, for instance, acknowledged that the right of bequest was an extension of the right of property. As such, endowments for education were to be accepted as a fact of life. If, however, they were held to cause serious imperfections in the private market for education, then economists had the duty to devise newer methods of allowing public endowment financing to operate. The main trouble with endowments arose, Mill argued, when they were made in perpetuity. The wishes of the original donor often became impractical with a change of conditions centuries later. The trustees, meanwhile, often became so corrupted that they eventually began to think of the funds as their own property. The need was for some impartial body to interpret the appropriate use of the funds with the passage of time. Those who wanted to abolish endowments because of the problems, were too extreme. To prevent misuse, endowments made in the distant past, Mill contended, ought, at least ultimately, to be under the complete control of the government.[21]

The 19th century disciple of Adam Smith, Sir Robert Lowe, agreed with Mill but endeavored to be more specific in devising conditions.[22] Following Smith he thought it was important to try to work into endowments "the merits of the free system." This could be done by incorporating bequests into a system of "payments by results." An educational institution should be rewarded with a flow of funds from endowments according to its proficiency and according to the number of students taught. Clearly, Lowe's system approached that of the modern voucher scheme proposal.

It is useful to keep Lowe's position in mind when considering the history of university education. In the 19th century especially, the endowment was typically administered so as to end up serving the interests of the faculty and administration rather than of the student. Stanford University, for example, which, although established to provide undergraduate education, seems to have quickly deviated from the ideas of the benefactors to become like other institutions. Similarly disturbing was the attempt by the Rockefeller Foundation to shape higher education into a comprehensive system and to discourage unnecessary duplication and waste. In fact, it is usually untrue that "duplication and overlapping" means waste; for competition to exist there must, in most cases, be at least two suppliers who "overlap" each other.

On a consistent view of property rights it is arguable that benefactors should be allowed to make their own conditions on the endowments they leave. Nevertheless, it is difficult not to be disturbed by the practice of the Carnegie Foundation in discriminating against church colleges from the beginning of the 20th century. It may be contended that, so long as there is free entry, different benefactors will cancel out the idiosyncracies of others. This contention, however, could not have been so reassuring in the 1930s when the trusts set up by Carnegie and Rockefeller contained over three-fourths of the known assets of foundations.

If the proposals of Sir Robert Lowe had been implemented from the mid-19th century, a free and more competitive system would have emerged even though Carnegie and Rockefeller had dominated the endowment "market." Lowe recommended that foundations and wealthy individuals have their endowments channelled through a special central agency (such as, in Britain, the Charity Commissioners) to educational institutions *simply according to their enrollments*. Although this does not constitute a voucher system in the direct sense, the result is the same. The student or his family triggers off an incremental portion of the grant that goes to the school or university by his decision to choose one particular institution in preference to others. Subsidies follow the student, therefore, just as they do with the conventional voucher. In this way the system embraces all the advantages of competition, free choice, and efficiency that are associated with voucher plans.

It is reasonable to conjecture that if Lowe's mechanism had been adopted there would have been less chance for universities and other institutions to manipulate endowment funds for the purposes of the administrators and faculty. Whether the Carnegie Foundation could have discriminated against church colleges would have depended on the design of the constitutional body that was to have had the responsibility of allocating all the funds to universities. Compromise arrangements could have been introduced of course whereby, for instance, for every endowment dollar going to particular universities for such items as buildings and research, two dollars had to be devoted to the common pool of "voucher" funds. The latter would have to be allocated in proportion to enrollments at the college of the student's choosing and would, therefore, be spent according to teaching efficiency as perceived by students and their families.

PRIVATE UNIVERSITIES AS A SAFEGUARD AGAINST A MONOPOLY PUBLIC SYSTEM

The effect of tenure systems is probably more pernicious in public than in private universities. Because of stronger union representation in public institutions there is less variance in rewards to faculty members since, in effect, the less productive members redistribute from their more efficient colleagues towards themselves.[23] What needs to be cautioned against, however, is the temptation to believe that, because private universities exist, their presence will provide all the necessary correctives to the shortcomings of the public sector. One necessary condition must be fulfilled for this view to be valid: a reasonably sized private sector must be maintained in the future. The trouble is, as we have shown, that the presence of a strong public undertaking is a continuous threat to the number of its competitors.

One is reminded of the contrasting views of the classical economists on this question. In the early 19th century some of them were beginning to be attracted to the idea of government-as-enterprise, that is, to the idea that the government should be allowed to enter at any level of a market-provided service and "compete" with existing private establishments. The position in the early days was treated as fairly innocuous since the proposed interventions were seen merely as marginal experiments.

Of all the advocates, the name of John Stuart Mill stands out. In his *Principles of Political Economy*, published in 1848, he distinguished what he called undesirable or *authoritative* interference that controlled the free agency of individuals, from the non-authoritative intervention designed to promote the general interest. An example of the latter would be intervention that, while leaving individuals free to use their own means of pursuing any objects of general interest, "the government, not meddling with them, but not trusting the objects solely to their care, establishes, side by side with their arrangements, an agency of its own for a like purpose."[24]

Under this rubric, Mill attempted to justify governments participating both in education and in business generally. With respect to education he argued "though a government, therefore, may, and in many cases ought to, establish schools and colleges, it must neither compel or bribe any person to come to them."[25] A public (government) college should exist: "as one among many competing experiments, carried on for the purpose and stimulus, to keep the others up to a certain standard of excellence."[26] The argument that the public institutions would always be superior pace-makers was of course entirely *a priori*. No substantial evidence on the matter was yet available.

Since Mill's time, experience has shown that when a government agent enters a profession or industry there are automatic or unavoidable restrictions placed on the private competitors. For one thing, the public enterprise has the extra advantage of reliance on government tax revenue and loans that rest on the public credit. Individuals connected with the public supply, moreover, often become a disproportionate political constituency in their own right and are able to press successfully for further degrees of protection and intervention.

PROPRIETARY ACADEMIES

The point has already emerged that the efficiency of academic institutions depends crucially on the structure of property rights surrounding them. So far we have examined (a) public colleges where most, if not all, of the costs are provided by government; and (b) independent colleges that are privately endowed. We have also emphasized that, before the state-run higher educational institutions, the universities such as Oxford and Cambridge which operated without government support throughout the 18th century and well into the 19th century were certainly not monumental successes. It is reported by Winstanley, for example, that by the mid-19th century there was in Cambridge a growing resort by students to the services of private tutors (at a fee) as an escape from the inefficient teaching provided by the university and colleges.[27] Luminaries such as Edward Gibbon and Jeremy Bentham, as well as Adam Smith, were all highly critical of the privately endowed universities.

And again it was Adam Smith who diagnosed the source of the problem: inappropriate property rights specifications.

> If the authority to which the teacher is subject resides in the body corporate, the college, or university, of which he himself is a member, and in which the greater part of the other members are, like himself, persons who either are, or ought to be, teachers; they are likely to make a common cause, to be all very indulgent to one another, and every man to consent that his neighbour may neglect his duty, provided he himself is allowed to neglect his own. In the University of Oxford, the greater part of the public professors have, for these many years, given up altogether even the pretence of teaching.[28]

The only ultimate cure of the US university's "cost disease" today is the gradual but planned withdrawal of government finance from the academic industry. Without this event the crowding out effect will always make it difficult for new *proprietary* academic establishments to prosper. In Britain it is probably true to say that the unique case of the sole independent university at Buckingham is maintaining a threshold mainly because of the recent retrenchment of public spending on the "conventional universities." And it is remarkable that the Buckingham institution is the only one hitherto to have introduced such innovations as two-year degree courses, the substitution of 2–5 year contracts for the old tenure system, and academic years consisting of four 10-week terms.

CONCLUSION

The debilitation of typical universities in today's environment stem from years of oversupply of public funds. The argument by some economists that government intervention has been justified by the existence of public (external) benefits has been based on assertion rather than evidence. One part of the argument contains the *implicit* assumption that intervention will significantly expand educational output. Having applied the analysis of Peltzman (with our own modifications) we have reached the conclusion that significant educational output expansion following intervention has never been demonstrated. Meanwhile we have witnessed a substantial expansion in the costs of an increasingly inequitable and monopolistic public establishment and the slow demise or crowding out of a competitive private system.

This is not to say that any form of privately funded education institution will do much better. The authority of Adam Smith and others provides testimony to this. Private subsidies can be just as disruptive or enervating as public subsidies. The main requirements are proprietary enterprises whose main source of revenue derives directly from the market and its system of payment by results. Such institutions only will experience the salutary feedback mechanism of the stock market, a mechanism that will constantly keep proprietary establishments progressively up to standard. Administrators' and professors' sovereignty should go. The consumer should be reenthroned.

NOTES

1. Elchanan Cohn, *The Economics of Education* (Cambridge, Massachusetts: Ballinger Publishing Co., 1975), p. 24.

2. Sam Peltzman, "The Effect of Government Subsidies-in-Kind of Private Expenditures: The Case of Higher Education," *Journal of Political Economy* 81:1, January, 1973.

3. Charles L. Ballard, *et al.*, "General Equilibrium Computations of the Marginal Welfare Costs of Taxes in the United States," *American Economic Review* 75(1), March, 1985. Other fairly recent estimates are to be found in: A.B. Atkinson and N. Stern, "Pigou, Taxation and Public Goods," *Review of Economic Studies*, 1974, pp. 119-128; Edgar K. Browning, "The Marginal Cost of Public Funds," *Journal of Political Economy*, 1976, pp. 283-298; Dan Usher, "Tax Evasion and the Marginal Cost of Public Funds," *Economic Inquiry*, Vol. XXIV, October, 1986.

4. Dan Usher, "The Private Cost of Public Funds: Variations on Themes by Browning, Atkinson and Stern," *Economic Research*, Queen's University, 1982.

5. US Department of Education, *Digest of Education Statistics 1985–1986* (Washington, D.C.: Government Printing Office, 1986), Table 139.

6. Adam Smith, *The Wealth of Nations, Book V*, Edwin Cannan, ed. (London: Modern Library, 1950), p. 265.

7. US Department of Education, *op. cit.*, Table 87.

8. Martin M. Frankel and Deborah E. Gerald, *Projections of Education Statistics to 1990–1991* (Washington, D.C.: National Center for Education Statistics, US Department of Education, 1982), Table 20.

9. William Orzechowski, "Economic Models of Bureaucracy: Survey, Extensions and Evidence," in Thomas E. Borcherding, ed., *Budgets and Bureaucrats: The Sources of Government Growth* (Durham, North Carolina: Duke University Press, 1977).

10. David Sisk, "A Theory of Government Enterprise: University Ph.D. Production," *Public Choice* 37, No. 2, 1981, pp. 357–363.

11. Alfred Marshall, *Principles of Economics*, 9th edition (London: The Macmillan Company, 1961).

12. John Rawls, *A Theory of Justice* (Cambridge, Massachusetts: Harvard University Press, 1971).

13. See, for, instance E.L. Hansen and B.A. Weisbrod, *Benefits, Costs and Finances of Higher Education* (Chicago: Markham Publishing Co., 1969).

14. Milton and Rose Friedman, *Free to Choose: A Personal Statement* (New York: Harcourt Brace Jovanovich, 1980).

15. *Ibid.*, p. 177.
16. *Ibid.*
17. Adam Smith, *op cit.*, p. 283.
18. *Ibid.*, p. 284.
19. *Ibid.*
20. E.G. West, *Adam Smith, The Man and His Works* (Indianapolis: Liberty Press, 1976), p. 44.
21. John Stuart Mill, "Endowments," *The Jurist*, 1833.
22. Sir Robert Lowe, *Middle Class Education: Endowment or Free Trade?* (London: Hartwell, 1868).
23. Richard Freeman, "Unionism and the Dispersion of Wages," Harvard University Discussion Paper No. 629, June, 1978.
24. John Stuart Mill, *Principles of Political Economy* (New York: Augustus Kelley, 1969), p. 942.
25. *Ibid.*, p. 956.
26. John Stuart Mill, *On Liberty* (Everyman's edition, London, 1972), p. 240.
27. D.A. Winstanley, *The University of Cambridge in the Eighteenth Century* (Cambridge, Massachusetts: Cambridge University Press, 1922).
28. Adam Smith, *op. cit.*, Chapter 1, Part III, Article II.

ELEVEN

ACCREDITATION OF HIGHER EDUCATION
A CASE OF MISREPRESENTATION

Robert J. Staaf

Parts II through V of this paper examine the institutional structure of how colleges and universities are accredited.[1] Part II presents an overview of accreditation in terms of the number and types of accrediting associations, the amount of federal funding tied to accreditation status, and the role of the U.S. Department of Education. Part III examines "institutional" accreditation and the incentives of evaluators. Part IV examines specialized or "program" accreditation. Part V considers the demand for accreditation by students, businesses, institutions, and governments.

Parts VI and VII analyze accreditation as a mechanism to assure quality. Part VI is a brief summary of recent advances in the economic literature on quality assurance as applied to for profit firms.[2] Part VII applies this literature to nonprofit firms in higher education. It is apparent from this analysis that the accreditation process does not provide quality assurance. Given current institutional arrangements, quality assurance will be provided, if at all, at the institutional level. The accrediting process creates, if anything, negative incentives to monitor or assure quality. Moreover, accrediting associations, as independent agencies, do not have brand-name capital at risk to assure quality. The conclusion in Part VIII suggests that accreditation is primarily a means of organizing higher education interest groups to engage in lobbying for certain types of government funding and the avoidance of regulation.

OVERVIEW OF ACCREDITATION

There are four national accrediting associations, six regional associations, and at least thirty-eight specialized associations recognized by the U.S. Department of Education and the Council on Post-secondary Accreditation (COPA).[3] COPA is an umbrella organization in which each association has membership on the council.[4] The regional and specialized associations represent the most comprehensive accreditation for purposes of this paper.[5] The Middle States has 485 accredited and 22 candidate institutions, New England has 194 accredited and 4 candidate institutions, North Central has 915 accredited institutions, Southern has 722 accredited institutions and the Western has 133 accredited and 10 candidate institutions.[6] The following associations are the major specialized accrediting associations in terms of membership as of 1983:

The Accreditation Board for Engineering and Technology has accredited 1302 engineering and 670 engineering technology programs; the American Assembly of Collegiate Schools of Business has accredited 231 business administration and 18 accounting programs; the American Bar Association has accredited 173 law schools; the American Dental Association has accredited 60 dental schools, 479 specialty programs, 276 general practice residency programs, 9 advanced general dentistry programs, 292 dental assisting programs, 201 dental hygiene programs and 56 laboratory technology programs; the American Psychological Association has accredited 126 clinical, 31 counseling, 19 school, 5 combined, and 242 internship programs; the Association of Theological Schools has accredited 167 units; the Committee on Allied Health Education and Accreditation has accredited 3,125 various programs; the

National Accrediting Agency for Clinical Laboratory Sciences accredited 644 medical technologists, 172 medical laboratory technicians-associate degree, 74 medical laboratory technicians-certificate and 51 histologic technician programs; the Council on Social Work Education has accredited 88 graduate and 320 baccalaureate programs; the Liaison Committee on Medical Education (AMA) has accredited 142 programs; the National Association of Schools of Art and Design has accredited 114 programs; the National Association of Schools of Music has accredited 522 institutions; the National Council for Accreditation of Teacher Education has accredited 517 elementary (BA), 524 secondary (BA), 338 elementary (graduate), 309 secondary (graduate), 247 elementary administration, 245 secondary administration, 144 superintendent, 209 curriculum and instruction, 231 counselor, and 103 school psychologist programs for a total of 561 institutions; and the National League of Nursing has accredited 492 BA and MA programs, 408 associate programs, 280 diploma programs, and 123 practical nursing programs.[7]

The U.S. Department of Education does not approve or accredit institutions. Rather, the Department is the accreditor of accreditors and the Secretary has been referred to as the national commissar for education.[8] The Department's list of nationally recognized accrediting bodies is published in the *Federal Register*. This procedure has been in existence for about 30 years. There are at least 15 different pieces of federal legislation that require accreditation standing in order to participate. There are also 40 separate statutory references to the Secretary's list of approved agencies that involve not only the Department of Education, but a total of 10 federal agencies, other departments and independent agencies in the government.

As of 1983, the Department recognized 47 organizations as reliable accrediting bodies. There are 77 components of these 47 organizations that include 13 commissions that are units of the six regional associations and 64 other bodies of national scope characterized as institutional or specialized or a combination of both.[9] There are five standards that institutions must satisfy in order to participate in programs of federal financial assistance. The most important standard is that an institution must be accredited by a nationally recognized accrediting agency. There are several alternatives to comply with this standard. An institution can be approved if it can be certified that its credits will be accepted by three other fully accredited institutions. Some state agencies, such as the New York State Board of Regents, have also been designated as nationally recognized accrediting bodies. The Department may also directly approve an institution or program upon a finding that there are no nationally recognized accrediting agencies qualified.[10]

The criteria, policies and regulations used by the department in order for accrediting associations to be on the approved list has been criticized on the basis that the Department has exceeded its statutory authority. It has been argued that the Department is constrained by statute to ministerial functions with little or no discretionary authority in the area of accreditation.[11] As an example of the Department exceeding its statutory authority, it has taken the position that it is unlikely that more than one association or agency will qualify for recognition for a defined geographic area or in a given field or program. But the major criticism has been directed at the criteria that must be satisfied in order for accrediting agencies to be put on the approved list. The first criterion is that the agency "foster ethical practices" such as equitable student tuition refunds and nondiscriminatory practices in admission and employment. Second, that accrediting agencies encourage "experimental and innovative programs." Third, a requirement that the agency take into account the rights, responsibilities, and interests of students, the general public, the academic, professional, or occupational fields involved, and institutions. Fourth, a requirement that accrediting agencies include "representatives of the public" in its decision-making process, and to assure that the composition of its policy and decision-making bodies reflect the community of interests directly affected by the scope of its accreditation.[12]

The academic community has argued that the Department is constrained by statute to simply list nationally recognized accrediting agencies without regulating their activities or functions. The Department has justified its regulations on the basis, *inter alia*, of conditional grant making powers. That is, institutions and accrediting associations are not required to be approved by the Department unless they desire federal assistance. Those who choose to be listed voluntarily agree to conditions established by the Department to ensure proper use of the funds.[13] This argument has been used in numerous instances such as the National Fair Labor Standards Act to expand the scope of national power beyond its constitutionally delegated powers and has been upheld by the courts. It is not clear why there should be an exception in the field of education despite rhetoric to the effect that the government is an investor and not a purchaser of education or that First Amendment rights are involved. Indeed it can only be the political naivety of educators to be surprised by the intrusion and regulation of government when federal assistance becomes pervasive.

Because most accrediting agencies require that institutions also be approved by their respective state agencies, there is a two tier standard of governmental regulation (e.g., see Appendix A).[14] State regulation primarily affects private institutions since public institutions are by definition approved when public funds are appropriated.[15] The importance of accreditation can be illustrated by the growth in federal student loan programs. The Guaranteed Student Loan Program has increased from $1,015 million in 1970–71 to $8,288 million in 1985–86. The National Direct Student Loan Program increased from $240 million in 1970–71 to $751 million in 1985–86.[16] The following 1986 appropriations are representative of other federal funds tied to accreditation: College Work study-$567 million; Pell Grants-$3,578 million; Supplemental Grants-$395 million; Academic Facilities-$51 million; Developing Institutions-$135 million; Disadvantaged Students-$176 million; and International Education-$25 million.[17]

The importance of accreditation status is further illustrated by controversial Rev. Jerry Fallwell's Liberty Baptist College prominent feature in advertisements that the institution is fully accredited. Given current demographics, accreditation status is likely to be essential for institutional survival with substantial declines in college age population occurring in the next decade.

INSTITUTIONAL ACCREDITATION

Institutional accreditation, compared to program accreditation, is far more important in qualifying for direct or indirect federal assistance (e.g., student loans and grants). For example, if a college lost its specialized accreditation status, in say journalism, it is unlikely there would be any effect on its eligibility for federal student loan programs provided it was accredited by the regional accrediting association.[18] Regional accrediting commissions have emphasized institutional inputs in the past as critical factors in approving institutions (e.g., faculty qualifications, faculty/student ratio, facilities, etc.). There have been criticisms of the input approach. Presently there is a greater emphasis placed on institutions stating their goals or objectives in conjunction with plans to achieve these goals. The most progressive or modern view is an emphasis on educational outputs. This approach has not met with success as there is very little agreement on what outputs should be in post-secondary institutions or how they are measured.

Accrediting associations do not attempt to rank or compare institutions. Moreover, evaluation reports by accrediting association are confidential and not made public except in unusual circumstances.[19] Accreditation status is generally granted for a period of 5 to 10 years before a renewal evaluation is required. Evaluations are made by a team of volunteers drawn from the ranks of faculty and administrators of member institutions. The team is generally drawn from states other than the state of the evaluated institution. Thus the evaluation is appropriately called a peer group evaluation. It can be expected that members of the evaluating team have little incentive to give an unfavorable evaluation that could result in the loss of accreditation. For example, the Southern Association of Colleges and Schools has four divisions ranging from Level I (associate degree) to Level IV (bachelor, master and doctoral degrees). Evaluation members usually come from comparable institutions. An unfavorable evaluation may mean reduced job opportunities for members of the evaluation team.[20] Moreover, an unfavorable evaluation may result in team members being tied up in protracted litigation. Thus, there would seem to be a free-rider problem of teams giving an unfavorable evaluation as its members are not in a position to capture any gains from an unfavorable report, but risk incurring private costs. This may explain why very few institutions have lost their accreditation status.[21]

In summary, it can be argued that institutional accreditation means very little unless it is withdrawn. The inputs approach is similar to the Marxian labor theory of value and probably represents a more binding constraint than the goals-planning approach. The goals-plan approach is flawed by being a vague prediction or forecast about the future with no guarantees of realization. Its emergence may be explained by the expansion and diversity of the membership of accrediting associations in which a total reliance on an inputs approach would exclude too many institutions within any accrediting association, changing and unanticipated market conditions, lack of incentives to adapt within the institutions to change and the inherent difficulties associated with measuring educational outputs given the diversity of students and faculty.[22]

PROGRAM ACCREDITATION

The importance of program accreditation lies in the relationship that exists between accreditation and state licensure or certification. In most states, graduates of an unaccredited program such as law, medicine, nursing, or teaching are ineligible to become licensed or certified. Moreover, some specialized associations have been accused of using their U.S. Department of Education approval status as leverage with state agencies to require graduation from an accredited institution as a condition for a license or certificate.[23] In addition, specialized associations have been accused of interfering with the internal governance of institutions by making demands concerning course content, number of faculty and qualifications, higher faculty salaries and more facilities. It is argued that the demands of specialized accrediting associations comes at the expense of non-accredited programs and overall institutional autonomy or self-governance.[24]

The incentives of a visiting specialized team are different from those of a visiting institutional team. Because most evaluators are professors, they have an incentive to create and enforce rigorous standards (i.e., input requirements) that may increase the demand for and salary of existing professors. Because institutions do not price discriminate among programs on the basis of cost, it may be possible for faculty of accredited programs to gain at the expense of non-accredited programs. The team members of a licensed group may want to restrict or make it more costly to gain entry into the vocation or profession to increase the overall market salary in the profession.[25] That is, a team may capture the benefits of an unfavorable evaluation of a program that may supply a significant number of entrants to the licensed or certified profession or occupation. As discussed previously, the U.S. Department of Education has a policy of not approving more than one accrediting agency in any given geographic area or program area thereby creating a cartel arrangement that can extract rents.

In summary, program accreditation would seem to impose more constraints on institutions that offer such programs than does institutional accreditation. Moreover, it is likely that program accreditation has restricted actual and potential competition among institutions. It can be argued that equal opportunity and equal and open access goals, that began to be articulated in the 1970s have influenced institutional accreditation. The open admissions policy and other practices of Parsons College would not be criticized today and indeed is often mandated. If direct or indirect student, faculty and staff quotas are used regardless of qualification or abilities, then it is difficult to deny accreditation on the basis of some quality measure.

DEMAND FOR ACCREDITATION

The arguments of why accreditation is demanded can be categorized by examining the demands of students, businesses, institutions, and governments. It has been argued that accreditation allows students to transfer credits among accredited institutions. That is, transferable credits permit easy entry into and exit from institutions by students that foster competition. Credits that are transferable are more valuable property than credits that could not be transferred. Thus, transferability benefits students and institutions. This argument must be qualified.

First, an accredited institution is not required to accept a student or a student's credits earned at another accredited institution. Moreover, there is no prohibition on an accredited institution from accepting student's credits earned at an unaccredited institution, and indeed this is done at many institutions. For example, it is unlikely that a student who earned credits at Harvard University or at any number of major universities would have difficulty in transferring credits if these universities were to lose accreditation status. Of course, students of unknown unaccredited colleges have a more difficult time in transferring. But, a student's admission to another school under these circumstances is more likely to depend on factors such as his or her SAT scores or residency status if a public institution. Unfortunately, there are no data on the number of transfers that occur from unaccredited schools. Even if there were data, it would likely be misleading in today's environment because of the requirement that a school be accredited to be eligible for federally assisted student loan and grant programs. Many students are unlikely to be aware of accreditation unless he or she is denied federal assistance to attend an unaccredited institution.

Another reason given for accreditation is that it is similar to a consumer protection agency for students. This argument will be discussed more fully in Parts VI and VII. The consumer protection argument is questionable. Accredited institutions do not provide guarantees or warranties to students, nor are the institutions or their faculty subject to malpractice liability.[26] Nor does the accrediting association make any warranties to students about quality. Presumably what is meant here is that accrediting associations protect the student against fraud or misrepresentations. But the common law protects students in these cases by allowing them to bring a private action against the institution that engages in such practices. If there is a concern about fly-by-night operations, then a requirement that institutions post a bond would be more efficient than accreditation.

It has been argued that businesses demand accreditation. This is also dubious. Poorly qualified students hired as employees would be terminated within a short period of time. Because of continuing dealings or purchases by firms, it is unlikely that an institution would survive if the quality of its graduates were deceptive, with or without accreditation status. There may be a demand by businesses for certain programs that provide training specific to that business or industry and use accreditation to constrain the program to meet their needs. In these cases it is likely that the specialized accrediting association will be captured by the industry. These businesses also have an interest in governments subsidizing such specific human capital if it results in a lower wage bill. Thus, some firms may favor program accreditation by the U.S. Department of Education. But in the absence of such subsidies, it is likely that businesses would provide their own training to monitor and insure quality.

Even before extensive government involvement in higher education, institutions voluntarily joined accrediting associations. Certainly the costs of not being accredited are much higher today than they were several decades ago. One explanation for institutional demand for accreditation was and is to ward off state government interference. It is interesting to note that institutional accreditation is at a regional rather than state level although there is deference to the state authority by requiring the institution be approved by the appropriate state agencies (see appendix A). There would seem to be no inherent reason for regional association other than as an attempt to reduce the various types of state regulation.[27] Compared to other state agencies, public higher education institutions and their employees have a great deal of autonomy. In the absence of some apparent external observer or evaluator, it is likely that state agencies would exercise more control.

Another reason institutions may desire accreditation is that accrediting associations provide lobbying services. While presidents of institutions often lobby state government officials for their own benefit, an association is a more effective lobbyist for general programs that effect higher education in general. This would seem to be especially important at the federal level. For example, three of the four national institutional accrediting associations[28] and sixteen of the thirty-eight specialized accrediting associations are located in the Washington D.C. area. The President of the American Council on Education has expressed concern that higher education is simply viewed by Congress as another special interest group. For example, besides federal programs, higher education has enjoyed a number of advantages in tax and retirement laws.[29]

QUALITY ASSURANCE IN THE PRIVATE SECTOR

There are a number of reasons why colleges and universities seek accreditation from an independent agency or agencies as noted above. But accreditation as quality assurance is not one of the reasons. If accreditation was taken seriously as a measure of quality assurance, then Harvard, Yale, or the University of Chicago would have their respective brand-name capital at risk if the claimed quality of other members of the accreditation association to which they belong is deceptive. Just as McDonalds, Sears, or IBM do not lend their name to other firms because they would incur considerable wealth losses in the form a diminished value of their trademark if the claimed quality of these other firms were deceptive or not of equal quality, so would recognized colleges and universities lose the value of their trademarks if their name was associated with other colleges that were not of equal or better quality. That is, a regional or specialized association is not like a brand-named franchise which has a considerable investment in its trademark and exercises considerable control over those licensed to use the name. Indeed accrediting agencies have very little capital and charge modest fees for membership.

It is useful to examine the recent quality assurance literature that has been applied to profit making firms. Certification in any form, such as a trademark, would have zero value in a world of perfect information as consumers could costlessly determine variations in quality and performance among products and services.[30] Most products and services have the characteristic of not being subject to costless determination of quality before purchase.[31] Moreover, for many goods and services, the seller's statements (or advertisements) about the quality or the warranties associated with a good or service require enforcement costs (e.g., time and legal costs) that may exceed the value of performance if such statements should be deceptive. Under these circumstances, a firm or organization will have an incentive to sell a product or service that is of lower quality than its represented or advertised quality. If a consumer receives a product or service of a quality at least as high as implicitly contracted for, he will continue to purchase from the seller. On the other hand, if quality representation is deceptive, consumers will cease to purchase from that firm. But if there is a return to the seller from deception (i.e., receipt of a high price for a low quality/low cost product) each firm will have an incentive to be deceptive. In equilibrium, the only producers that will survive are those that produce a low quality product or service with low quality assurances. Consumer information and enforcement costs will limit the availability of high quality products.

There may, however, be a price higher than the perfectly competitive price of high quality. Such a price creates a price premium over and above the *costs of production* including a normal profit. These price premia represent the return to brand-name (trademark) capital investments.[32] These investments typically take the form of specific capital investments. Specific capital is defined as having a very low or zero *salvage* value in alternative uses. Thus the returns (price premia) to investments in brand-name capital (e.g., college name or trademark) depend on *repeat* sales. If future sales are not realized because the trademark loses its reputational value (e.g., the firm is deceptive), then the salvage value of the trademark capital is very low or zero.

Specific capital investments by firms selling trademark goods or services signal information to consumers on what firms have at stake if quality assurance is deceptive. That is, specific capital investments can be interpreted as a "performance bond" that is forfeited if future (repeat) sales are not realized.[33] Specific capital investments simultaneously serve to insure "market" performance of quality assurances that would not be necessary in a world of costless enforcement of quality claims. Besides brand-name advertising, other forms of specific investments may be made such as luxurious storefronts, thick carpeting, and ornate displays and signs, even though they yield little or no direct service flows to consumers.[34]

The price premium or specific quality assuring capital investments for any good or service depends on a number of factors. Fewer quality assurance expenditures are required the more frequent a good or service is purchased because consumers can discipline a deceptive seller more quickly. Durable goods will require higher quality assurance expenditures. Because the quality assurance argument is premised on a market enforcement mechanism (rather than legal enforcement through the courts) of implicit and explicit agreements, the cost of legal enforcement relative to the cost on nonperformance is important as a determinant in the level of quality assurance expenditures. For example, the consequential damages that may be realized by a defective drug may explain why low priced "generic" drugs, despite legislation intended to promote them, have not been as successful against higher priced brand-name drugs.

The price premia for quality assurance are net of other price premia used to cover the costs of other functions the seller may perform. For example, the total price premium or mark-up is often expressed as percentage of the manufacturer's suggested retail price. Part of the mark-up will be used to cover such things as the cost of shelf space and inventory costs. The price premia for such functions is competitively determined in the market and not unique to the trademark. That is, there are a large number of buyers (distributors of goods) and sellers (retailers) of, say, shelf space. If the margin offered is not competitive (does not cover the cost of providing shelf space), then the retailer will turn to competitive buyers. The capital utilized in providing shelf space has alternative uses and its value is not dependent on the reputational value of a trademark.[35] Moreover, mark-ups will be used to compensate retailers for post sale services such as the cost of handling refunds or warranty repairs. The capital used in providing such services may also be of a general nature (i.e., has alternative uses) and not trademark specific.[36]

To summarize, investment in quality assurance provides information to consumers that they can rely on the promised or claimed quality of the product or service. The reliance stems from an explicit or implicit consumer recognition that a firm that is deceptive will forfeit its specific capital investments in the trademark if future (repeat) sales are not realized because of deceptive quality. Trademark capital depreciates similar to other capital investments and requires continual investments.[37]

Free-riding on a trademark can occur in several ways. First, as discussed above, a price premium over and above the cost of production is necessary to provide a return to specific investments in brand-name capital and cover the costs of such services as shelf space, inventory, refunds and warranties. If unauthorized sellers are able to purchase trade-marked items at a cost less than the cost of production plus the price premium, then they have a competitive advantage over authorized sellers by being able to sell at a lower price. Authorized sellers have two options. They can either maintain their price and experience a reduction in quality sold, or reduce their price to be competitive thereby reducing the price premium. Either alternative represents a decrease in the seller's gross revenue defined as total revenue minus the cost of goods sold. As long as gross revenues are sufficient to cover variable costs including a return on general capital, authorized sellers will stay in the market even though revenues are not sufficient to provide a normal return to specific investments. As the price premia declines, the value of trademark capital falls.[38] In the limit, if unauthorized sales capture a significant share of total trademark sales, the value of the trademark will fall to zero.[39]

A second type of free-riding can take the form of unauthorized sellers selling lower quality products that are imitations of the brand-name good. Unauthorized sales that are inferior to authorized goods may disappoint consumer expectations and/or increase the costs of consumer information. For example, an unauthorized sale may be last year's model or it may not have been properly stored or shipped or may not be suitable for use in this country (e.g., different electric currents). Lower quality products diminish the reputational or trademark value in manner similar to the first case of free-riding. Consumers who receive lower quality products will perceive them as being of deceptive quality. If authorized products cannot be distinguished from unauthorized products, consumers will either stop purchasing the trademark good regardless of its source or will not pay a price premium for the trademark good. The net effect is the same as the first case in that the price margin for authorized sellers will narrow, the reputational value of the trademark will fall and there will be less incentive to make future investments in quality assurance.

A third form of free-riding is the failure of sellers to provide post-sale services (e.g., warranties) that consumers expect because of the claims of the trademark owner. It is important to distinguish between pre-sale services and post-sale services. Pre-sale services usually take the form of marketing or promotional program aimed at creating an awareness of the product and differentiating the product from its competitors. The previous discussion of quality assurance captures much of what may be called pre-sale services for trademark products. That is, differentiating one product from another or creating consumer awareness is of little benefit unless the consumer can be assured of the claimed difference in quality. As discussed, unless the trademark owner or its authorized sellers can exclude other sellers from quality assurance, the potential exists for free-riding. A good or service where exclusion is costly or not possible has been defined as a "public" good. Once the service has been provided, others may take advantage of the benefits of the service without paying any of the costs.

Post-sale services, however, can be excluded or quantity adjusted by the sellers. For example, a product could be sold with no warranty, a one year warranty or a lifetime warranty. A warranty can be conditioned on proof of purchase from an authorized seller. There is no clear line distinction between "public" and "private" characteristics for some services. For example, a retailer's inventory of goods can be considered a public good in the sense that a consumer may physically inspect the good at one store (receive information) and purchase the good from a mail order house. That is, an authorized retailer's inventory can create a spill-over benefit to a mail order house. But an inventory also provides an excludable service in the form of consumer convenience and utility derived from having immediate delivery and possession, a benefit not provided by a mail order house.

Because of the potential for free riding, trademark owners carefully control or monitor sellers of their product or service. Such control can take the form of vertical integration of the manufacturer through retailers within the distributional chain or vertical restraints such as franchise agreements or other contractual agreements between the trademark owner and sellers. These agreements often impose significant sanctions on sellers who breach these agreements (e.g., free-ride) such as the forfeiture of a bond or termination of an agreement with the result of a loss of the specific capital invested in the trademark by sellers.

QUALITY ASSURANCE APPLIED TO COLLEGES AND UNIVERSITIES

A college or university name is much like a trademark and faces the same problems as firms in maintaining or enhancing reputation. It is apparent from the above discussion that an institution is not going to lose its identity or tie its reputation to another agency, such as an accreditation association, over which it has minimal control, and from which it may be subject to free-riding by other members of the agency. That is, an accrediting association and its members are not like members of the Holiday Inn chain, where reputational value is inextricably tied to the behavior and quality services of its franchisees (members). Harvard and Yale are not going to be tied with the quality of Massasoit Community College even though they all belong to the same accrediting association. Nevertheless, there are some similarities between non-profit and profit institutions in terms of quality assurance.

Public and nonprofit institutions in higher education do not charge price premiums as discussed above. However, quality institutions do charge non-pecuniary premiums such as high admission standards. That is, given the nonprofit nature of higher education, there is little incentive to maximize the residual between revenues and costs. The absence of a price system to allocate university resources necessarily involves some non-price rationing mechanism. Excess demand, in the form of the number of admission applications less those applicants admitted, is clearly taken as a signal of quality in higher education. Of course, it is necessary to distinguish schools in terms of the tuition charged. For example, the excess demand at Stanford University may be less than that of the University of Virginia because of the higher tuition charged at Stanford. Thus, the University of Virginia is not necessarily a higher quality school than Stanford because of the different mix of price and non-price rationing mechanisms. But, if both schools were to suddenly have an open admissions policy, and select students randomly, the perceived quality would certainly fall. The non-price premium in higher education is similar to the price premium for quality goods. This measure, however, is an *ex post* measure of quality. It does not explain the behavior of institutions in assuring quality.

Consider the costs of enforcing contracts. As discussed above, if contracts could be costlessly enforced, firms that made deceptive claims of quality would be sued thereby eliminating any return from deception. This problem of enforcing contracts would seem to be especially acute in colleges and universities relative to the private sector, not because of the direct costs of enforcing contracts (e.g., hiring a lawyer or court costs), but because rights and liabilities are not well defined or non-existing. For example, it is not likely a graduate could successfully sue a college for his failure to read or write. There are reasons one might argue for the absence of such rights or liabilities.[40] Similarly, college professors, unlike professionals such as lawyers and doctors, do not have to worry about malpractice suits. The essential point is that colleges and universities should want some self-enforcing mechanism to assure quality other than the legal system which is essentially not available.

Consider the resources of colleges and universities in terms of whether they could be classified as specific capital. Generally the campuses would not be considered specific capital as these resources may have a higher alternative use value whether in an educational use under another brand name or other uses (e.g., campuses in major cities). But it is interesting to note that at many private and public quality universities, the buildings are often ornate structures that would have a low alternative use value in many other activities. In addition, considerable investments are made in landscaping the campus, including the location of buildings, that are likely to have a low alternative use value. Besides buildings and landscaping, endowments are often conditioned on educational use thereby making these assets specific capital. Many junior colleges and lower quality institutions, by contrast, are often designed efficiently to accommodate a number of uses or have used facilities that were built to accommodate another use.

Unlike the private sector, non-profit institutions have very little specific capital in the form of *direct* advertising expenditures.[41] But institutions do have mass mailings of glossy brochures and bulletins to potential students such as the National Merit scholars. Institutions also have news staffs and alumni offices that engage in advertising. Perhaps the most important indirect advertising are the expenditures on an athletics program that can result in national exposure as well as providing revenues.[42] The success of an athletic program often depends on repeat purchasers (i.e., alumni) who form the boosters club. Similar to landscaping and buildings, an 80,000 seat stadium is likely to have a low salvage value if the alumni should lose interest.

The most difficult problem in applying the quality assurance literature of firms is that there are no owners or residual claimants in non-profit institutions and therefore little incentive to maintain or improve the brand-name capital. Such an environment should lead to free-riding off the brand name.[43] There is, of course some incentive to maintain brand-name capital, but whatever gain or income associated with the brand-name capital of a school cannot be *capitalized* or *transferred*. Indeed at major universities, most professors do research and publish to enhance their own human (brand-name) capital and any enhancements of the university brand-name is simply an indirect spill-over.

Now consider repeat purchases by students. If quality were deceptive, then the student would drop-out. Of course, for most students, it may be difficult or costly to judge quality until graduation when job or graduate school opportunities are realized.

Moreover there may be significant quality variations across departments and colleges within a university. The fact that a majority of students transfer majors at least once within a four year period, and that most schools have a general core curriculum, suggests that most students seek a very general quality measure of the university. Quality is used here in a very broad sense. That is, the social life or consumption aspects may be as important as the human capital aspects in choosing a school. Thus a successful athletic program with regional or national media coverage, or the ability to make social contacts that payoff in later life, is likely to attract students as does hiring Nobel Prize winners.

From an entering student perspective, the human capital demanded is likely to be of a general nature and not specific to a particular brand-name (school) in the sense of transferability. For example, if a student were unable to transfer courses to another school or gain entry into graduate schools, then the costs of attendance or deceptive quality would be high relative to free transferability among a group of schools. But as discussed previously, it is not clear how important accreditation is in terms of transfer although it may be essential in terms of licensure.

Unlike a franchising arrangement such as Holiday Inn, an institution is not going to submit to quality control measures that make it indistinguishable from competitor institutions. That is, there is an inherent conflict in quality accreditation among competing institutions with separate brand names. Harvard is not going to claim it has the same quality as Yale. Of course some institutions may *claim* that they are the same quality as Yale or Harvard. But belonging to the same accrediting agency is not going to do anything in terms of assuring the same quality.

CONCLUSIONS

The principal conclusion of this paper is that whatever accrediting associations do, it is not to assure quality of its member institutions. Accrediting agencies or their evaluating teams do not have any specific capital at risk in the form of a trademark or brand name that provides quality assurance. As discussed, the incentives may be perverse in terms of monitoring quality. What has become at risk for accrediting agencies is the loss of approval status by the U.S. Department of Education. As federal funding of higher education expands, it can be expected that accrediting agencies will distance themselves from being simply private associations when they were formed at the turn of the century to become more and more entrenched quasi-governmental agencies of the department.[44] Perhaps such an arrangement is a second best alternative to direct regulation of institutions by the federal government.

Accreditation and its nexus with state and federal governments effectively precludes accredited institutions from viable competition from the private sector in the form of for profit colleges and institutions. In addition it can be argued that accrediting agencies act to prevent radical departures in such areas as advertising for students, university governance, and incentives, such as occurred at Parsons College, that threatened all aspects of the higher education structure. Finally, it can be argued that accrediting associations are the organized constituents of the U.S. Department of Education that lobby Congress for general benefits in the form of student grants and loans as well as research grants. That is, accrediting associations seek rents for its members from federal and state legislators at the expense of taxpayers and unorganized potential entrants. Whether the accrediting associations will be able to appropriate some of these rents from its members will depend on the extent of future government funding.

APPENDIX A

It is difficult to generalize the criterion and process of the accrediting associations. The Southern association is somewhat representative of regional accreditation; an institution must have (1) a charter and/or formal authority from the appropriate governmental agency or agencies to award a degree, certificate and diploma it may offer; (2) a governing board which includes representation reflecting the public interest; (3) offer one or more degree programs of at least one academic year in length or the equivalent at the post-secondary level with clearly defined educational objectives as well as a clearly defined statement of its means for achieving them; (4) a general education at the post-secondary level as a prerequisite or essential element in its principal programs; (5) admission policies compatible with its stated objectives; (6) publish and make available to the public a summary of its latest audited financial statements which indicates fiscal resources adequate to support its offerings; (7) completed a major portion of at least one cycle of its principal programs prior to on-site evaluation; (8) possess candidacy for accreditation status; and (9) submit an updated application form.

The accrediting process involves (1) an institutional self-study of every institution seeking re-affirmation of accreditation, including an application form for every institution applying for initial application; (2) a visiting committee is scheduled to visit the institution following the submission of a satisfactory self-study report (the average committee consists of approximately nine members, appointed by the commission staff); (3) the visiting committee report is sent to the executive officer of the commission and to the chief executive officer of the institution: (4) the admission committee makes recommendations on initial accreditation and the committee on standards and reports makes recommendations or reaffirmation to the Executive Council of the commission; (5) the executive Council makes recommendations to the commission which takes final action; (6) the institution may appeal an adverse decision according to established policies and procedures. The annual fees for belonging to the Southern Association of Colleges and Schools range from $870 to $2610 depending on the enrollment in the institution. The visiting Committee serves without compensation and expenses average about $500 per committee member. Thus, direct costs to member institutions of belonging to an association are nominal.

NOTES

1. Accreditation is an important link in examining "Intellectual Freedom and Government Sponsorship of Higher Education." The principal issue to be addressed by this conference would seem to be the nature and extent of government influence brought about by its largess and not whether there is an influence. As James Buchanan has stated several decades ago, we should not expect government officials to be bifurcated individuals who are self interested in their private endeavors and then become publicly spirited or minded, whatever that term means, when they act in their official capacity.

   It is naive to think that politicians or government officials, who control purse strings of student subsidies or sponsored research, have preferences that are focused on an unbiased competition of ideas or a search for the truth or will sacrifice their own self interest for the public interest. The lessons learned from the economics of bureaucracy and rent seeking literature are no less applicable when applied to higher education. Government funding leads to government regulation and control. Similarly, it can be expected that support from private foundations, on both sides of the political spectrum, also leads to regulation and control. Thus, this paper is not premised on a normative view of what should be the extent of government regulation or control, but rather to examine the extent and nature of such regulation or control.

2. *Webster's New Collegiate Dictionary* defines the term accredit as: "(1) to consider or recognize as outstanding, (2) to give official authorization to or approval of: a: to provide with credentials; esp: to send (an envoy) with letters of authorization b: to recognize or vouch for as conforming with a standard c: to recognize (an educational institution) as maintaining standards that qualify the graduates for admission to higher or more specialized institutions or for professional practice."

3. The national associations are: American Association of Bible Colleges, Association of Independent Colleges and Schools, National Association of Trade and Technical Schools and the National Home Study Council. The Association of Independent Colleges and Schools represent a large number of private proprietary business schools that offer non-degree programs. Most major colleges and universities belong to a regional, rather than a national accreditation association. The regional associations are: Commission on Higher Education/Middle States Association of Colleges and Schools, Commission on Institutions of Higher Education/New

England Association of Schools and Colleges, Commission on Institutions of Higher Education/North Central Association of Colleges and Schools, Commission on Colleges/Northwest Association of Schools and Colleges, Commission on Colleges/Southern Association of Colleges and Schools, and the Accrediting Commission for Senior Colleges and Universities/Western Association of Schools and Colleges. Among the more popular specialized accrediting associations are: the American Bar Association, American Assembly of Collegiate Schools of Business, Accrediting Board for Engineering and Technology, and the American Medical Association.

4. The Council was formed in 1975 by the merger of the National Commission on Accrediting and the Federation of Regional Accrediting Commissions on Higher Education. The approved list of the U.S. Department of Education is slightly larger than COPA's accredited members because some specialized associations by-pass COPA and go directly to the U.S. Department of Education.

5. The number of accredited programs and institutions listed below was taken from a 1983 report entitled "A Guide to COPA Recognized Accrediting Associations (1983)."

6. New England and Western Associations have separate associations for vocational, trade, junior colleges, and schools.

7. Only the major specialized accrediting associations are listed. Most of the other specialized associations have less than 100 accredited programs or institutions.

8. See "Statement of Boyer, Ernest L., President, Carnegie Foundation for the Advancement of Teaching," *Hearing before the Subcommittee on Post-secondary Education of the Committee on Education and Labor, House of Representatives, Ninety-Eighth Congress, 1st session,* Feb. 8, 10, 1983, p.23; hereinafter referred to as the *Ninety-Eighth Congress.* Accrediting associations are critical of this arrangement and recommend that COPA perform this function independent of any government agency. The criticism stems from the regulations or pressure employed by the Department in approving accrediting associations that would have the effect of using the associations as enforcers of federal laws such as equal opportunity and for repayment of student loans.

9. The National Advisory Committee on Accreditation and Institutional Eligibility advises the Secretary on the criteria and procedures for recognizing accrediting bodies, the designation of state agencies as reliable concerning the approval of public post-secondary vocational education and nurse education, and developing and recommending standards and criteria for specific categories of educational institutions for which there are no recognized accrediting bodies for state agencies.

10. *Ninety-Eighth Congress, op. cit.,* p.4.

11. Finkin, Mathew W. "Federal Reliance on Educational Accreditation: The Scope of Administrative Discretion," The council on Post-secondary Accreditation, Wash. D.C. 1978.
12. *Ibid.*, p. 5.
13. An alternative public choice explanation is that the criteria is designed by the Department of Education to maximize the size of its constituency to permit continued expansion of congressional programs and thus the Department's budget.
14. There are several recent court cases that deal with the state's power to regulate higher education. In *Nova University v. Board of Governors of the University of North Carolina*, 287 S.E. 2d 872 (N.C. 1982), the N.C. Supreme Court held that the board of governors could not prohibit Nova University, licensed in Florida, from establishing a program in North Carolina that would lead to a doctor of education degree in Florida. In commentary, the N.C. court also discussed constitutional issues of state regulation of non-degree granting branch institutions and concluded that North Carolina could not constitutionally prohibit Nova University from teaching in-state. As a side note, Florida and North Carolina both belong to the Southern Association of Colleges and Schools with Nova University being an accredited member. This suggests that the transferability argument of accreditation is over emphasized.

   Restrictions on the state's right to regulate was reached by two New Jersey courts in which the New Jersey Board of Education denied degree granting authority to a small Christian college and the right to teach in another case. In *New Jersey State Board of Higher Education* v. *Directors of Shelton College*, 48 A2d 988 (N.J. 1982), the State Supreme Court found that the states denial of the right to grant degrees or credits would not unconstitutionally burden the right of freedom of religion as the state has the right of protecting students as potential consumers of education whereby minimum state standards must be met. However in *New Jersey-Philadelphia Presbytery* v. *New Jersey State Board of Higher Education*, 482 F.Supp. 968 (D.N.J. 1980), a federal district court upheld the state's right to regulate the granting of degrees, and credits and advertising but prohibited the state from taking any action to prevent the college from teaching or engaging in other educational activities. See Belsches-Simmons, Grace, 1983, "Regulation of Post-secondary Institutions: Model Legislation," *ECS Issuegram* no. 22, Education Commission of the States (Mar. 1).
15. For example, the Ohio Board of Regents has warned four Bible colleges that action to shut them down will proceed unless they prove they existed prior to 1967 or seek certification which entails a review of such things as curriculum, faculty and support services.

1986. *The Chronicle of Higher Education* 33 (Oct. 8):3.

16. 1987. *The Chronicle of Higher Education* 33 (Jan. 7):1.

17. 1986. *The Chronicle of Higher Education* 33 (Oct. 8):28.

18. Boston College lost its accreditation status with the Accrediting Council for Education in Journalism and Mass Communications over the failure to satisfy the required percentage of liberal arts courses which students must take (i.e., 75%) and the unit rule which requires 50% of the journalism student body be enrolled in accredited sequences. The 25/75 rule requires students to take these courses outside the department or college. 1983. *The Chronicle of Higher Education* (Feb. 2):3. There was also a dispute over whether the Council could require the University to disclose salary information. *Ninety-Eighth Congress*:81–82. Because journalists are not licensed because of the first Amendment, the loss of accreditation probably had little effect on Boston College graduates. It is interesting to note that journalism programs at Northwestern, Stanford, Michigan, University of Pennsylvania, and Baylor are boycotting the Council accrediting process because of its lack of flexibility. Guzda, M.K. 1983. "ACEJMC Struggles to Find Fair Guidelines." *Editor & Publisher* (Dec. 24):8. On the other hand, there may be federal assistance programs such as nursing grants that require enrollment in an accredited program.

19. If an institution selectively makes public a portion of the evaluation for self-serving purposes, then the association may make the entire report public.

20. Note also that because the team is drawn from outside the state, the evaluated institution is not a competitor for state funds of the team members' institutions.

21. The most notable case is that of Parsons College. Parsons College, under the leadership of Dr. Millard Roberts, adopted practices during the period 1955–1967 that included: open-door admission for students who either could not be accepted by or were dismissed from other colleges, a set of core courses, a preceptor system, a system that allowed students to charge their meals and other expenses, the use of modern computers, offering attractive employment benefits to faculty members, and using a prominent public relations firm and law/accounting firms. Enrollment during this period increased from 200 to over 5,000 in 11 years. Problems developed between the college and North Central Association of Colleges and Secondary Schools between 1963–1967. Parsons College finally lost its accreditation in 1967 with an immediate dramatic decline in enrollment.

   These practices were criticized during the period but are commonplace today. Dixon, Terry. 1983. "Parsons college: Innovative

Ideas or Unethical Practices." *EDRS MF01/PC01* (Dec. 12): 12. It should be noted that Dr. Roberts evidently used a College owned plane to travel throughout the country to give speeches in which he received fees. Parsons was the topic of a *Life* magazine article in 1966 which portrayed the College as a school for "flunkies." Dixon has suggested that it was the adverse national news coverage that caused the extra scrutiny by the association and its eventual withdrawal of Parson's accreditation status.

22. It is interesting to note that in the area of athletics where outcomes are clearly measurable (i.e., win, loss or tie), the regulations of the accrediting association (NCAA) are far more extensive than any other accrediting association. If educational outcomes could be measured as they are in football, then it is likely that there would be far more regulation as the outcomes would then present an inter-institutional means of comparison. Of course, an institution could withdraw its membership, but at a cost of losing its eligibility for federal funding.

23. *Ninety-Eighth Congress*: 25 and 40.

24. Standards differ among specialized accrediting associations. For example, the following lists some of the requirements of the American Assembly of Collegiate Schools of Business (AACSB). What is surprising is the extent of these standards since most students with a degree in business would not need to be licensed or certified. AACSB Standard III-Personnel prescribes an explicit ratio of the number of student credit hours to the full-time teaching equivalent (FTE) necessary to generate these hours. AACSB standard for faculty qualification are: "...As a measure of the faculty's teaching, research, applied knowledge, and overall scholarly capability, at least 80 percent of the full time equivalent academic staff...will possess qualifications such as the PhD, DBA, JD, or LLB...the percent of full time equivalent academic staff holding the Phd, DBA, or other appropriate doctoral degree shall not be less than the sum of 50% (of the total faculty)...required at the under-graduate level..."

The AACSB also requires that faculty offices "...should provide sufficient privacy and space to carry out the faculty's responsibilities" and that classrooms "should be appropriate in size and design to the courses offered." Admission and retention standards should compare favorably to those of the university or college as a whole. AACSB also calls for "regional articulation agreements" and seeks assurance "that the overall education experience of the transferring student is comparable to that of the student taking all of his or her work at an accredited school." See Schnur, James O. 1982, "Of Swans and Ducklings...Business and Education Program Accreditation

Compared," *Journal of Business Education* (Oct.):31-33. Schur seems to be arguing that education accrediting agencies should have more rigorous standards similar to the AACSB so that their faculty would also be protected against the sharp declines of institutional resources experienced by many education programs.

25. A report by the Council on Post-secondary Education stated that "Accreditation is too often based on minimal statistical standards without insistence on higher quality in the process of teaching and learning and general education...Accreditation, particularly of specialized professional and occupational programs, is sometimes perceived as self serving at times with justification." Accrediting organizations sometimes are "perceived as promoting a self-protective system to control a market in one way or another, as it is believed that the specialized programs in our nation's colleges and universities are in league with their professional colleagues from the national profession in a back-scratching kind of relationship." Accrediting sometimes "focuses too narrowly on a particular program" without taking into account the needs and mission of the college or university of which it is a part. 1986. "Accreditors Urged to Gauge Quality, Not Just Compliance with Minimum Standards." *The Chronicle of Higher Education* 33 (Oct. 8):4.

26. For example, football players and other students at some major universities have alleged that they received degrees without being able to read. Similarly, public elementary and secondary schools are also accredited by the same regional associations. Yet no successful action has been brought against the accrediting associations or schools for the decline in SAT scores and other achievement scores of students nationwide. Education is one of the few areas where *caveat emptor* (let the buyer/student beware) has not been replaced by *caveat venditor* (let the seller/professor or university beware).

27. Historically, with limited migration, the transfer of credits may have been another reason for regional associations.

28. Only the American Association of Bible Colleges is located outside of D.C.

29. Palmer, Stacy E. 1987, "Higher Education Losing Credibility in Congress, Council Chief Warns," *The Chronicle of Higher Education* 33:8. It is not likely that accrediting associations are registered lobbyists, but lobby indirectly by appearances in hearings, etc. Indeed Dupont Circle in Washington D.C. seems to be a favored location for higher education associations that extend beyond accreditation. A number of schools have hired professional lobbyists for specialized interests. For example, in 1986, Congress appropriated $98 million to 12 universities that included five that were clients of Cassidy and Associates, a professional lobbyist. The schools

Cassidy represents are private and public universities ranging from Northwestern U. and Indiana U. to Atlanta U. and Catholic U. Cordes, Colleen, 1987, "Controversial Lobbyist Cajoles Congress into Giving Funds to College Clients," *The Chronicle of Higher Education* 33:23.

30. The discussion is based on Klein, B. and K. Leffler. 1981. "The Role of Market Forces in Assuring Contractual Performance." *Journal of Political Economy* 89:615. Also see Shapiro, C. 1982. "Consumer Information, Product Quality and Seller Reputation." *Bell Journal of Economics* 13:20.; Knoeber, C. 1983. "An Alternative Mechanism to Assure Contractual Reliability." *Journal of Legal Studies* 12:333; Klein, B., R. Crawford and A. Alchian. 1978. "Vertical Integration, Appropriable Rents, and the Competitive Contracting Process." *Journal of Law and Economics* 21:297.

31. For some products, generally not associated with a trademark, consumers can determine quality prior to purchase at a low cost (e.g., fresh fruits or vegetables, lumber, grains, etc.).

32. In the case of colleges and universities which are subsidized, the price premium may be thought of as the amount of excess demand that permits these institutions to employ other rationing mechanisms than price (e.g., a very selective admissions policy), that provides benefits to faculty or administrators and alumni who want to see the school perform well. While one can make an analogy between profit and non-profit institutions, the analogy should not be carried too far as there are no residual claimants or means to capitalize the premium in a non-profit institution.

33. In competitive equilibrium, specific capital investments in the trademark equal the present value of the price premium stream charged for quality products.

34. For example, the frequent use of noted personalities or entertainers in commercials may be attributed to consumer perception of the high cost of these endorsements rather than their being more effective in presenting advertisements. Pepsi made no secret of the fee paid for the Michael Jackson commercials. Local advertisements often refer to other expensive advertisements such as advertised on the "Tonight" show. Klien, B. 1981. "The Role of Market Forces."

35. This is not to say that the price of shelf space or the cost of inventory will be the same for all retailers. Shelf space is much more costly on 5th Ave. than in Hoboken.

36. For example the cost of refunds is simply the cost (interest rate) of capital. However, warranty repair may require specific human capital investments (specialized training associated with a particular good) that cannot be transferred to other goods.

37. Continued investments are observed in the market for well established trademarks. In part, this may be attributed to an atrophy in

consumer information about prior investments and/or the price premium stream may have covered prior specific investments thereby creating an incentive to be deceptive. See Klein, B. 1981. "The Role of Market Forces." for a discussion of the end period problem. Further, specific investments (e.g., advertising) cannot be priced separately, even if it were possible to do so by say pricing them separately, and still serve as a mechanism for quality assurance. If it were possible to separate the information from advertising from the good or service itself, and independently price the two, the expenditures on advertising would not serve as a performance bond assuring the quality of the good. For example, if IBM sold the use of its name without any control over the use of the name, then the quality assurance value of the name IBM would likely fall.

38. That is, the present value of the price premia decreases as the retail price decreases.

39. In the long run, without quality assurance investment the demand for the trademark product will decrease.

40. See Meiners, Roger and Robert Staaf. 1987. "Property Rights in Academe." *mimeo*, Clemson University (March).

41. In the case of public institutions, there may be statutory prohibitions. But even in the absence of such prohibitions, academics frown upon advertising as being degrading and commercial whether in the public or private sector.

42. See McCormick, Robert and M. Tinsley. 1986. "Athletes Versus Academics." The Center for Policy Studies Working Paper No. 19, Clemson University for an excellent discussion of this point.

43. See McCormick, Robert and R. Meiners. 1986. "University Governance: A Property Right Perspective." The Center for Policy Studies Working Paper No. 24, Clemson University for a discussion of free-riding and the absence of rights to claim the residual. They argue with empirical support that the more democratic the governance structure is the less productive the university is in research and teaching.

44. In earlier times, accrediting agencies were interpreted by the courts and government agencies as private associations. A consensus has now developed that accrediting agencies and the interests they affect are more public than private. Indeed, the courts have increasingly interpreted them as either quasi-governmental or quasi-public. See Kaplin, William A. 1983. "Accrediting Agencies' Legal Responsibilities: In Pursuit of the Public Interest." *Journal of Law and Education* 12, 1983, p. 87.

TWELVE

On Universities and the Wealth of Nations

THE MARKET IN IDEAS AND THE ENTRENCHMENT OF FALSE PHILOSOPHIES

W.W. Bartley III

Unpopular views have largely vanished from American campuses...because there are strong sanctions against the hiring and promotion of holders of unpopular views.... Of all monopolies, that of opinions is the worst.[1]

—George Stigler

Erroneous beliefs may have an astonishing power to survive, for thousands of years, in defiance of experience, and without the aid of any conspiracy.... One example is the general conspiracy theory itself...the erroneous view that whenever something evil happens it must be the evil will of an evil power.[2]

—Sir Karl Popper

> The academic community should not assume that the university is an indispensable institution in contemporary society. All of its functions could be performed elsewhere.... As many historians have pointed out, history is littered with the ruins of allegedly indispensable institutions.[3]
>
> —*W. Glenn Campbell*

> Kuhn's ideas...legitimize the social formations in which the science of his time is temporarily housed. Popper...offers an explanation of the success of science that not only transcends the particular social formations of his time, but which happens also to be inimical to and critical of these formations, and thereby of those ideas of Kuhn which legitimate these formations.... The American academic and scientific Establishment...has naturally preferred to embrace Kuhn and to hold Popper at a distance.... So far from legitimating an establishment and its perquisites, Popper threw doubt on all expertise and made challenging establishments integral to the scientific endeavour.[4]
>
> —*I.C. Jarvie*

> It is completely in accord with the etatist thinking prevalent everywhere today to consider a theory to be finally disposed of merely because the authorities who control appointments to academic positions want to know nothing of it.[5]
>
> —*Ludwig von Mises*

> The most characteristic trait of modern epistemology is its entire neglect of economics, that branch of knowledge whose development and practical application was the most spectacular event of modern history.[6]
>
> —*Ludwig von Mises*

My topic[7] is based on an approach developed mainly in three places. The first is my old book, *The Retreat to Commitment*.[8] The second is my book, *Evolutionary Epistemology, Rationality, and the Sociology of Knowledge*.[9] The third is a long manuscript as yet unfinished, entitled *On Universities and the Wealth of Nations*, which was an unintended consequence of the biographies I am writing of Karl Popper and F.A. von Hayek. The talk itself is mainly drawn from a fragment of this manuscript. Since this long manuscript is itself a kind of aerial survey of a large field, my remarks here should perhaps be described as an aerial survey of an aerial survey. They omit detail but show the general contours of my position.

My position, in a nutshell, is this: an epistemologist needs to be concerned with the growth of knowledge, and an epistemologist who works in a university may well be concerned with how universities contribute to such growth. Yet universities, as constituted at present, often work against the growth of knowledge. I try to make this claim a little more plausible, and to show why matters should be so, in terms of the economics of knowledge.

I

The central concern of epistemology—that is, of the theory of knowledge—is the growth of knowledge.[10] It does not seem to have been noticed that this makes the theory of knowledge a branch of economics. It must study and seek to understand the expansions and contractions, the booms and slumps, in the generation of knowledge, and in our understanding of the world in which we live. *Knowledge is a primary component of capital; and epistemology is the economics of knowledge.*[11]

This is not merely a matter of classification. The classification of university disciplines and departments is largely a matter of convenience for administrators, and of little theoretical importance;[12] whereas the identification and solution of theoretical problems is of prime importance to the advancement of learning —and such work often leaps disciplinary borders. Economics and epistemology are both concerned with growth and contraction in wealth, and are further connected in that the advancement of knowledge often goes arm in arm with increase in other forms of wealth.[13] Nor does the story end there. Both in turn form part of a larger undertaking that as yet has no agreed name (though some call it ecology[14]): that broad investigation of the general conditions nurturing growth, hindering it, and leading to contraction, not only among organisms and their products, but even in the inorganic realm. Biology, the theory of evolution, and general systems theory would also be part of this larger undertaking.[15]

II

That epistemology and the growth of knowledge have had something to do with economics has of course been *sensed* from very early days, long before Adam Smith, Adam Ferguson, and David Hume founded the science of economics. So much one can tell from some of the metaphors philosophers have used. Thus Lucian (A.D. 120–c. 180), in an exceptionally funny satire that hardly anyone reads any more, wrote of "The Auction of Philosophers"; Kierkegaard, in *Fear and Trembling*, wrote of the "clearance sale of ideas"; and William James repeatedly sought to reckon the "cash value" of philosophical notions. But the most popular economic metaphor—that of the "free market of ideas"—seems to originate with John Milton, who, in his *Areopagitica*, wrote thus of "Truth": "Let her and falsehood grapple: who ever knew Truth put to the worse in a free and open encounter?"

Epistemologists are sometimes uncomfortable about Milton's declaration, but rarely identify the mistake in it. The mistake has, for instance, nothing to do with Gresham's Law. We begin to identify the mistake if we notice that Milton's declaration —that Truth is never put to the worse in a free and open encounter—is itself unfalsifiable. Ironically, this watchword of critical debate shields itself from refutation by deflecting critical examination. It is easy to appreciate how this works, for we all have been in situations where truth seems to have been bested: indeed, most of us have ourselves occasionally lost arguments yet remained convinced that we were right. Such an experience never need force one to jettison Milton's dictum, but may even serve—or at least may be used—to confirm it. In defeat, one may hang on desperately to the dictum itself—not in order to concede that truth did win, but in order to maintain, in excuse, that *the encounter was not free and open*, and that one *would* have won had it been so. This way of shifting the blame or burden of proof to an opponent or circumstances makes those employing it ever right in their own eyes, even if at the cost of tending to render them practicing paranoiacs.

The mistake in Milton's view of the inevitable triumph of truth in a free market of ideas lies in its being dressed out in, and usually understood in terms of, the presupposition that truth is naturally "manifest"[16]—an assumption that, in turn, leads to *an interventionist or conspiracy theory of error*: to the idea that if what is true is not obvious, then some party must have intervened to prevent its being seen. That is, it presupposes that error arises only from deliberate intervention or conspiracy to suppress the truth, whereas in fact error and ignorance are omnipresent regardless of intentions, and do not have to be "explained" as due to any conspiracy.[17] These hard facts about truth and error are due chiefly to the *unfathomable* character of knowledge—a theme (indeed, in my view the most important thing one needs to know in epistemology) I discuss elsewhere.[18]

In F.A. von Hayek's use of the same metaphor, or in that of Ronald H. Coase,[19] Milton's assumption is (although tacitly) dropped. Thus when Hayek, as a fallibilist, writes of market competition as a "discovery process,"[20] he presupposes error, ignorance, and limited information—rather than knowledge —as a natural state of being. This is so whether or not any conspiracy or deliberate suppression of information is, additionally, at work, and hence even in the most "free and open encounter."

Such writers, of course, do see unfettered markets as the best means not only to generate more ordinary forms of wealth, but also to uncover knowledge and better identify, even if never fully to eliminate, error. Such markets are, however, not perfect. Nor can they become so, for error and ignorance—*and consequently occasional market failure even in the marketplace of ideas*—are there regardless of intervention: regardless of its presence and regardless of its absence.[21] It is well to remind ourselves that error walks always with us, that fallibility is our lot, and that any marketplace of ideas (or indeed any marketplace at all) can function only in such a dismal setting. Knowledge, like wealth, is hard to obtain, and even when won, may easily be lost again.[22]

Others see matters differently, supposing that knowledge, unlike other forms of wealth, always keeps growing—or at least never diminishes. Thus Arthur Koestler once declared that "We can add to our knowledge, but we cannot subtract from it."[23] And on the occasion of Harvard's 350th anniversary, President Derek Bok stated that "In most other walks of life, institutions come and go. Institutions that seem to be doing very well in one generation decline in the next. *That's not true of universities.*"[24] (Italics added.) Being a Stanford man, the President of Harvard is easily impressed.

This essay asks what role a market plays in our current generation of knowledge, and where growth of knowledge in fact now mainly occurs.

III

Two facts need to be considered. First, Western intellectuals, and especially university professors, advocate, and usually believe themselves to enjoy (in, for example, the intellectual exchange occurring within our universities), a free market of ideas. It is simply taken for granted.[25] Second, they tend to follow, or at least to praise, the sociology of knowledge of Thomas S. Kuhn. *But these two positions are incompatible.*

Analogies are often drawn between a free market in ideas and free markets in goods and services. But professors tend to dislike such comparisons: they see the free market in ideas as something on a higher plane, qualitatively different from free markets in commodities and such like; many of them indeed even hate the marketplace as traditionally conceived, and would want nothing to do, even analogically, with a free market in coal, housing, fish or petroleum.

Take a few examples from the work of several distinguished scholars whose work I admire. My colleague, Sidney Hook, and also Edward Shils, strongly protested the analogy when it was drawn by Michael Polanyi at the Congress for Cultural Freedom.[26] Hook called Polanyi's comparison between free markets in goods and in ideas "clever but questionable" in that a man who offers commodities in the free market "is not bound by anything," whereas in science one is bound to an objective method. Supporting Hook, Shils added that members of the scientific community, by contrast to businessmen and traders, act in accordance with overriding standards, a "common law" above and beyond individuals.

Such a position does not withstand examination, and I do not know that Hook would still want to maintain his casual remark. Someone offering commodities in a market—far from being "not bound by anything"—is governed by *enforceable* law relating to fraud, credit, contract, and such like. To be sure, the analogy does have limits, but of a different sort: in the marketplace of ideas, fraud, plagiarism, theft, false advertising (including false claims to expertise and the whole mystique of expertise), "conspiracies of silence," casual slander and libel, breach of contract, deceit of all sorts is *more* common than in business—simply because there are few readily enforceable penalties.[27] This is especially so in those areas (the humanities, economics, social sciences, the arts—as opposed to profitable fields)—where transaction costs of enforcing such things as property rights, priority claims (or even accurate reporting) usually outweigh or undermine any real advantage to doing so, and where the transaction costs of trying to defend oneself against such things as slander are prohibitive.[28] Robert K. Merton has noticed the roughneck character of academic behavior, although he does not put it in economic terms, in his "Priorities in Scientific Discovery: A Chapter in the Sociology of Science."[29] W. Glenn Campbell has noted the casual character assassination that takes place on American university campuses, where "verbal pollution has reached a dangerously high level."[30] Further recent, even shocking examples are reported by William Broad and Nicholas Wade in their book, *Betrayers of the Truth: Fraud and Deception in the Halls of Science.*[31] And there is an enlightening economic treatment of the "predatory behavior" of academics in Richard B. McKenzie, *The Political Economy of the Educational Process.*[32]

Not only do Hook and Shils ignore such facts; they also take an inaccurate view of scientific as opposed to business "communities," implying (although not explicitly stating) that there is no sense of community in the world of business, that commercial activity is no more than "a mere collection of separate individuals." Businessmen are, of course, not saints. But this idealization of academics at the expense of businessmen conflicts with Montesquieu's wise remark that "Ou il y a du commerce, il y a des meurs douces" (1748, i.e., roughly, "Wherever there is commerce, there one finds gentlemanly behavior"). It conflicts with most psychological and sociological studies of the priestly and scholarly mentality undertaken ever since Nietzsche wrote on ressentiment; and it conflicts also with the conclusions of the public choice school about the contrast between the moral pretense and the actual behavior characteristic of politicians, bureaucrats, and academics. Public choice theorists, such as Buchanan and Tullock, would insist that academics, like public "servants," act as much in their own interest as do businessmen. In a similar vein, Karl Popper cautions against the "civil servants" who would be our "uncivil masters."[33] There is little hope of achieving such educational aims as the advancement of learning and the growth of knowledge until it is acknowledged, as Shils does not, that individuals working in educational institutions are as self-interested as businessmen, but that the organizational framework in which they operate—the network of incentives, constraints, and sanctions—tends to work against, rather than to further, public benefit, and does so just because educational and professional institutions work contrary to market principles.

Ronald H. Coase may have been the first to notice the contradictions embedded in the positions of such academics. In a series of essays,[34] Coase gently exposes and chides their self-servingly contradictory behavior in typically insisting on government regulation in the market for goods, and deregulation in the market of ideas. He sums up: "The market for ideas is the market in which the intellectual conducts his trade.... Self-esteem leads the intellectuals to magnify the importance of their own market.[35] That others should be regulated seems natural, particularly as many of the intellectuals see themselves as doing the regulating. But self-interest combines with self-esteem to ensure that while others are regulated, that regulation should not apply to themselves.... It may not be a nice explanation but I can think of no other for this strange situation."[36]

Our first lesson, then, is that professors are as self-serving as business folk (if not more so), and that many intellectuals—like many business folk—seem to construe a free market chiefly as freedom for themselves. Our second lesson is more sobering, since it passes beyond belief to action; it is that the record of many intellectuals suggests that, whatever they may *say*, in practice they tend to work against free markets of *any* kind— including free markets in ideas—at least wherever they have the opportunity to *enforce* their own ideas with relative impunity, or low cost, on others, including fellow intellectuals. What they call intellectual freedom often means, in practice, protection from intellectual competition. For example, in several studies[37] Mikhail Bernstam has drawn on two areas of his expertise, Soviet studies and American welfare programs, to argue that 20th-century intellectuals (that is, producers and distributors of ideas) have, in both cases and places, designed transfer programs—based on supposedly altruistic ideological notions that dictate economic relations—that internalize the benefits of their ideas (i.e., they appropriate the benefits of those ideas for themselves) but which deftly shift to other members of the community (externalize) virtually all the costs (costs that include terror and genocide in the first case; and in the second, milder case with which we are all familiar, costs in terms of current unemployment and indefinitely perpetuated unemployability, poverty, broken homes, welfare dependency, and induced illegitimacy). In plain terms, they implement their own ideas, and profit from them, at the expense of others. As Bernstam so nicely puts it: *"Intellectuals die for, but not of, their ideas. Somehow, it turns out, intellectuals never happen to be where the costs of their ideas strike people."*

One way for such intellectuals to reduce their production costs is to attempt to obtain various sorts of security for themselves (the security of tenure, for example, which is not available in markets). This security may be justified by appealing to "academic freedom," "intellectual freedom," or even "the free market of ideas."[38] Often, however, the freedom sought is the freedom to secure their own positions and to corner the market, and thus to remove, not create, a free market in ideas.[39]

IV

Some will not only dispute this, but will accuse me of taking a shockingly cynical if not pathological view of my fellow academics; they may admit that something like this happened to some intellectuals in Russia, and perhaps even to some *other* intellectuals in this country, but would stoutly deny that anything of the sort happens with them.[40]

If one were going to argue this issue on the empirical evidence (where, of course, it must ultimately be decided), one would have to be prepared for a long discussion. There is no time for that here, so I would like to do a kind of end run around any empirical dispute. My argument may leave you unconvinced, but it should at least startle you. The argument is simple, and it is not new. Ian C. Jarvie and I began to develop the background for it in two separate and independent studies published in the same anthology in 1982;[41] and Jarvie developed the argument to a smashing crescendo in an essay read in 1984 Washington, D.C., which will be published shortly.[42]

The sociology of science of Thomas S. Kuhn, as developed in his *The Structure of Scientific Revolutions*[43] and elsewhere, is the most influential account of life in the knowledge industry. If one enters into the spirit of sociology[44] and appeals to a sociological measure—the citation index—one finds that Kuhn is one of the most frequently cited contemporary authors. And if one bears in mind that the basic Kuhnian ideas come from Ludwig Wittgenstein[45]—who is also among those most often cited—one gains, if only in sociological terms, some impression of the influence of Kuhnian ideas. Many people praise Kuhn not only for having described life in the universities, and in the various scientific disciplines, realistically, the way it is, *but also for having appreciated that it could not be otherwise.* What sort of report does Kuhn give? Is it of a marketplace of ideas? *Hardly.* It reports a milieu in which nothing resembling such a market operates. Perhaps this is why he ignores economic explanations almost entirely. Kuhn might have investigated institutions of learning from an economic rather than a sociological point of view, but he did not.[46]

As Kuhn's contribution is usually reported, he is supposed to have attacked "idealized" accounts of science (such as Popper's) —accounts that, emphasizing the parallel between the growth of science and biological evolution and natural selection, claimed that scientific ideas are subjected to sharp competition, that science is a revolutionary activity dedicated to pursuing truth by overthrowing error, and that unsuccessful ideas are weeded out by confronting them with contrary facts—that is, by falsification. By contrast, so it is maintained, Kuhn described how science really proceeds: on his account, most of science is bound by precedent, tradition, and commitment to reigning paradigms guarded, licensed, and franchised by scientific elites, elites that are concerned to train, indoctrinate, supervise, and socialize initiates into the scientific enterprise. Its main activity, and the activity for which initiates are to be trained, is the solving of relatively minor problems—or "puzzles"—set by, and in conformity with, the reigning "paradigm." Intellectual revolution is a rarity, likely to be more disruptive than enlightening, something against which the guardians of the paradigms should protect themselves—even weeding out dissidents and outsiders—for the sake of the larger enterprise. In any case, the shift from one paradigm to another is irrational; nor does it indicate progress towards the truth—on the contrary, the entire account is relativistic, asserting that paradigms are incommensurable. Scientists constantly rewrite their textbooks not in order to chart progress towards the truth, to record what really happened (the interesting errors together with the gains, or the current controversial state of critical discussion), but, rather, to suppress resurgence of ideas already overthrown and to reinforce those in fashion or in power. Thus the history of science is not the story of a battle for truth among competing frameworks in a marketplace setting; for competing frameworks are excluded by reigning hegemonies. Rather, the history of science is the story of *successive* ideological hegemonies and the irrational ways in which they have seized the whiphand of power in the halls of learning. Kuhn has written: "It is precisely the abandonment of critical discourse that marks the transition to science."

But this *report* of the problem situation is deeply misleading. Kuhn and his followers systematically misdescribe their opponents; thus they misdescribe the problem situation, and prevent it from being seen in an economic light. In denouncing *idealizing philosophers,* Kuhn and his followers have *interpreted recommended ways to attain stated ends as descriptive claims.* Thus Popper never offered an idealized description of what scientists actually do or claimed that, in practice, scientists always try to falsify their claims; indeed, he outlined in detail some stratagems to which they resort to avoid refutation. Rather, after analyzing the logic of the situation, he *recommended* that, to advance knowledge, that situation be made as competitive as possible, that every attempt be made to falsify or otherwise expose theories and frameworks to critical examination.[47] He advocated that competitiveness be furthered by embedding it in a system of rules—what one might call a "constitution of learning"—that would hinder ideas from being entrenched either by means of sharp practice or by built-in devices for deflecting criticism.[48] I do not know whether anyone ever attacked Adam Smith for idealizing the marketplace on the ground that real markets, as we know them, are not free. Such criticism would be exactly parallel to the one Kuhnians mount against Popper. Smith, seeing clearly the character and defects of the markets of his time, recommended freer and more competitive markets in order to increase wealth; similarly Popper recommended attempting to overthrow existing theories in order to increase knowledge. In both cases we are given a methodology or an economics for increasing wealth, not a sociological description of the way things are usually done.

While claiming to attack idealized descriptions of the scientific process, Kuhn thus actually presents an idealized, uncritical estimation of the actual results achieved in science—and neglects to consider the possibility that such results might have been much improved had methodological norms been more closely approximated.[49]

Such distortion is essential to Kuhn and all Kuhnians.[50] Otherwise his ideas would be less appealing to American academics. For what function do Kuhnian ideas serve in contemporary academic life? It is to legitimate the existing structures of our reigning academic institutions. As Jarvie puts it so well:

> Kuhn's ideas legitimate the system from which he benefited so much; a system moreover, that was relatively new and sorely in need of a legitimating ideology. *Kuhn's ideas...legitimize the social formations in which the science of his time is temporarily housed.* Popper...offers an explanation of the success of science that not only transcends the particular social formations of his time, but which happens also to be inimical to and critical of these formations, and thereby of those ideas of Kuhn which legitimate these formations. Kuhn's ideas legitimate science's current social embodiment, Popper's undermine it.... The American academic and scientific Establishment...has naturally preferred to embrace Kuhn and to hold Popper at a distance.[51]

V

My "end run" is nearly completed, and it is time to return to the contradiction with which I began this meditation. That is, Western intellectuals, and especially professors, advocate, and usually think that they enjoy, a free market of ideas; yet they tend to recommend the sociology of knowledge of Thomas Kuhn. If it is now clear why these two positions are incompatible, it is also now easy to understand why they are nonetheless held. Professors need Kuhnian ideology in order to legitimate what they do in practice—for no doubt Kuhn is, on the descriptive level, largely right. What they do in practice is to attempt to control the intellectual landscape. If they can—by means of an ideology such as Kuhn's—convince themselves and their patrons, whether private or public, that their anti-competitive activities are socially necessary, they greatly reduce the production costs of their views, more firmly entrench themselves, and better enforce their ideas on others—whatever the effects on the real development of science and on the community. Moreover, what began by claiming to be hard-headed realistic description of the way science really works takes on a strongly normative function. For in Kuhn's world, *what is is right.* As one of his admirers expresses it, the truth of a scientific theory reflects or is a projection of the *consensus* of the scientific community, and a theory is false when it is rejected by that community; and if the scientific community has made no commitment, then the theory is neither true nor false.[52] What is true, that is, is what we experts agree to be true; what is open is that on which we have no opinion. The continuing, almost raging popularity of Kuhn's relativistic ideas among academics is strong evidence that, in fact, the marketplace of ideas is severely regulated. Like Wittgenstein, Kuhn told professionals what they wanted to hear.[53]

VI

If our educational and research institutions are not free market, how then should one describe them in economic terms? That their structure is economically peculiar has been noticed before. Thus James M. Buchanan has described universities as place where the consumers (students) do not buy, the producers (faculty) do not sell, and the owners (trustees, etc.) do not control.[54]

So simple a description is perilous, as Buchanan would at once agree, for these institutions, whatever their economic character, are set in—and interact with—a complex social and legal network in which relatively free markets coexist with extensive state controls and regulations, state subsidies, and private and public cartels. This context may, in fluctuating circumstances, either enhance or mitigate the effects of the particular forms of organization that one finds in education.

Yet Buchanan's description is also all too accurate. A trivial example from my own experience helps to illustrate this. In the past 15 years, enrollment in philosophy courses has plummeted in almost all universities, public and private, for, among other things, there was little market for the philosophical goods produced by the cartel—or unholy alliance consisting of phenomenology, so-called analytic philosophy, and the remnants of logical positivism—that had come to dominate and control most departments.[55] As a result, in most state institutions, and in many private ones, where funding was related to faculty/student ratio, all hiring of philosophers stopped around 1971, and even tenured philosophy professors were, for a time, in real danger of being laid off.

But the philosophy professors were rescued, as it were, by a national catastrophe. For at just this time the test scores of enrolling students had fallen badly, and many students were indeed barely literate. Throughout the country, the latter problem has been used to "solve" the former by one simple device: the creation of compulsory remedial courses in "Clear Thinking" and "Critical Thinking" taught chiefly by philosophy professors. This creates—or rather, legislates—a large demand for philosophy professors; and their jobs are saved.[56] Yet there is hardly any evidence that clear thinking can be taught; or that—even if it can be taught—philosophy professors are particularly good at clear thinking or at teaching it; or that there even is any such thing as "clear thinking" in the abstract, divorced from subject matter. There is also little evidence that courses in clear thinking actually succeed in remedying illiteracy of students, or that students would—if not required—enroll in such courses.

The situation is even worse: many such courses consist largely in the teaching of a theory of learning called "inductive logic"—despite the fact that Popper showed, as long ago as 1934, that there is no such thing as inductive logic.

The professors do not sell: they impose their services to preserve their jobs; the students do not buy but are compelled to purchase (and often unwittingly to waste their time learning a theory of learning that is both psychologically and logically impossible—a theory which, if students did actually "learn" in "inductive" terms, they could not learn); and the trustees have evidently been convinced by the self-serving experts they consulted (their own endangered faculty) that the legislation serves the learning task of the university and the public good. There is no market here. Nor any education. What there is, is what James Buchanan rightly calls a "public bad."

While this may be a nice illustration of the self-interested and all too "realistic" behavior of our faculties, I am mainly concerned not with the teaching task of our institutions of learning, one that they occasionally perform surpassingly well, nor with their role as museums for the care and occasional display of some of the records of our intellectual heritage and traditions— a task that they also perform remarkably well. What concerns me more is their research tasks: those of their functions that do not simply generate fluctuations in the temporary store of information in the heads of students, but are supposed to swell the storehouse of knowledge.

The chief institutions of contemporary research—especially those connected with faculty hiring, graduate research and disciplinary professions—are late feudal in character.[57] These departments and professions consist in arrangements more closely resembling fiefdoms, guilds, cartels, and mutual protection rackets than any free-market arrangements; and they are primarily concerned not with the production of innovative knowledge, but with the control of entry, the gaining of "livings," the placements of vassals, and the controlled production and protection from competition of non-innovative alleged knowledge—ideas that would perish if not endowed with the intellectual equivalent of price supports, which I take to be the real function of incorporation as requirements in university catalogues. Thus the university becomes a virtually ideal setting for those who want to gain a sheltered pulpit (i.e., credibility) and to reduce their own production and transaction costs, those who want not only to protect themselves against competition but even to stifle it, and not only to control markets in the sense of eliminating or forcing out competitors but also to force their own products on the population.

If this is so, what is surprising is not (as Kuhn and Robert Merton have reported) that innovations have difficulty in spreading, but that revolutions in knowledge ever take place at all in such institutions. Significant *economic* growth is not nurtured in comparable institutions; why should growth in *knowledge* occur in them?

VII

Actually, it does so less often than commonly supposed, and only under special circumstances. The impression to the contrary is created, first of all, by the expansion in the allegedly necessary apparatus of knowledge production, such as the proliferation of state universities and related institutions, and the creation and growth of the national research foundations (institutions that may work against the growth of knowledge).[58]

Also contributing to the impression of growth is the so-called publication explosion. There is, indeed, an information explosion, as well as its accompanying publication explosion; but its size is exaggerated, it is wrongly interpreted, and much of it contributes to the advancement, not of knowledge but, of professors who must (or think they must) publish or perish. The bulk of this publication is of little worth, consisting chiefly of misreadings, and is well known to be so by those immersed in it.[59] Which is one of several reasons why it is in fact, for the most part, not read.[60] Thus Claire Friedland and George Stigler report, after studying the record of doctors in economics of major universities, that in the first 15 years after receiving the Ph.D., one-third do not publish a single article and the median journal output of those who do publish is about two articles. "For the profession as a whole, the output of articles is probably one per economist per 20 years."[61] Reskin, and also Price, report that "many scientists do no original research after leaving graduate school and rarely or never publish."[62]

VIII

All this suggests that our universities are in the midst of an intellectual slump; they are, in terms of the generation of new knowledge, in a depression.[63] I expand on this claim in a longer version of this talk. To defend it adequately in the time remaining would be impossible, for it goes against a good bit of surface evidence. I shall, therefore, leave you with no real evidence, but only, again, with a few examples, briefly sketched, and some dismal thoughts for meditation.

It would, of course, be foolish to deny that innovative research does occur in our academic institutions, or that productive geniuses do spend their lives within university walls. My own experience leads me to think that there are fewer of these than commonly supposed. Only because the university exists in and interacts with a larger, more competitive culture is there as much innovation in it as there is. The most successful associations between university departments and innovators seem to occur in those areas that impinge directly on engineering and medicine;[64] and many scientific and medical breakthroughs have been associated, at least initially or in part, with university departments and laboratories.[65] Such collaboration is in the news, particularly when associated with genetic engineering and engineering technology, and has been particularly important at about five or six prominent research centers. But such things have happened in only a few places, and *mainly* under special conditions in which commercial and entrepreneurial interests collaborate with universities in business-like ways to create conditions in which innovators can flourish, and gain credit and profit from their work—and in which they are relatively protected both from university bureaucracies and from the harassment of unproductive colleagues.

In most other areas the situation is far bleaker. In the longer version of this lecture, I argue, with examples, that in the humanities, the arts, the social sciences and psychology, and in several areas of the natural sciences, the greatest advances in knowledge of the present century have come from outside the university[66]—just as they did in the two preceding centuries; and that universities themselves tend to serve as bastions for resistance, and for the entrenchment of false philosophies— just as, not so long ago, they served as bastions for more explicit forms of entrenched religion.

This is not surprising. For certain kinds of groups, universities are handy places in which to have a strong redoubt. They are handy for any groups that are not competitive, that are peddling ideas for which there is little demand, ideas that do not work, that fail to explain, and whose proponents are consciously or unconsciously tempted to turn them into ideologies in order to perpetuate themselves. After all, funding is provided, and internal scrutiny is more or less in their control. As David Riesman (who has obviously been "socialized" by his experience with universities) put it in one of his sociological investigations, "A college generous enough to open itself to scrutiny should not suffer harm as a result."[67] Why not? Why should educational institutions be closed to scrutiny?

I shall mention just a few examples to argue the claim that our universities serve for the entrenchment of false philosophies—not to prove anything but only to show where I stand.

The false philosophies that I have in mind (which sometimes present themselves as sciences rather than philosophies) are found not only in departments of philosophy, but in most of the arts and in some of the sciences: they include Wittgensteinian "analytic" philosophy,[68] logical positivism, phenomenology and hermeneutics, behaviorism, pragmatism, determinism, and scientism. The academic disciplines that they shape most deeply include physics (especially in the Copenhagen Interpretation of quantum mechanics); psychology; sociology; history and especially intellectual history and the history of science; anthropology; economics—even Austrian economics;[69] and also literary criticism and the theory of art.

These false philosophies, or only slightly variant predecessors, have dominated thinking in university departments for some 40 years, and there is no sign of their early demise.[70] There has been no growth or even much change in fundamentals in these departments despite an avalanche of devastating criticism. It seems that Eugen von Böhm-Bawerk was wrong when he wrote that "Science progresses through the old professors dying off."[71] For the old professors have died off; and there is still little progress. Far from dying out, these departments and professions have in recent years begun to consolidate and extend their influence: they have, literally, formed intellectual cartels. This is possible because there are deep underlying structural similarities, and thus common interests, among them. Despite different points of departure, different historical and geographical origins, they enjoy "family resemblances" in Wittgenstein's sense. There are deep structural similarities[72] among behaviorism, positivism, hermeneutics, linguistic philosophy, determinism, and scientism—even if some of these present themselves occasionally as opponents of one another. These structural similarities include, especially, justificationism, which in turn spawns relativism.

What could be called a common "style" also contributes to the resemblances: the style of obscurantism, a style that presents itself in two main forms, forms that are sometimes combined: first, in the conspicuous deployment of mathematical formalism in places where it serves no purpose; and second, obscurantism in speech and presentation, the most ostentatiously obscurantist being Wittgensteinian and Heideggerian philosophy. One understands this from an economic point of view: the production cost of obscurantist philosophy is particularly low: those who must listen to it, to learn it, and to think in terms of it are those who pay the price. Such philosophies are hard to criticize, and thus are all the better protected, being not only shielded behind a barricade of symbolism and jargon but also infused with the doctrine that that which appears difficult must be deep, whereas whatever is clear must be superficial.

IX

Take as an example the ritual practice of mathematics. Before doing so, lest I mislead anyone, I should mention that my doctorate is in mathematical logic and scientific method, and that I regard the discoveries of this century in mathematics and meta-mathematics as among the greatest human achievements of all time. I am not opposed to mathematics; nor do I blame those who have fallen under its spell, for it is a most wonderful enchantress.

Yet two fields that especially concern me have impoverished themselves by an addiction beyond all reason, or even an enslavement, to mathematics. These are philosophy and economics.

Contemporary British and American philosophy focus chiefly on mathematical logic and on an activity known as "meaning analysis" that is as vague and undisciplined—and unanalytical— as logic itself is precise. There is a reason for this: it was discovered that many of the old logical paradoxes could be resolved through a kind of meaning analysis that involved metamathematical techniques. And philosophers were understandably inspired by the thought that they could, in exactly the same way, resolve the ancient problems of philosophy. It was a brilliant idea, and has now become a program controlling much research in philosophy. But there is a catch to it: the parallel does not hold. It is their self-referential character that enables the ancient logical paradoxes (e.g., the liar paradox: "I am lying now") to be treated in such ways. But the traditional problems of philosophy (as opposed to the paradoxes of logic) do not involve self-reference; the entire program is thus beside the point and—despite being practiced for nearly 50 years now, by some three generations of philosophy professors—has produced no result except to drive bored undergraduates out of philosophy courses at a moment when the world is sharply divided on ideological and philosophical lines.[73]

A similar enchantment reigns in economics, although the details are different, and the original idea was less brilliantly inspired. I have in mind the elaborate mathematics connected with the Walrasian idea of general equilibrium—a state in which all markets and economic agents are simultaneously in balance with regard, for example, to supply and demand. Equilibrium, a concept taken from classical mechanics and denoting a balance of opposing forces, has a limited analogical usefulness in economics; but many economists, wanting to make far more of it, have taken it as the basis of a mathematical apparatus employing simultaneous equations that is alleged to be a powerful analytical tool useful in understanding real life situations. Thus Jevons, usually a more sensible man, declared that the "Theory of Economy...presents a close analogy to the science of Statical Mechanics, and the Laws of Exchange are found to resemble the laws of Equilibrium of a Lever."[74]

So close an analogy is dubious: for it has always been widely assumed—and was assumed at Jevons's time—that classical mechanics can describe physical processes only to the extent that they are reversible in time. It is assumed, that is, that any film taken of a classical process would be reversible in the sense that, if it were inserted into a projector with the last picture first, it would again yield a possible classical process.[75]

When economists took over the notion of equilibrium from classical (non-statistical) mechanics, they evidently did not understand it; for it is unlikely that they could really have wanted to import such an assumption. In economics, as in the life sciences generally, one deals with processes assumed from the outset to be irreversible. Not, of course, that economists assume that any state of equilibrium will be long preserved, but they do not expect or allow for a return to an earlier state. Rather, economics treats open systems and the evolution of higher structures; and, if there were any doubt about the possibility or potentialities of such systems, Prigogine has now shown[76] that open systems far from equilibrium can build up new structures rather than moving towards entropy.

Of course, many contemporary economists will welcome such developments. Unfortunately, however, they will not be able to do so consistently while retaining much of the theory of general equilibrium; for the processes mentioned—being intrinsically unpredictable—are incompatible with the assumption of "perfect knowledge" that lies at the heart of general equilibrium theory and which is, in turn, an import (usually not recognized or acknowledged) into economics from now obsolete Laplacean physics and its perfectly informed "demon" (no doubt an ideal social manager) that is able to predict any state with any required degree of precision.[77] In addition to this difficulty from physics, there is the epistemological and logical point that the objectively unfathomable character of knowledge is incompatible with perfect knowledge.[78]

Actually, such historical points may be academic except in showing that the "scientistic" analogy used here was faulty from the start: for it is now known that the old assumption of the reversibility of all classical mechanical processes is false, and that irreversible classical processes do exist. A simple example is that of the propagation of a wave from a center. A film taken of a large surface of water initially at rest into which a stone is tossed will, if reversed, show contracting circular waves of increasing amplitude, and a circular region of undisturbed water will close in towards the center. Such processes are not possible in classical mechanics as usually understood.[79] And even in non-classical statistical mechanics, such processes are, although physically possible, extremely improbable.

There are many other problems too: general equilibrium as often conceived by economists would also involve instantaneous adjustments to change involving action at a distance—which (whatever may eventually be decided about Bell's theorem and the world of the quantum)[80] could hardly apply in economic exchange.

These simple objections—ones that any physicist might raise —are strong ones, but many other objections as well have been raised by economists themselves. There are, for instance, the familiar (and related) Austrian objections that the theory assumes perfect competition, takes no account of and is unable to handle time, and is incompatible with methodological individualism.

Thus, while I agree that the leading characteristic of general equilibrium theory in its effect within economics "has been the endless formalization of purely logical problems without the slightest regard for the production of falsifiable theorems about actual economic behavior, which, we insist, remains the fundamental task of economics,"[81] the real faults of the theory are, from the point of view of logic, physics, and the life sciences, more serious: the project of general equilibrium theory is not just useless and irrelevant, it is incoherent.

In sum, the bulk of mathematics used in philosophy and economics fails to advance knowledge, and functions chiefly (apart from providing employment for mathematicians) as a rite of initiation. Anthropologists report that among the most effective initiation devices for generating commitment is the practice of compelling one to master and to adopt an absurdity—and the more highly complicated and difficult of mastery the absurdity, the better its effectiveness in generating commitment. And so, I believe, it is here.

X

These ritual practices aid the formation of intellectual cartels: the prior adoption of common ceremonies eases the formation of coalitions. But let us return to the cartels themselves. The cartelization of the originally separate philosophies mentioned above began some time ago. Morton White pointed the way in his *Toward Reunion in Philosophy* in 1956.[82] Hubert Dreyfus and Richard Rorty have continued the task, with only slightly different examples, more recently.[83] White, Dreyfus and Rorty are not critics of these philosophies; rather, they enter the scene as facilitators and mediators to enable the cartels to be formed. Far from seeing their wares as problematic, they sense their similarities, and try to elicit from them a core in terms of which reconciliation and cooperation may be achieved—reconciliation and, with it, further domination of the intellectual marketplace,[84] further exclusion of rival points of view.

I suggested earlier that universities are as innovative as they are due chiefly to the competition they still face from other institutions. To the extent that university disciplines must compete with independent organizations, institutes, multiple and overlapping professions, newspapers and periodicals, their power to inhibit the growth of knowledge is lessened. But they resist such diminishment of their power, and attempt to reduce such competition from without as well as competition from within. How they engage in going about this is another long story that I shall not have time to explore here.

Cartels, professions and guilds, when found in the ordinary marketplace, often present themselves and their interests to government as lobbies. The cartels entrenched in universities have devised ways to obtain support that many lobbyists might envy: they have infiltrated the government. They have brought pressure to create (and then they have virtually captured control of) such bodies as the National Endowment for the Humanities and the National Endowment for the Arts.[85] Where there exists a strong profession backed by government agencies, it becomes more cost-effective for academic groups to attempt to manipulate or even take over the government or professional apparatus, and more expensive to engage in the competitive behavior that creates social surpluses such as the advancement of knowledge. In the circumstances, one may wonder how much separation of ideology and state still exists in American education.[86] National research agencies tend to be staffed by members of the same professions, guided by the same presuppositions, as those whom they fund. In those areas that deal with the mind, the dwelling place of human freedom—psychology, education, and philosophy—control, funding, and licensing is in the hands of departments, academies, and professional guilds whose directorates interlock with state bureaucracies. With such support they can last for a long time, whereas business cartels usually fall apart after a relatively short period.

Not just state control is involved. Entrenched ideologies posing as the only legitimate producers of professionals, and exercising exclusive power to license and grant credentials through universities, gain control of institutions formally independent of universities, such as professional associations, and from there—appealing to the credentialing and licensing power that they already control—gain even greater access to state power and funding (which is itself usually the source of professional licensing power) the better to police, through rewards and punishments of various sorts, their own domains. The tentacles of the ideologies extend outward to tap the power of the professions and of the state, and then turn back upon their members to enforce conformity. Eventually, in the course of the expansions and contractions that mark this process, few uncontrolled sources of ideology (apart from the uneducable freethinking individual, on whom all hope rests) remain to staff whatever independent positions may remain for a time—such as those provided by the platforms of occasional newspapers and periodicals. But how long can *these* be independent? And if they can be independent can they *also* be taken seriously by those who grant credibility—or must whatever they say, at least if it is critical, be dismissed?

XI

Representatives of the sociology of knowledge often claim that it can replace epistemology. Rather, I maintain, the sociology of knowledge needs to be replaced by the economics of knowledge, a subject of which epistemology is a crucial branch. What are some of the ways in which they differ?

1. The sociology of knowledge—which pretends to be the theoretical arm of intellectual history—is concerned with the description of current social arrangements, and even its best proponents, such as Robert Merton play down, or hardly attend to, the content of ideas. It is interested in the *acceptance* of ideas, not in the *content* of ideas. Whereas the economic value of ideas, their wealth-generating power, cannot exist apart from their unfathomed content (which is so risky to estimate), and does not depend on the historical arrangements or costs that attended

their production. Moreover, most sociology of knowledge is written as if there is no cost—no transaction, information or opportunity cost—in the revision of "paradigms"; whereas, if these costs were taken into account, scientific revolutions and revolutionary failures, which Kuhn and his followers allege to be irrational, would often appear as all too rational. *Kuhn never asks what it would cost to overthrow a paradigm*—and no wonder, then, that he is a relativist.[87]

2. Due to its scientistic and Marxist background (even when this background has been repudiated, as by Merton), sociology of knowledge tends to be deterministic and relativistic. Thus, as an unintended consequence, it legitimates existing structures (as does Kuhn's theory) and neglects the aims of those operating within these structures, just as it neglects the content of the ideas produced by those so operating. One of the most important aims in science, one which is almost wholly neglected (where it is not denied) by the sociology of science, is the growth of knowledge and the advancement of learning—just as one of the most important aims in economic activity is the increase of wealth. Economics is also interested in social structures, but it is concerned with the way in which different such arrangements (and the law that attends them) further or hinder the expansion of wealth.

3. The key doctrines of economic theory as they relate to these aims—marginal utility theory, the subjective theory of value, methodological individualism, analysis of the logic of the situation, and transaction and opportunity costs—are little more than rumors in the sociology of knowledge. The key doctrine of epistemology as it relates to economics—the theory of unfathomed objective knowledge—is completely unknown to the sociology of knowledge, and contradicts virtually all its premises.

Perhaps these brief programmatic suggestions may point the way to some fruitful discussions among philosophers, economists, educators and intellectual historians—ones in which they may at least contemplate the possibility that, from the point of view of the academy and the professions as now constituted, a truly free market of ideas would be a black market in ideas—one that would be most unprofessional.[88]

NOTES

1. George J. Stigler, "The Intellectual and the Marketplace," *The Intellectual and Marketplace* (Cambridge, Massachusetts: Harvard University Press, 1984).
2. Karl R. Popper, *Conjectures and Refutations* (London: Routledge & Kegan Paul, Ltd., 1962).
3. W. Glenn Campbell, "The Universities and National Priorities," Mimeographed speech given at the Stanford Campus Conference on Relevance, Stanford, California, May 22, 1971.
4. I.C. Jarvie, "Explanation, Reduction and the Sociological Turn in the Philosophy of Science—or Kuhn as Ideologue for Merton's Theory of Science," in Gerard Radnitzky, ed., *The Search for Unity in the Sciences* (New York: Paragon House, 1989).
5. Ludwig von Mises, *Epistemological Problems of Economics* (New York: New York University Press, 1981).
6. Ludwig von Mises, *The Ultimate Foundation of Economic Science* (Kansas City: Sheed Andrews and McMeel. Inc., 1978).
7. For delivery in the "Distinguished Scholars Interdisciplinary Lecture Series," Institute for Humane Studies, George Mason University, Fairfax, Virginia, December 1, 1986, and at the conference on "Intellectual Freedom and Government Sponsorship of Higher Education," Bermuda, February 12–15, 1987. I am grateful to conversations on these themes with Mikhail Bernstam, Donald T. Campbell, Timothy Groseclose, Robert Hessen, Sidney Hook, Ian C. Jarvie, Leonard P. Liggio, Naomi Moldofsky, Stephen Kresge, Sir Karl Popper, Phil Salin, and Dorothy and Günter Wächtershäuser.
8. W.W. Bartley III, *The Retreat to Commitment*, 2nd edition (LaSalle and London: Open Court, 1984).
9. Gerard Radnitzky and W.W. Bartley III, eds., *Evolutionary Epistemology, Rationality, and the Sociology of Knowledge* (LaSalle: Open Court, 1987).
10. Karl R. Popper: *The Logic of Scientific Discovery* (London: Hutchinson, 1959), p. 15: "The central problem of epistemology has always been and still is the problem of the growth of knowledge. *And the growth of knowledge can be studied best by studying the growth of scientific knowledge.*" The epistemology usually taught in universities is not directly concerned with the growth of knowledge, but rather with other matters such as "justified true belief," attempts fruitlessly to calculate probabilities of theoretical statements on the basis of observation statements, and the related attempt to construct worlds out of sense perceptions. However large a role such investigations

played in the history of philosophy, they have no contemporary or scientific relevance, are Lamarckian in presupposition rather than Darwinian, are contradicted by the achievements of evolutionary epistemology, and also stand in conflict with both economics and biology. This view I have argued in *The Retreat to Commitment, op. cit.;* and it is a view that is elaborated, and applied to questions of evolutionary theory, sociology and economics, in *Evolutionary Epistemology, op. cit.*

11. There are, of course, other senses of economics apart from the one I have stated—that in which economics is the study of the booms and slumps in the generation of wealth—senses in which epistemology is not, or only very indirectly, or in a different sense, a branch of economics. There is the sense, for instance, in which economics is seen as the allocation of scarce resources to satisfy competing ends; as a problem of choice in a situation of scarcity; as confined to the market or to the study of the allocation of material goods to satisfy material wants; as a confrontation of conflicting ends, or in Pareto's sense in which one has an economic problem whenever one has a goal and obstacles to its achievement. I am concerned not with names, nor with establishing new definitions, but with underlying problems.

12. See Karl R. Popper, *Realism and the Aim of Science,* Vol. I of *Postscript to the Logic of Scientific Discovery* (London: Hutchinson, 1983), p. 5.

13. I make no concession, however, to philosophers who might be willing to see economics as a branch of epistemology, but not the other way around. Economics has always been concerned with the growth of knowledge, whereas epistemology has rarely concerned itself with those other kinds of growth that interest economists.

14. On ecology in such contexts see W.W. Bartley III, *The Retreat to Commitment, op. cit.,* Appendix 1.

15. Among efforts to integrate economic and epistemological thinking, special note should be taken of Gerard Radnitzky's recent papers: "Towards an 'Economic' Theory of Methodology," *Methodology and Science* 19, 1986, pp. 124–147; "Evolutionäre Erkenntnistheorie, Epistemische Ressourcen, und die Ökonomie des Handelns," in R. Riedl and F. Wuketits, eds., *Die Evolutionäre Erkenntnistheorie* (Berlin: Paul Parey, 1987), "Cost-Benefit Analysis in the Methodology of Research: The 'Economic Approach' Applied to Key Problems of the Philosophy of Science," in Gerard Radnitzky and P. Bernholz, eds., *General Economy: The Economic Approach Applied Outside the Traditional Areas of Economics* (New York: Paragon House, 1986); and "Über die Nützlichkeit des 'Economic Approach' in der Wissenschaftstheorie: Handlungsrationalität, Basisproblem und Theorienpräferenz," in R. Born and J. Marschner, eds., *Festschrift für Rudolf Wohlgenannt,* in the

series "Linzer Universitatsschriften. Festschriften, Monographien, Studientexte" (Berlin: Springer Verlag, 1987).

16. Unfortunately, the fallacious assumption that truth is manifest is closely linked to the understanding that many people have of Adam Smith's "invisible hand."

17. On Milton, see Karl R. Popper: *Conjectures and Refutations, op. cit.,* pp. 8, 16; and J.W.N. Watkins, *The Listener,* January 22, 1959. On the unfathomable character of knowledge, see W.W. Bartley III, "Knowledge Is a Product Not Fully Known to Its Producer," in Kurt Leube and Albert Zlabinger, eds., *The Political Economy of Freedom* (Munich: Philosophia Verlag, 1985); and W.W. Bartley III, "Alienation Alienated: The Economics of Knowledge *versus* the Psychology of Knowledge," in Gerard Radnitzky and W.W. Bartley III, *op. cit.* This idea, which stems from Popper, is the theme of W.W. Bartley III, *Unfathomed Knowledge, Infinite Ignorance* (LaSalle: Open Court, 1989). The idea is presented in Karl R. Popper, *Unended Quest* (LaSalle: Open Court, 1977), section 7, and is developed briefly with regard to Hobbes in J.W.N. Watkins, *Hobbes's System of Ideas* (London: Hutchinson, 1965), pp. 22ff.

The conspiracy or interventionist theory of error did not, of course, die with Milton: a variant of it, what could be called the "conspiracy theory of humorlessness" undergirds the plot of a recent popular book and movie, Umberto Eco's *The Name of the Rose,* wherein it is assumed that the intervention of a fanatical priest, suppressing a lost treatise by Aristotle on laughter, is required to preserve philosophical grimness and lack of humor. I shall wager that, in case such a work is ever discovered, philosophers will examine and debate its tenets in the most humorless possible way. See an essay written long before Eco's work, namely Walter Kaufmann, "Why Most Philosophers Cannot Laugh," *Critique of Religion and Philosophy* (Princeton: Princeton University Press, 1958/72), section 8.

18. See W.W. Bartley III, "Alienation Alienated: The Economics of Knowledge *versus* the Psychology and Sociology of Knowledge," *op. cit.* See also W.W. Bartley III, *Unfathomed Knowledge, Infinite Ignorance, op. cit.*

19. Ronald H. Coase, "The Market for Ideas," *The National Review,* September 27, 1974, pp. 1095–1099; and Ronald H. Coase, "The Market for Goods and the Market for Ideas," *Private Higher Education: The Job Ahead* (Malibu, California: AAPICU, 1976), pp. 17–21. See also Ronald H. Coase, "The Nature of the Firm," *Economica 4,* 1937; Ronald H. Coase, "The Problem of Social Cost," *Journal of Law and Economics 3,* 1960; and Ronald H. Coase, "Adam Smith's View of Man," *Journal of Law and Economics,* 1976.

20. See Freidrich A. Hayek *The Fatal Conceit,* W.W. Bartley III, ed., (Chicago: University of Chicago Press, 1989), Vol. I of *The Collected Works of F.A. Hayek.*

21. Freidrich A. Hayek, *The Constitution of Liberty* (Chicago: University of Chicago Press, 1960), pp. 22, 29. See also *supra* note 20. See also Friedrich A. Hayek, Congress for Cultural Freedom, *Science and Freedom* (London: Martin Secker & Warburg Ltd., 1955), pp. 53–54.

22. Fallibilists such as Hayek and Coase, of course, do favor "free and open encounter" and oppose intervention and conspiracy, but this is because the latter bring a more abundant yield of error, and make it easier to eradicate. But error is there in any case.

23. Arthur Koestler, *The Sleepwalkers: A History of Man's Changing Vision of the Universe* (London: Hutchinson, 1959). p. 19.

24. Interview with Derek Bok, President of Harvard University, published in "John Harvard's Journal," *Harvard Magazine,* September-October, 1986, p. 207. I was comforted, in my dismal and dissident view that knowledge too can be lost and that even one's own *alma mater* may decline, by a dissenting observation made on the same anniversary occasion by Jacob Neusner, a fellow Harvard alumnus and a University Professor at Brown. "Like the rest of the Ivy League," Neusner declared, Harvard "sets too comfortably on its ivy laurels. Believing your own press releases is not the way to achieve excellence, and in field after field Harvard simply does not excel." Is my poor *alma mater* rusting on her laurels? If it is true, as Douglass North writes, that "stagnation has been more characteristic of economic societies than growth throughout history," the allegations of Bok and Koestler need defending. Douglass C. North, in Michael Flinn, ed. *Proceedings of the Seventh International Economic History Congress,* (Edinburgh: University Press, 1978), p. 212.

    Another who, like them, believes that knowledge can be won but not lost may be Thomas Kuhn, who holds "that the sequence of conceptions espoused by a scientific community is irreversible, and that there is, therefore, something like progress involved—but this is progress away from confusion, rather than toward any antecedent reality." See Thomas L. Haskell, *ACLS Newsletter* 36, Summer-Fall, 1985, p. 15.

25. Much (fortunately not all) of what they construe as manifestations of such a free market is, in fact, one of two sorts of behavior. The first is the genteel, bitchy but amiable, chatter of the ordinary common room. But this is anything but characteristic of the marketplace; for in a market, people are seriously selling and buying, whereas the genteel common room intellectual will hesitate to "sell" his ideas lest he look pushy, and hesitate to "buy" anyone else's—unless it is already in fashion—lest he appear susceptible of being

gulled. Common room chatter does not usually put money on ideas; it is not serious business. It is rarely more than gossip and hearsay *about* a market somewhere else. The conventions of the common room are often such that, if one does take argument seriously, if one does attempt seriously to buy or sell arguments in the common room, one is dismissed as one who is "not a good conversationalist" in Rorty's sense, or as a "difficult man." (See the first section, "A Difficult Man" in W.W. Bartley III, "A Popperian Harvest," in Paul Levinson, ed., *In Pursuit of Truth: Essays in Honour of Karl Popper's 80th Birthday* (New York: Humanities Press, 1982), and W.W. Bartley III, "Ein Schwieriger Mensch: Eine Porträtskizze von Sir Karl Popper," in Eckhard Nordhofen, ed., *Physiognomien: Philosophen des 20. Jahrhunderts in Portraits* (Königstein/Taunus: Athenäum, 1980), pp. 43–69.)

A second sort of academic behavior that may be mistaken as a manifestation of a marketplace of ideas is the bad-tempered squabbling and disagreement (usually not about ideas but about perquisites of various sorts) that Nietzsche associated with the "priestly" mentality—behavior that thrives even in totalitarian societies.

26. Congress for Cultural Freedom, *op. cit.,* p. 47. Another statement of the difference between the university and business organizations appears in the Association of American Universities, *The Right and Responsibilities of Universities and Their Faculties,* March 1953, reprinted in the *University Bulletin,* University of California, Vol. I, No. 33, April 20, 1953, pp. 162–164.

27. One of the few thinkers willing to pay the transaction costs of claiming and attempting to enforce priority and intellectual property rights has been Sir Karl Popper. And he has had to pay dearly—through "retaliation by conspiracy of silence," by further plagiarism, and, especially and perhaps most damaging, by deliberate, systematic misreporting of his ideas—for his priority controversy with Neurath (which Neurath started), for helping to defend Tarski against attempts to plagiarize his work; and for his own accusations of plagiarism against Carnap, Lakatos, and Reichenbach. See W.W. Bartley III, "A Popperian Harvest," *op. cit.* In practice, the social convention that one not make claims about the merits or originality of one's own contributions outweighs the sense of proper ownership, and very much increases the cost of enforcing any claim to ownership.

28. From this fact alone, it follows that educational institutions, as structured at present, are unlikely to contribute as much as they are expected to the growth of knowledge. For, as Douglass North writes:

> The reason that property rights are the determinants of performance is that they provide the basic set of incentives which encourage or discourage economic activity. Savings and investment in human capital, invention and innovation, are all fundamentally influenced by the way in which property rights are specified.

As North also points out, many of those who discuss such matters wrongly assume perfectly and costlessly specified and enforced property rights, i.e., they assume zero transaction costs and no externalities. See Michael Flinn, ed. *op. cit.,* p. 211.

29. *American Sociological Review* 22, December, 1957, pp. 635–659.
30. See *supra* note 3.
31. William Broad and Nicholas Wade, *Betrayers of the Truth: Fraud and Deception in the Halls of Science* (New York: Simon & Schuster, Inc., 1982).
32. Richard B. McKenzie, *The Political Economy of the Educational Process* (The Hague: Martinus Nijhoff, 1979), chapter 7.
33. See Karl R. Popper and Konrad Lorenz, *Die Zukunft ist offen: Das Altenberger Gespräch mit den Texten des Wiener Popper Symposiums,* Franz Kreuzer, ed. (Munich and Zurich: Piper Verlag, 1985). On the development of the commercial morality and traditions that created the conditions for civilization, see *supra* note 20.
34. See *supra* note 19.
35. This is often so even of proponents of the free market. Thus one of the Keynesian sentiments generally approved by free marketeers is Lord Keynes's declaration, in the famous closing passage of *The General Theory,* that "the ideas of economists and political philosophers, both when they are right and when they are wrong, are more powerful than is commonly understood. Indeed the world is ruled by little else." (John M. Keynes, *The General Theory of Employment, Interest and Money* New York: Harcourt, Brace and World, 1964.) Those who support free-market scholars, just like everyone else, do not hesitate to quote the devil when useful. But are ideas really so influential? Almost all economists are in favor of free trade, and the evidence is all on their side; yet the idea of free trade has, recently, faltered more than it has for many decades. What are we to conclude? That the marketplace of ideas has not been free and open? Or that decisions are being made elsewhere, without much reference to that particular market?
36. Ronald H. Coase, *National Review, op. cit.,* p. 1096. See also Aaron Director, "The Parity of the Economic Market Place," *Journal of Law and Economics* Vol. 7. October, 1964, pp. 1–10. Note also Thomas L. Haskell's revealing discussion *op. cit.,* p. 11. "In this country," Haskell writes,

[T]he educational reformers who played the key roles in establishing the academic disciplines within which we work today...regarded the establishment of specialized professional disciplines as a way of defending certain ideas of the good, the true, and the beautiful *against what they perceived as corrosive competition.* In their eyes, academic professionalization was a defensive and culturally conservative measure, though also an immensely hopeful one, for it was designed to create safe havens for sound opinion in a mass society that threatened to withhold deference from even the highest values.... Many of the academic professionalizers in this country saw professionalization as a conservative cultural reform, a way of ameliorating what might be described as an 'epistemological crisis,' or, at any rate, a 'crisis of authority.'"

(Italics mine.) Further evidence of antipathy to competition within universities comes from "Collegiality and Responsibility in Academic Governance," a statement (opposing awards to faculty based on scholarly merit) prepared by the Executive Committee of the Academic Senate of the California State University and presented to the Board of Trustees, July 9-10, 1985:

In order to function as a community of scholars, the faculty within its own ranks must necessarily practice collegiality, grounded in mutual respect for their diverse professional and disciplinary expertise.... The introduction of collective bargaining into matters of salary, benefits, and related aspects of faculty employment has brought with it a procedure that, because of industrial precedents, is adversarial. That adversarial characteristic must not permeate the remaining areas of educational policy development, which cannot be achieved in an atmosphere of polarization or an administrative hierarchy modeled on hierarchy.

Quoted from *The Academic Senator: Newsletter of the Academic Senate, The California State University,* November, 1985, p. 3. Quite: there is little of the market (here misdescribed as "industrial precedent") in the university setting. And *when the faculty unionizes,* as it has done here, it is to make it *more* guildlike, less threatened by competition from within or without. Adversarial, i.e., competitive, activity for "merit awards" is to be punished not rewarded.

37. Mikhail S. Bernstam, "Bleeding Hearts and Liquid Assets: Seeking Rent on Public Goods," *Modern Age,* Spring-Summer, 1986, and Letter, *Commentary,* June, 1985, pp. 9–13.
38. See the discussion by Armen A. Alchian, "Private Property and the Relative Cost of Tenure," in Philip D. Bradley, ed., *The Public Stake*

in Union Power (Charlottesville: University Press of Virginia, 1959), pp. 350–371.

39. "Academic freedom," as developed in 19th-century Germany, was quite different from what is understood by that term today. There, professors, who were civil servants, paid by the state, were granted freedom to teach their subject matter as they wished—provided they refrained from questioning the faith, morals, and politics of their society. See Walter Kaufmann, *The Future of the Humanities* (New York: Reader's Digest Press, 1977).

40. Thus Warren O. Hagstrom once wrote that "The American university system is intensely competitive...universities and their component departments compete in a relatively free market for faculty, students, research facilities, and glory." See Warren O. Hagstrom, "Inputs, Outputs, and the Prestige of University Science Departments," *Sociology of Education* 44, 1971, pp. 375–397. See also Warren O. Hagstrom, "Competition in Science," *American Sociological Review* 39, February, 1974, pp. 1–18. A more plausible statement from the same period, concentrating on competition in physics rather than in universities in general, is found in Jerry Gaston, "Secretiveness and Competition for Priority of Discovery in Physics," *Minerva 9*, October, 1971, pp. 472–492.

41. Ian C. Jarvie, "Popper on the Difference between the Natural and the Social Sciences," in Paul Levinson, ed., *In Pursuit of Truth: Essays in Honour of Karl Popper's 80th Birthday* (New York: Humanities Press, 1982), pp. 83–107; and W.W. Bartley III, "A Popperian Harvest," *op. cit.*, pp. 249–289.

42. See Ian C. Jarvie, "Explanation, Reduction and the Sociological Turn in the Philosophy of Science—or Kuhn as Ideologue for Merton's Theory of Science," *op. cit.* See also Ian C. Jarvie and Joseph Agassi, "Indexes, Footnotes and Problems," *Philosophy of the Social Sciences* 16, 1986, pp. 367–374.

43. Thomas S. Kuhn, *The Structure of Scientific Revolutions*, 2nd edition, (Chicago: University of Chicago Press, 1970).

44. Which I do not recommend: but two can play this game.

45. See W.W. Bartley III, *Wittgenstein*, 2nd edition, (London: Hutchinson, 1986). See also the section on "The Wittgensteinian Problematic" in W.W. Bartley III, "A Popperian Harvest," *op. cit.*

46. At least two things—his personal association with the sociologist Robert Merton, and the deep influence exerted on him by Wittgenstein, as purveyed to him by his colleague Stanley Cavell—must have led him to prefer sociological to economic explanations.

47. Falsification is not the only way to do this. See W.W. Bartley III, "Eine Lösung des Goodman-Paradoxons," in Gerard Radnitzky and Gunnar Andersson, *Voraussetzungen und Grenzen der Wissenschaft*

(Tübingen: J.C.B. Mohr (Paul Siebeck) Verlag, 1981), pp. 347–358.

48. My hero Ronald H. Coase, in another lecture, finds it "strange" that such a normative theory should be offered, objecting (although to Milton Friedman not Popper) that "What we are given is not a theory of how economists, in fact, choose between competing theories but...how they ought to choose." (See Ronald H. Coase, *How Should Economists Choose?, op. cit.,* p. 8.) That Friedman and Popper both speak of "the aim of science" in this connection in no way conflicts, as Coase suggests, with the principle that only individuals have goals—after all Popper is an ardent champion of methodological individualism (see Karl R. Popper, *The Poverty of Historicism* (Boston: Beacon Press, 1957)). Thus he opens his classic article on "The Aim of Science" with these words: "To speak of 'the aim' of scientific activity may perhaps sound a little naive; for clearly, different scientists have different aims, and science itself (whatever that may mean) has no aims. I admit all this. And yet...." For Popper's defense of his usage, see Karl R. Popper *Objective Knowledge* (London: Oxford University Press, 1972), Chapter 5. One may, without violating the principle of methodological individualism, attempt to describe the practices and institutions that would be needed in order for individuals who wanted to maximize their understanding of the world to be able to succeed—just as one may describe the law and institutions needed for individuals wanting to maximize other kinds of wealth to succeed. If the thesis with which I opened this essay is correct, these descriptions would overlap greatly—or be part of a common enterprise.

On some other occasion, I should like to analyze Coase's argument in *How Should Economists Choose?* more thoroughly. Meanwhile, the reader is referred to Ian C. Jarvie's review of M. Blaug, *The Methodology of Economics* (Cambridge: Cambridge University Press, 1980), in *The British Journal for the Philosophy of Science* **34**, 1983, pp. 289–295, especially p. 294.

49. Ronald H.Coase, *How Should Economists Choose?, op. cit.,* p. 16, does not see matters this way, but argues, with Kuhn, that ignoring discrepancies between theory and fact is "more efficient." Efficient for what purpose? To perpetuate the profession? Or to advance knowledge? This is a wholly uneconomic suggestion, and also countered by some of the evidence that he himself, in this same lecture, brings from the history of economics. That it is also anti-competitive can be seen from Kuhn's remark that "It is precisely the abandonment of critical discourse that marks the transition to science." See Thomas S. Kuhn, *The Essential Tension* (New York, 1977). It is true (and a part of Popperian normative methodology) that one *should* not immediately abandon an apparently enlightening and

powerful theory when a contradiction or other difficulty in it appears—particularly when this appears early in the life of the theory, before its content and power have seriously been investigated. After all, the differential calculus, when first put forward by Newton and Leibniz, was full of contradictions, and had scientists abandoned it—as Bishop Berkeley had urged in his *Analyst*—the loss to science would have been great. But scientists and mathematicians did not *ignore* these contradictions; they did not *suppress* them: they did not "abandon critical discourse" relating to them. Rather, they developed *and changed* the differential calculus so as to avoid such difficulties.

Josef Poschl and Gareth Locksley adopt a more balanced attitude to Kuhn in their "Michael Kalecki: A Comprehensive Challenge to Orthodoxy," in J.R. Shackleton and Gareth Locksley, eds., *Twelve Contemporary Economists* (London: Macmillan, 1983, p. 143, where they write:

> Post Keynesians have consciously attempted to formulate a complete theoretical complex influenced by the heated discussions following the publication of Kuhn's *Structure of Scientific Revolutions*.... The problem was that important criticisms of some aspects of orthodox economics (for example studies of monopolistic competition, or the work of Veblen and even that of Keynes) could not break its hold over the profession and policy making. *Typically the criticisms would be translated into 'common terms,' i.e. they were filtered and their emphases changed; then they were treated as an example of a special case, a slight aberration from the powerful general line. Certainly they were not discussed as an alternative to the orthodoxy; rather they were destined for incorporation in a modified form or to be forgotten.... Such a process ensures the continuation of orthodoxy as all isolated criticisms will be translated or transformed and thereby made to appear a mere footnote.*

(Emphasis mine) This may be "efficient" if one's aim is to perpetuate an orthodoxy, but not if one's aim is to advance knowledge.

Henri Lepage, on the other hand, in *Tomorrow Capitalism* (LaSalle: Open Court, 1982), p. 217, also falls for Kuhnian notions, failing to recognize that to do so contradicts the thesis of his own book (in which he champions the *resurrection* of free-market economics over the Keynesian and socialist views which had swamped them). Lepage writes, citing Kuhn, that "the history of science is essentially the history of a succession of paradigms that replace one another as a function of their greater efficacy...." If that were so, how could a Hayekian (or Austrian) outlook loom both at the beginning *and* at the end of the Keynesian era? Did it stop being "efficacious" and then 40 years later start being efficacious again? On the other hand, if one allows that an orthodoxy may take over and suppress a more adequate view (as recognized by Popper, and also by Poschl and Locksley, as cited above), then the situation, and the questions one must ask, change entirely.

50. We could put this distortion in terms familiar to Austrian economists by noting how closely the situation resembles that which set the debate between the historicism (*Historismus*) of the German historical school and the ideas of Carl Menger.

51. Ian C. Jarvie, *op. cit.*, Italics mine.

52. Harold I. Brown, *Perception, Theory and Commitment: The New Philosophy of Science* (Chicago: Precedent, 1977).

53. On Wittgenstein, see W.W. Bartley III, "A Popperian Harvest," *op. cit.*

54. James M. Buchanan and Nicos E. Devletoglou, *Academia in Anarchy: An Economic Diagnosis* (London: Basic Books, 1970).

55. See W.W. Bartley III, "Facts & Fictions," *Encounter*, January, 1986, pp. 77–78.

56. Use of curriculum requirements to manipulate supply and demand is explicitly endorsed by Howard Bowen and J. Schuster, of Claremont, in a study financed by the Carnegie and Ford Foundations, and by Exxon, TIAA and CREF. See the report in *The UPC Advocate* XVII, November, 1986, p. 4.

57. In short, they remain as Adam Smith described them in *The Wealth of Nations*, Book V (London: 1950), Part III.

58. One of the first to remark that the increase in size of the academic establishment did not imply a necessary increase in quality, in "pushing back the frontiers of knowledge," or in other public benefit was W. Glenn Campbell, *op. cit.* Campbell asked the crucial question whether the university sets an example for other sections of society to imitate and to follow. The answer suggested in the present paper is, like Campbell's, an emphatic "No." For our financial and market institutions to follow or imitate the protectionist and monopolistic example of the university would be catastrophic.

59. The best evidence of this is that it is not read. See W.W. Bartley III, "Facts & Fictions," *op. cit.* 60. Studies have shown that only about half of one percent of the articles in journals of chemistry are read by any one chemist. Studies of reading among psychologists give closely comparable results. See Robert K. Merton, "The Matthew Effect in Science," *Science* 159, January 5, 1968, pp. 56–63.

61. See George J. Stigler, *The Economist as Preacher and Other Essays* (Chicago: Chicago University Press, 1982), p. 61. Thus the doctrine of "publish or perish" is another myth of a community in which the free market of ideas and competition are given lip service but not practiced. Minimal publication is usually not only acceptable but in

one's real self interest, provided loyalty or a certain homage is rendered to the guild or professional chieftain who wields the keys of appointment and promotion. This is less true in very great universities, but even there any number of professors who have given little evidence of original research, by publication or otherwise, are nonetheless regularly promoted.

The findings of Stigler and Friedland do not vary much from a variety of similar studies in other professions. A study of the publication record of sociologists shows that, among members of the sample studied (the sample consisted of all those who earned their doctorates between 1945 and 1949), for the period 1940 through 1959, six percent had no periodical publication, 31 percent had one to three articles, 12 percent had four or five articles, another 12 percent had from six to nine articles, 7 percent from 10 to 14 articles, and 3 percent had 15 or more. See Nicholas Babchuk and Alan P. Bates, "Professor or Producer: The Two Faces of Academic Man," *Social Forces,* May, 1962, pp. 341-348. Similarly, in an earlier study Logan Wilson reports (*The Academic Man* (New York: Oxford University Press, 1942), p. 108) that:

> A survey of 35 lesser institutions found...that only 32 percent of all staff members made any contribution to printed literature over a five-year period, and that the median number of contributions was only 1.3 items. An inquiry conducted by the American Historical Association...revealed that only 25 percent of the doctors of philosophy in history are consistent producers. Similarly, 'among 1,888 persons in the United States who took the Ph.D. in mathematics between 1862 and 1933, after graduation 46 percent prepared no published papers; 19 percent only one paper; 8 percent only two papers; 11 percent three to five papers: 6 percent six to 10 papers; 2 percent 21 to 30 papers; and 2 percent more than 30 papers.' These figures indicate that if the average academician in the typical college or university depended on his quantitative scholarly output for employee advancement, in rank and status, the hierarchical pyramid would show very few members at or near the top. The actual situation in such institutions proves, therefore, that the research function is not participated in extensively by most faculty members.

See Babchuk and Bates, as cited above, footnote 8, for further figures.

See also Yoram Neumann and Lily Neumann, "Research Indicators and Departmental Outcomes: A Comparison of Four Academic Fields," *International Social Science Review,* Spring, 1982, pp. 94–97; and Michael H. MacRoberts and Barbara R. MacRoberts, "A

Re-evaluation of Lotka's Law of Scientific Productivity," *Social Studies of Science* 12, August, 1982, pp. 443–450.

62. See also Derek J. de Solla Price, *Little Science, Big Science* (New York: Columbia University Press, 1963), and Barbara F. Reskin, "Scientific Productivity and the Reward Structure of Science," *American Sociological Review* 42, June, 1977, pp. 491–504, especially p. 492. By mentioning these examples, which relate chiefly to publication, I do not want to endorse the uneconomic assumption, so often found in sociological studies of research, that one's goal should be "output" and "production." For output often represents no development at all, and output for its own sake—regardless of demand, interest, or usefulness—can be pointless or even counterproductive, rather like the continuing manufacture of steel where steel is a glut on the market or the continuing mining of unproductive mines for the sake of keeping miners in the jobs that they are used to.

Nor should this counting of publications be taken too seriously. For example, Reskin, just cited, excluded from her study of scientific productivity among chemists (as she reveals in passing, and explains only in a footnote) unpublished work, books and patents. She explained that "books represent a very small part of sample members' publications." No doubt: comparatively few persons publish books. But to ignore such a paramount example of productivity, even among chemists, distorts understanding of scholarly activity. That the omission of patents distorts her findings she herself acknowledges. (See "Where Scientists Fear to Tread: Peter Medawar Accuses his Colleagues of Lacking the Nerve to Write Books—and Tells of Those Which have Most Influenced Him," *Times Higher Education Supplement.*)

Nor do I want to endorse the use made by such sociologists of "citation counts," for citations are biased towards those who agree with one, or are a part of "accepted and acceptable" sources *from one's own point of view,* and thus frequently omit reference to creative challengers to one's point of view. In the case of extremely threatening rival viewpoints, there may even occur what can only be described as a conspiracy of silence. For a study of some of these issues, see Ian C. Jarvie, *op. cit.*

63. This does not mean that this is widely recognized. On the contrary, one often hears claims of new "revolutions" in the humanities. Thus one might bear in mind Walter Kaufmann's admonition that what has increased in the humanities is "the presumption, the loss of self-perception, the delusions of grandeur about progress, about a revolution in philosophy, and about working on the frontiers of knowledge." See Walter Kaufmann, *The Future of the Humanities, op. cit.,* p. 38.

64. This includes chemistry. See *Science*, June 10, 1977, p. 1184.
65. See Joseph Ben-David, "Scientific Productivity and Academic Organization in Nineteenth Century Medicine," *American Sociological Review* 25, 1960, pp. 828–843. Ben-David argues that "the competitive structure of medical research in the United States was the basis of its eminence in the twentieth century." See also Stigler's comments in *The Economist as Preacher, op. cit.*, p. 117 & n. On the other hand, it is worth rereading John Rae's *Life of Adam Smith* (London, 1895), pp. 273–280, to recall Adam Smith's worries about the damaging results of regulation granting medical monopolies, and his advocacy of free-lance medicine. It is also worth recalling the attempt by the National Institute of Health (NIH) National Cancer Institute to monopolize credit for the identification of the AIDS virus. This is a complicated and interesting story that needs to be investigated and analyzed in detail. The virus was first identified in the Pasteur Institute in Paris and announced in May 1983—at a time when the NIH claimed itself unable to locate a virus. But American and British scientific publications were reluctant to publish French reports of their discovery, and organizers of American medical symposia failed to invite the French to discuss their findings. Then nearly a year later, in April 1984, in a blaze of hype, the National Cancer Institute proclaimed its own discovery of the AIDS virus (which turned out to be identical to the French one), and the American secretary of Health and Human Services, Margaret Heckler, proclaimed that "Today we add another miracle to the long honor roll of American medicine and science." There is competition here, but no free market, for American and British institutions controlled the main vehicles of scientific reporting, and thus appear to have been able, if only for a time, scandalously to suppress the dissemination of vital information.
66. This claim is one for which I have the authority of Paulsen. See Friedrich Paulsen, *The German Universities: Their Character and Historical Development* (New York: Macmillan and Co., 1895), pp. 6f.
67. David Riesman, "Ethical and Practical Dilemmas of Fieldwork in Academic Settings: A Personal Memoir," *op. cit.*, pp. 210–231, especially pp. 223, 225.
68. Wittgenstein's philosophy frees individual disciplines from competition with one another. See my discussion of the "Wittgensteinian problematic" in W.W. Bartley III, "A Popperian Harvest," *op. cit.*
69. It is curious to find Austrian economists embracing hermeneutics. Hermeneutics has some of its most important roots in, as well as sharing some of the fundamental theses of, *Historismus*, which was the main object of Menger's methodological attack, and the main subject of the *Methodenstreit*, the well-known controversy between

the Austrian and German Historical Schools. It is relativist, idealist (anti-realist), authoritarian, and romanticist in many of its manifestations. And most of its major proponents have embraced political opinions radically opposed by the founders and traditional leaders of Austrian economics. Thus Herbert Marcuse and most of the members of the Frankfurt School were Marxists; Jürgen Habermas and Paul Ricoeur are socialists; and Heidegger was, for a time, a leading Nazi. When, after Hitler's rise to power, Lord Beveridge (then Sir William, and Director of the London School of Economics), negotiated a contract with the Frankfurt School that would bring them and their Library to the L.S.E., Lionel (later Lord) Robbins (then a follower of Austrian economics) learning of this at the very last minute when he, by chance, went into Beveridge's office, ran to Hayek's office at the L.S.E. to enlist his support, and these two leading Austrian economists acted successfully to thwart Beveridge's plan. There is only one intellectual ancestor of any importance that Austrian economics and hermeneutics could be said to share; this is Max Weber; and Weber can be construed as an ancestor of hermeneutics only by neglecting most of his later methodological writings, whereas most of contemporary hermeneutics would be deeply antithetical to the entire thrust of his thought.

For criticisms of hermeneutic philosophy from the point of view of the Popperian position, or "critical rationalism," see Hans Albert, *Treatise on Critical Reason*, translated by Mary Varney Rorty (Princeton: Princeton University Press, 1985), and the essays by Peter Munz and Gerard Radnitzky in G. Radnitzky and W.W. Bartley III, eds., *Evolutionary Epistemology, Rationality, and the Sociology of Knowledge*, op. cit. On Hans-Georg Gadamer, see Jonathan Barnes, "A Kind of Integrity," *London Review of Books*, November 6, 1986, pp. 12–13; on Habermas, see Roger Scruton, "Thinkers of the Left: Jürgen Habermas," *Salisbury Review*, October, 1984, pp. 22–27.

70. I mean *control:* it is often said that one man, Gilbert Ryle, the editor of *Mind* and formerly Waynflete Professor at Oxford, controlled all university appointments in philosophy throughout the former British Empire for nearly 20 years in the sense that no one could be appointed without his agreement. In the post-war years Heidegger exerted a similar power in West Germany.

71. See J. Schumpeter, *History of Economic Analysis* (Oxford: Oxford University Press, 1984), p. 850.

72. See W.W. Bartley III, *The Retreat to Commitment, op. cit.*, and W.W. Bartley III, "Rationality versus the Theory of Rationality," in Mario Bunge, ed., *The Critical Approach to Science and Philosophy* (New York: Free Press, 1964), Chapter 1.

73. See my discussion in W.W. Bartley III, *Lewis Carroll's Symbolic Logic*, 2nd edition (New York: Clarkson N. Potter, Inc., 1986); and in W.W. Bartley III, *Wittgenstein, op. cit.*

74. W.S. Jevons, *The Theory of Political Economy* (New York: Kelley & Millman, 1871), p. viii.

75. For this assumption see Max Born, *Natural Philosophy of Cause and Chance* (Oxford: Oxford University Press, 1949), especially pp. 25ff. For criticisms of the position, see Karl R. Popper, "The Arrow of Time," *Nature*, March 17, 1956, p. 538; Karl R. Popper, "Irreversibility and Mechanics," *Nature*, August 18, 1956, p. 382; and E.L. Hill and Adolf Grünbaum, "Irreversible Processes in Physical Theory," *Nature*, June 22, 1957, pp. 1296–1297.

76. Ilya Prigogine, *From Being to Becoming: Time and Complexity in the Physical Sciences* (San Francisco: 1980), especially pp. 88–89. See also A. Einstein, *Annalen der Physik 17*, 1905, pp. 549–560; and A. Einstein *Annalen der Physik 19*, 1905, pp. 371–381; and A. Einstein *Physikalische Zeitschrift*, 1919, p. 821. See Popper's discussion in *The Open Universe*, Vol. II of the *Postscript to the Logic of Scientific Discovery*, W.W. Bartley III, ed. (London: Hutchinson, 1983).

77. That even Newtonian physics was, contrary to what is usually supposed, *in*deterministic has been maintained consistently by Popper for the past 36 years (see, for discussion and earlier references, his: *The Open Universe: An Argument for Indeterminism* (London: Hutchinson, 1982), and *Quantum Theory and the Schism in Physics* (London: Hutchinson, 1982), being volumes 2 and 3 of the *Postscript to the Logic of Scientific Discovery*, ed. W.W. Bartley, III), but has now been confirmed by Sir James Lighthill, in "The recently recognized failure of predictability in Newtonian dynamics," *Proceedings of the Royal Society, A*, Vol. 407, 1832, September 8, 1986, pp. 35–47.

78. See W.W. Bartley III, "Knowledge Is a Product Not Fully Known to Its Producer," *op. cit.*, and my closing essay in Gerard Radnitzky and W.W. Bartley III, *op. cit.*

79. Incidentally, the irreversibility involved is independent of that other sense of equilibrium having to do with entropy increase. *Ibid.*

80. See J.F. Clauser and M.A. Horne, *Physical Review*, D 10, 1974, p. 526; T.D. Angelidis, "Bell's Theorem: Does the Clauser-Horne Inequality Hold for All Local Theories?," *Physical Review Letters* **51**, 1983, p. 1819; Anupam Grag and A.J. Leggett, "Comment," *Physical Review Letters* **53**, 1984, pp. 1019-1020; A. O. Barut and P. Metstre, "Rotational Invariance, Locality, and Einstein-Podolsky-Rosen Experiments," *Physical Review Letters* **53**, 1984, p. 1021; and "Angelidis Responds," *Physical Review Letters* **53**, 1984, p. 1022. See also James T. Cushing, "Comment on Angelidis's Universality Claim," *Physical Review Letters* **54**, 1985, p. 2059.

81. Mark Blaug, *The Methodology of Economics* (Cambridge Massachusetts: Cambridge University Press, 1980), p. 192. For a criticism of Blaug's book, see Ian C. Jarvie, *The British Journal for the Philosophy of Science* **34**, September, 1983, pp. 289–295.
82. Morton White, *Toward Reunion in Philosophy* (Cambridge, Massachusetts: Harvard University Press, 1956).
83. Richard Rorty, *Philosophy and the Mirror of Nature* (Princeton: Princeton University Press, 1979). See Peter Munz's brilliant dissection of Rorty's work in Gerard Radnitzky and W.W. Bartley III, eds., Hans Albert's *Treatise on Critical Reason, op. cit.*, can be seen as a reply to the cartel. He writes (pp. xiii–xiv):

> This book...was devised to present critical rationalism as an alternative to the philosophical views characteristic of the German situation: the conception of the Frankfurt School; hermeneutic thinking as represented by Hans Georg Gadamer, a former student of Martin Heidegger; analytic philosophy, which—foremost under the influence of the posthumous writings of Ludwig Wittgenstein—began to gain a foothold here; and logical empiricism, which had then influenced philosophy of science through the writings of Wolfgang Stegmuller.... Gadamer's hermeneutic thinking has spread to America, as has the thinking of the Frankfurt School.... But when I tried to discuss these views with people outside of Germany, I found that many know nothing at all about the criticisms that are available in Germany.

It is interesting that Albert, whom Popper has described as "by far the most important contemporary German social philosopher," began his career as an economist and continues to hold economic views of a generally "Austrian" perspective. See Hans Albert, *Marktsoziologie und Entscheidungslogik* (Neuwied am Rhein und Berlin: Luchterhand, 1967). See also Hans Albert, "Hermeneutik und Realwissenschaft," *Plädoyer für kritischen Rationalismus* (Munich: R. Piper & Co., 1971); Hans Albert, *Theologische Holzwege* (Tübingen: J.C.B. Mohr (Paul Siebeck) Verlag, 1973); Hans Albert, *Transzendentale Träumereien: Karl-Otto Apels Sprachspiele und sein hermeneutischer Gott* (Hamburg: Hoffmann und Campe, 1975); Hans Albert, "Geschichte und Gesetz," in K. Salamun, *Sozialphilosophie als Aufklärung: Festschrift für Ernst Topitsch* (Tübingen: J.C.B. Mohr (Paul Siebeck) Verlag, 1979); Hans Albert, *Traktat über rationale Praxis* (Tübingen: J.C.B. Mohr (Paul Siebeck) Verlag, 1978); and "Münchhausen oder der Zauber der Reflexion" and "Transzendentaler Realismus und rationale Heuristik," both in Hans Albert, *Die Wissenschaft und die Fehlbarkeit der Vernunft* (Tübingen:

J.C.B. Mohr (Paul Siebeck) Verlag, 1982). In his "Hermeneutik und Realwissenschaft," Albert argues that valid elements of the older hermeneutical school can be "continued within the framework of critical rationalism (i.e., Popperian thought) by taking into account the linguistic work of Karl Bühler." See also Jürgen von Kempski, "Die Welt als Text," *Berechungen. Kritische Versuche zur Philosophie der Gegenwart* (Hamburg: Rowohlt, 1964), pp. 585ff. On Heidegger see also Walter Kaufmann, *Discovering the Mind: Nietzsche, Heidegger, and Buber,* Vol. II (New York: McGraw-Hill, 1980).

84. A nice example, again, is that of "Clear Thinking," where American philosophers have tried to establish themselves as *those who must be consulted* in this area. See Gareth B. Matthews, American Philosophical Association letter to Departmental Chairman, September, 1985: "The Board of Officers of the A.P.A. believes that it is important for professional philosophers to be consulted in the development of curricula and tests in critical thinking."

85. See Edward C. Banfield, *The Democratic Muse: Visual Arts and the Public Interest* (New York: Basic Books, 1984).

86. The *lack* of separation begins, of course, in the secondary schools, for which an elaborate system of state control of belief has been created. See the superb studies collected by Robert B. Everhart, *The Public School Monopoly: A Critical Analysis of Education and the State in American Society* (San Francisco: Pacific Institute, 1982).

87. The sociology of knowledge is a theory of non-market choice with regard to ideas. In this connection, see Theodore Suranyi-Ungar, Jr., "The Role of Knowledge in Invention and Economic Development," *The American Journal of Economics and Sociology* 22, 1963, pp. 463–472. Suranyi-Ungar writes (p. 471) that "competition, the phenomenon upon which the entire functioning and efficiency of a free enterprise economy rests, is more likely to harm than benefit fundamental scientific research." Such an argument leads to a justification of "social" or state intervention into scientific activity.

88. See Pascal Salin, "Can Democracy be Tamed?," paper for the Mont Pelerin Society, St. Vincent, Italy, September, 1986, p. 5.

THIRTEEN

WHAT IS HIGHER EDUCATION?

Gordon Tullock

In China from the end of Tang until about 1900, higher ranking officials were all extremely well educated. Indeed, if you read accounts of officialdom you get the impression that you are reading about the faculty of a distinguished university. Almost all officials had fairly profound intellectual interests with production of books on history, philosophy or poetry quite common. This high level of intellectual activity was obtained without any institutions of higher learning.

Most of these officials had gone to a primary level school where they had learned the Chinese equivalent of reading, 'riting and 'rithmetic, but almost without exception above that level they were self taught. The trick was accomplished very easily. There was a set of examinations, the passage of which was necessary for high official rank, and high officials were very, very, well paid. Under the circumstances, individuals had a motive to work hard in their studies and families had motives to provide leisure for study to promising young men. If the family was poor, some other well-off villager would normally be willing to gamble on a promising youth.

This is not the only case in which we observe high levels of education which result from radically different systems than ours. The Ulama were a collection of highly educated scholars in the Koran and the things that have developed out of the Koran. They have high status in Islamic states. There are, in this case, formal institutions, but these consist of little more than an opportunity for anyone who wishes to lecture and for anyone else to listen. Further, it is not necessary to have attended one of these institutions in order to be recognized as a person with adequate learning to hold the kind of positions which are reserved for members of the Ulama in Islamic countries.

If we look at the history of education in the West we observe that it used to be radically different from our present universities. A Roman who wanted to be thought of as an educated person and had enough money, went to Athens where basically he studied Greek and rhetoric. In the Middle Ages, he would go to one of the universities where he would take careful lecture notes. (When he left they would become his library. Printing had not yet been invented.) The subjects would mainly be Latin and theology, although other subjects were lectured on.

Latin, a subject of no practical value except communicating with other people who had studied it, remained an important part of Western education right up to the period between the wars. I do not know when students at Eton stopped learning to write poems in Latin; in fact, for all I know, they are still doing it. Indeed, education in the 19th century at a place like Harvard had relatively little resemblance to what it is today.

Most American universities were founded essentially by wealthy people who wanted to train pastors for their particular church. A required course in "ethical science" usually taught by the president of the university was intended to cap the whole educational process. Rhetoric remained an important part of universities up until very recently; indeed when Alexander Hamilton was attending Kings College in New York, students would periodically address the entire college.

In all of these institutions there was what you might regard as a core to the curriculum, although it is very hard to argue that this core had any particular reason for existing. High Chinese officials did indeed need to know something about hydraulic engineering, one of the minor subjects tested, and certainly would benefit from the study in philosophy and history because they were intended to implement a governmental system derived from that philosophy and history. Nevertheless there does not seem to be even the slightest reason why they should have been required to compose poetry and to have good handwriting.

What one can say about all of these systems is that they have produced a collection of educated people who, as a matter of fact, are rather similar. Whether these were good educations in the sense that the subject matter was well selected for their goals in life, or a poor education in that sense, it is nevertheless true that a graduate of Cambridge in the 19th century meeting another graduate of Cambridge would find that they had many things in common. It is not obvious that being able to discuss Thucydides would be of any practical help to a district officer in India; but it would give him something in common with other officials and military officers.

The immense diversity of the subjects studied in different cultures together with the fact that the kind of people who seemed to come out of all these systems were remarkably similar may be evidence that higher education has only three real goals. The first of these would be to simply select people who are bright and energetic enough to get through the procedure. This is sometimes referred to as a screening function. The second would be to generate among all of these people a somewhat similar set of interests and social talents so they could get along well with each other. Thus, the society will be integrated because all of the higher ranking members of the society have a good deal in common regardless of what that thing in common is. Lastly, and only subordinately, the individuals would be taught something which would be of practical use in later life.

If these are the goals of higher education, the modern higher education has concentrated on the first and third objectives whereas most previous educational systems have concentrated on the first and second. Modern universities are hard to get through, some much harder than others, hence they screen. (Some of them like Harvard, are hard to get into, but once you get in are not very hard to get through.) Their graduates will be bright hard-working people. Usually, the graduate of a modern university will also have learned something which is at least of potential value in whatever way of life he chooses to enter. Doctors, engineers, accountants, lawyers and economists have all gone through a training which fits them for their particular occupation. They may not have very much else in common.

The frequent criticism of our educational system, by people who are rather old-fashioned advocates of "liberal arts," in essence can be put down to a statement that objective two tends to be left out. It is not normally put in that language. What they usually say is that something in particular, let us say Shakespeare, should be part of everybody's education. They then normally make some false statements about the reasons why it should be a part of everyone's education. It may be claimed, for example, that it teaches psychology or improves the students' ethics, or something of that sort. Actually, its principal advantage would be that everyone would have a core of knowledge in common and hence something to talk about.

It seems likely that in the present day world, the core of knowledge which all college graduates have in common is more likely to be sports or TV programs. Indeed, most university faculties talk mainly about the performance of their football and basketball teams or faculty politics when they meet. They very rarely talk about matters of more intellectual significance except with other members of their own department.

If it is desired to produce some kind of core to our education at the university level, then this almost of necessity would have to be a matter of government policy. Indeed, the compulsory course in American government which almost every legislature in the United States has required of all undergraduates, is almost the only core that we now have.

It should be said here that that particular course is normally: A) a very poor picture of American government; B) quickly forgotten by all of its students; and C) not very much of a core because all the legislature has specified is the name of the course. Different teachers in different schools teach different things under that rubric.

It would be possible for the American government to make certain that everybody graduating from American universities knew Latin or geometry or for that matter the history of the

Inca empire. It would be at the cost of their knowing less about engineering, accounting, etc., than they now do. Cost benefit analysis would be extremely difficult. Indeed, it is not obvious that there would be either cost or benefit. Possibly any subject, as long as it has the necessary level of difficulty, has the same payoff.

I have a vague idea that most people at this conference, and indeed most modern American intellectuals feel that it would be desirable for everybody going to college to acquire a fixed core of knowledge. Different intellectuals would, of course, specify different things within that core. I think that most of us here also take the view that it is undesirable that the government impose this core on the population. (For some reason no believer in academic freedom seems to object to the compulsory course in American government.) I myself dissent from this local consensus.

Some government control over higher education, if it is going to fund it, seems reasonable. Indeed, if one assumes the purpose of higher education is to give the upper portion of society a common background, government controls would be desirable even if the government does not fund it. To take some very obvious examples, suppose a community college offered practical lock-picking for burglars or a drama school with a course on lying convincingly. Not only would the legislature not want to fund these courses, it might prohibit them. But these are extreme examples. Still if the government is going to pay for something, presumably it should make at least some effort to see that it gets what it pays for.

The problem we face here is that there does not seem to be any obvious reason why the government should be paying for higher education. Suppose, for example, that we feel that there are a lot of poor people who would not without help get a good start on life, which probably is true. Buchanan has suggested that we take whatever our annual subsidy for education is and simply divide it per capita among all 18-year-olds. They could then use it to fund their attendance at college or buy a part interest in a gas station, or some other form of investment. Indeed, I believe Buchanan would feel that if they just wanted to spend it that would be okay, but let us temporarily assume that they will invest it. Further, from the standpoint of the bottom two-thirds of the population intellectually, this would be better than our present system. There is no obvious reason why the people who will not do terribly well in life because they are stupid should be forced to pay taxes which will be used to make the income of the brighter people even larger than it otherwise would be.

It may be, however, that we feel that education is a capital investment and that society as a whole, including the poor, is benefited by the existence of highly educated people in the society. This would presumably require some restrictions on the type of education, but in any event, it is not at all obvious why this particular type of capital investment should be favored. Why not, to duplicate Buchanan's example, give everybody in the United States at the age of 18 a college board, give the best students a cash amount equivalent to the Harvard fellowship that they would otherwise get and so on down, with the people who would not be admitted to college getting nothing and the people who would go into a third-rate state institution getting only a little bit. They could then invest this money in whatever way they thought was optimal. This would be radically inegalitarian, but then so is our present method for subsidizing higher educational expenses.

Note here that currently, a lot of the subsidy that goes to somebody in Harvard comes from private donors. I am not sure that they would be happy about contributing to our new system of subsidizing bright people, but let us for the purpose of argument assume that they would in fact be willing to do so, so that from the standpoint of a bright student the only difference that this proposal would make from the present scheme is that he would have considerable freedom in investing the money instead of being compelled to invest it in higher education.

Is there any reason other than custom, tradition, and the fact that this proposal sounds radical and radical proposals are necessarily subject to great suspicion, that we should prefer our present method? I can think of only two, the first of which is that somehow or other we know that investment in education is better for the public than an investment of the same amount of money in material goods. It is not obvious how we could know that, but it is not certain that it is false.

More reasonably it might be argued that if we gave this money to a bunch of 18-year-old kids, who were permitted to invest it in anything, they would in fact simply spend it. For example, they would buy a gasoline station and then over the next three or four years, gradually run up debts against the gasoline station to the point where they lost it. If we force them to invest in intellectual capital, there is no way in which they can actually sell it off and spend the proceeds. Thus, by this, the second argument, recipients would be compelled to invest the money which was given them even if the investment was not optimal because we fear that if we give it to them in cash they will waste it.

I suspect that most of my readers will regard this discussion of alternatives to higher education as facetious. In a way, it is. The point of this joke is that there does not seem to be much justification for the system we now have. Nevertheless let us consider briefly what the system we now have is and the relationship of freedom to it.

The first thing to be said is that under present circumstances, although the bulk of the funds to support higher education, insofar as the support is institutional, come from the government; this amount is actually dwarfed by the cost incurred by the students who otherwise would be employed and obtaining significant incomes. (There are, of course, the private sources of support, but these are minor compared to either the government or the student contributions.)

It could then be argued that the subsidy to the formal institutions insofar that it has been passed on to the students (and a lot of it is glimmed onto by administrators, professors, research professors, etc.) may simply have the effect of lowering the cost to the student of this particular kind of capital investment. It is not obvious why we would want to do this, but nevertheless we must keep in mind that may be what is being done.

Having received his subsidy, the individual student has an absolutely immense menu of choices. He can go to a community college and study refrigerator repair, a leading university where he will study football, or St. John's where he will be converted into a "cultivated" gentleman. St. John's is of course not a public university, but many public universities have small elite courses with somewhat the same objectives. Superficially, it would appear then that the mere fact that the system is government-financed does not impose any restriction on what the student can study.

A little thought, however, immediately convinces one that this is not true. A whole series of points of view would jeopardize the appropriation of any university which presented them. It is not absolutely impossible to discuss possible racial differences in an American institution of higher education, but it certainly is dangerous and most government supported institutions would not dare even try.

I myself am a firm believer in evolution and have no objections to creationism being omitted from most educational systems. Nevertheless, it cannot be said that it has been omitted because the students do not want it. It has been omitted because the government does not want it taught. In this case, interestingly enough, it is the courts rather than the legislative and executive bodies who feel strongly about the matter.

Notably, this is not a question of science as opposed to non-science. Courses in astrology, and magic in which the subject matter is presented as true, rather than false, do exist in universities. Indeed, at the University of Iowa, there was a fairly lengthy squabble in which a member of the engineering faculty who wished to present a course attacking this kind of thing, which was being taught in the social science division, discovered that he could not. (This is from memory, I have not been able to track it down, but it was in the newspapers.)

What I think should be said here is we have really very little justification for government subsidy of higher education. This is not to say that there may not in fact be very good reason, it is to say at the moment they have not been offered. But if we are going to have higher education subsidized by the government, it seems that the government should have at least some idea as to what it wants taught. Thus, I am not convinced that we should have government subsidization of higher education (nor that we should not) but I think that, if we do, it is desirable that the government make sure that it is getting whatever it is attempting to purchase.

I should like, as a sort of addendum, to make some brief remarks about the way in which the government subsidizes higher education. Suppose that there are certain things which the government thinks that students should learn. A standard examination administered at the time when the student is leaving college, with awards distributed to those who do well, would seem a more efficient way of instilling this training than our present system. An alternative, which was in fact used in England in the late 19th and early 20th century, is a system under which the students are given such an examination, but the payment is made to the school rather than to the student. Both of these would seem more efficient than our present system.

If we look, however, at the Chinese and the English experience, we find that the students were highly specialized in the subjects covered by the exam. If we assume that the government wishes that some core of knowledge be taught and that in addition the students pick up accounting, law, etc., then it would be necessary to design the examination and prize system so that the students would not concentrate on the topic of the exam.

One way of doing this would simply be to make the core fairly easy. In other words, fix things up so that 80 percent of the students would pass the exam even though they only devoted, let us say, one-third of their time to studying for it. This would no doubt mean that some fairly dull students would receive the prize as a result of studying almost a hundred percent in the particular area, but it seems an inevitable consequence of providing any kind of reward.

This paper has been very diverse and I cannot claim that it has a definite theme. The reason is not because I have not thought about these matters, but because there does not seem to be very much in the way of a rational argument for the existence of the current type of higher educational institution. Hence the question of whether you have freedom in the institution should be preceded by the question of whether the institution should exist then, if it should exist, do we want freedom? I would be deeply depressed if I discovered that the medical schools were regularly teaching acupuncture as a major course. This would be regardless of what the professors and students thought about the matter. Of course, if the students and teachers were funding it themselves, I would not be inclined to interfere, but asking me to contribute is another matter.

Thus, I end up with a set of questions. 1) What is higher education? 2) Why do we want it? and 3) Assuming we do want it, will it work better if everyone is free to teach anything they feel like or if it is controlled by the people who finance it? Perhaps my listeners can provide answers.

EDITORS

Ryan C. Amacher is professor of economics and dean of the college of Commerce and Industry at Clemson University. He received his Ph.D. in economics from the University of Virginia. He has written *Yugoslavia's Foreign Trade, Principles of Economics* (co-author), and *The Economic Approach to Public Policy* (co-editor).

Roger E. Meiners is director of the Center for Policy Studies, College of Commerce and Industry, and professor of law and economics at Clemson University, Clemson, South Carolina. He received his Ph.D. from Virginia Polytechnic Institute and State University, Blacksburg, Virginia and his J.D. from the University of Miami School of Law. He has written *Victim Compensation, Legal Environment of Business* (co-author), and *Regulation and the Reagan Era* (co-editor).

CONTRIBUTORS

Peter H. Aranson is professor of economics at Emory University, co-editor of *Public Choice*, and former editor of *Supreme Court Economic Review*. He received the N. Ghoto Prize from the Mont Pelerin society in 1982 and the Lon L. Fuller Prize in Jurisprudence from the Institute of Humane Studies in 1987. He has written *American Government: Strategy and Choice* and *The Multiple Tax on Corporate Income*.

W.W. Bartley, III, is currently senior research fellow at The Hoover Institution on War, Revolution and Peace, Stanford University. He received his Ph.D. in philosophy from the London School of Economics and Political Science at the University of London. He is a fellow and member of the board of directors at The British Boltzmann Institute in London, fellow and adjunct scholar at the Institute for Humane Studies, George Mason University, general editor of *The Collected Works of F.A. Hayek*, and co-editor of *The Collected Works of Karl Popper*. He is a member of the Mont Pelerin Society, and Fulbright Scholar in the United Kingdom and New Zealand. He has written a number of books, the most recent being *Unfathomed Knowledge, Infinite Ignorance: A Philosophical Essay in the Economics of Knowledge and Education*.

Donald A. Erickson is professor in The Graduate School of Education at the University of California, Los Angeles. Called by colleagues "the father of modern research on public education" in *The American Education Journal*, he is former vice-president of the American Educational Research Association. Author of innumerable research reports and more than 100 articles, he has also written *Educational Organization and Administration, The Principal in Metropolitan*

Schools) (co-author), and *Public Controls for Non-public Schools*. He received his Ph.D. in education from the University of Chicago.

Michael T. Ghiselin is senior research fellow in the department of invertebrate zoology and geology at the California Academy of Sciences, San Francisco. He received his Ph.D. from Stanford and was a Guggenheim Fellow during 1978–1979 and a MacArthur Prize Fellow during 1981–1986. He has written *The Triumph of the Darwinian Method, The Economy of Nature and the Evolution of Sex*, and *Intellectual Compromise: The Bottom Line*.

Sidney Hook is professor emeritus of philosophy at New York University and senior research fellow at The Hoover Institution on War, Revolution and Peace, Stanford University. He received his Ph.D. in philosophy from Columbia University. A few of his nearly thirty books are *Education for Modern Man*, 2nd edition, *The Hero in History, Marx and the Marxists, The Quest for Being, Pragmatism and the Tragic Senses of Life,* and *Out of Step*, his autobiography and most recent publication.

Leonard P. Liggio is distinguished senior scholar and former president of the Institute of Humane Studies, George Mason University, Fairfax, Virginia. He received his Ph.D. in history from Fordham University and is an academic board member of the Center for Education and Research, Texas A & M University, and trustee of the Philadelphia Society. He is co-author of *Conceived in Liberty*.

Fred S. McChesney is professor of law at Emory University and visiting law professor and John M. Olin Fellow in law and economics at the University of Chicago Law School. He is general counsel of the Southern Economic Association. He received his Ph.D. in economics at the University of Virginia and his J.D.

from the University of Miami. He has published articles in the *Journal of Legal Studies, Economic Inquiry, Yale Law Journal,* and *Virginia Law Review,* to name a few.

E.C. Pasour, Jr., is professor of economics and business at North Carolina State University, a member of the editorial board of *The Review of Austrian Economics,* and of the advisory board of The James Madison Institute. He has written *The U.S. Economy and Agriculture* and articles in various popular and professional journals, including *The American Journal of Agricultural Economics, National Tax Journal, Public Choice, Southern Economics Journal, Minerva, Reason,* and *The Wall Street Journal.*

John W. Sommer is president of the Political Economy Research Institute and former dean of social sciences at the University of Texas, Dallas. He received his Ph.D. in geography from Boston University and is an adjunct scholar at the Cato Institute, and member of Sigma Xi. He is on the editorial advisory board of University Press of America, and has written *Human Geography in a Shrinking World, Games by Design,* and *Higher Education and the State.*

Robert J. Staaf is professor of law and economics at Clemson University, South Carolina. He received his Ph.D. in economics from Temple University and his J.D. from the University of Miami. He was a post doctoral fellow at the Virginia Polytechnic Institute and State University Center for Public Choice. He is a member of the Florida Bar Association, American Arbitration Association, and the Public Choice Society. He has written *Externalities: Theoretical Dimensions of Political Economy, American Economic Theory of Learning: Student Sovereignty and Academic Freedom* (co-author), and "Scholastic Choice: An Economic Model of Student Behavior," in *Journal of Human Resources.*

Robert T. Thompson, Jr. is a practicing attorney in Georgia, South Carolina, Washington D.C., New York and member of the American and Federal Bar Associations. He received his J.D. from the Emory University School of Law, where he later taught law. He is a member of the National Health Lawyers Association, American Judicature Society, The Association of Trial Lawyers of America, and the American Society of Law and Medicine.

Gordon Tullock is Karl Eller Distinguished Professor of economics and political science at the University of Arizona. Formerly a Holbert R. Harris University Professor at the Center for Study of Public Choice, George Mason University, he received his Doctorate of Law from the University of Chicago Law School. He is a member of the American Economic Association, American Political Science Association, and the American Academy of Arts and Sciences. He has written *Calculus of Consent*, co-authored with James Buchanan; *Logic of the Law*; and *Economics of Rent Seeking and Special Privilege.*

Ross L. Watts is a professor of accounting and finance, and Rochester Telephone Corporation Professor at the William E. Simon Graduate School of Business Administration of the University of Rochester. He graduated from the University of Chicago with a Ph.D. in economics, finance, and accounting. He is a member of the American Accounting Association and co-author of the book *Positive Accounting Theory.* Papers written by Drs. Watts and Zimmerman in that volume received the American Institute of Certified Public Accountants Award for Notable Contribution to Accounting Literature.

Edwin G. West is a professor of economics at Carleton University, and has been a visiting professor at the University of California, Berkeley; Virginia Polytechnic Institute;

Emory University, Atlanta; and the University of Chicago. He received his Ph.D. in economics from London University and has written more than a dozen books and 100 articles in scholarly journals in the areas of public finance, the economics of education, public choice, and the history of economic thought.

Jerold Zimmerman is faculty chairman, professor of accounting and finance, Alumni Distinguished Professor, William E. Simon Graduate School of Business Administration at the University of Rochester. He received his Ph.D. in business administration from the University of California, Berkeley. He is a member of the American Accounting Association and co-author of *Positive Accounting Theory*. Papers written by Drs. Zimmerman and Watts in that volume received the American Institute of Certified Public Accountants Award for Notable Contribution to Accounting Literature.

LIST OF TABLES

LIST OF TABLES

Index

recipients, 148
recommendations, 38, 45
redistribution, 154, 198, 231
redistributional policies, 156
redistributive scheme, 228
reef(s), 208, 211
 biology, 209
 limestone, 210
 structure, 207
reformative, 124
refutation, 304
regimes, democratic, 10
regional distribution, 167
regional transfer payments, 167
regression equation report, 153
regressions, 150, 152
regulation(s), 4, 11, 20, 107, 110, 114, 121,
 128, 131n, 133n, 136n, 139, 141, 145, 244
 avoidance of, 264
 attitudes toward, 104
 beneficiaries of, 113
 government, 114
 public interest model of, 104, 114
 system of, 107
regulatory
 affairs, 130n
 agencies, 159n
 attitudes, 110
 change, 104, 112-113, 115, 127
 interventions, 91, 104
 law, 118
 opportunities, 113
 power, 136n
 shift, 116
 system, 136n
relative prices, 155
religion(s), 17, 50, 204, 223
 entrenched, 310
 freedom of, 286n
 toleration of, 219
religious
 affiliation, 220
 diversity, 220
 fundamentalism, 159n
 institution, 223
 orders, 220
 requirements, 223
 toleration, 219
remuneration,
 monetary and nonpecuniary, 143
rent control, 156
rents, 100n
rent-seeking, 56, 64, 66, 143, 148, 154,

284n
repeat purchases, 280
replication
 of results, 141
 process of, 143
report, 34, 35
reporting
 accurate, 299
 system, 68
Republican Party, 151, 159n
Republicans, 159n
reputational value, 278
research, 2-5, 9, 11-12, 15, 20, 27, 29,
 33-35, 37, 40, 43, 47, 49, 58, 61, 64,
 72n, 184, 193, 196, 205-206, 208, 210,
 252, 255, 280, 307
 academics, 158n
Research and development (R&D), 170,
 176-179
 federal expenditure for, 172
research-and-development system, 166
research agendas, 98, 111, 141, 143, 145-
 146, 158n, 197
 nationally targeted, 197
research
 applied, 171, 195, 213
Research Applied to National Needs
 (RANN), 195
research
 approaches, 35
 areas of, 142
 award of funds for, 40
 basic, 5, 14-15, 23, 145, 169, 170-
 172, 183
 budgets, 47, 171
research capacity,
 proxies for, 174
research capability,
 cultivation of, 172
research
 centers, 43, 310
 choices, 140
 classified, 16
 concentration of, 174
 conduct of, 17
 conclusions, 146
 contemporary, 308
 decisions, 159n
 design, 29
 direction of, 183
 distortions, 158n
 "discipline specific," 197
 DNA, 142

laws regulating issue of, 100n
legislation, 87
trading of, 86
security
 analyst, 87
 holders, 124
 of tenure, 301
 sales, 100n
sediments, 208
segregate, 37
segregational policies, 18
selective
 advancement, 40
 dissemination, 45
self-reference, 313
self-referential character, 312
self-regulation, 135n
Semper, Karl, 208
Senator Proxmire's "Golden Fleece Award," 169
services, 15
 distribution of, 58
 pre-sale, 277
 post-sale, 277
 production of, 58
shape of islands, 207
shareholders, 90-91, 95, 124, 232, 235
 majority, 122
 minority, 122
 rights of, 123
shareholding employees, 252
shares, 236
 preferred, 122
skills, 213
 linguistic, mathematical and scientific, 12
slanting, 24
slumps, 295
Smith, Adam, 65, 253-254, 258, 296, 304
Smith-Lever Act of 1914, 224
Smith-Hughes Act of 1917, 224
Snell Exhibitions, 253
social
 benefits, 239
 control, 159n
 contacts, 281
 contract, 195
 customs, 62
 demand, 239
 embodiment, 305
 life, 145
 objectives, 252
 order, 119

programs, 121
policy, 145
unrest, 240
social science(s), 98, 111, 114, 150, 152-153, 155, 157n, 183, 225
social science
 disciplines, 175
 dummy, 152
 research, 225
social scientists, 110, 148, 152, 193
 analysis, 153
Social Security
 benefits, 237n, 249
 market, 234
 system, 232
social
 status, 36-37
 strata, 39
 stratification, 38
 structures, 318
 talents, 339
socialism, 147
socialist concept, 144
society, 10, 11, 14, 196, 239
socio-economic
 groups, 247
 status, 247
sociological
 description, 304
 studies, 300
sociology,
 spirit of, 302
source(s),
 of revenue, 259
 of support, 182, 218
 private, 17, 40
southern agriculture, 62
Southern Association of Colleges and Schools, 268, 283
southern congressmen,
 pressure from, 62
space science, 174
space station, 167
special interest, 242
 groups, 130n, 273
specialization, 16, 197
specialized interests, 175
specimens, 208, 211
 disposition of, 207
spill-over benefit, 277
sponsor, 16
sponsorship
 government, 14, 20

costs, 233
fees,
refunds, 266
tax credits, 26
Tullock, Gordon, 109

U

unanticipated tendencies, 33
underlying investment, 235
underpricing, 235
unemployment, 105, 155, 301
UK railroad regulation, 95
UK tax law, 96
Ulama, 337
unbelievers, 10
unified system, 111
unintended consequences, 212, 318
union(s), representation, 256
United States Department of Agriculture (USDA), 56, 191
    See also: Department of Agriculture
university(ies), 2, 6, 10-17, 40, 56, 59, 167, 169, 172, 174-179, 184, 197, 212, 218, 224, 245, 255, 257, 263, 278, 293, 298, 309, 316-317, 338
    administrators, 233
    autonomous, 10, 11
    autonomy, 12
    bureaucracies, 310
    debilitation of, 258
    departments, 13, 20, 310
university disciplines, 316
    classification of, 295
university
    education, 2, 254
    faculties, 340
    federal regime of, 229
    founding, 219
    free, 11
    governance, 282
    independent, 258
    land-grant, 56
    legal structure, 13
    life in the colonial period, 13
    managers, 245
    national interest, 171
    NSF-funded, 175
    opportunistic behavior on the part of, 233
    performance of, 235
    private, 11, 280, 306

private funding of, 218
privately-endowed, 258
programs, 6, 235
public, 223, 280, 306, 344
reputation of, 235
research, 175, 192, 225
resources, 278
role of, 218
schools, 20
state, 223
structure, 6
system, 175
US Constitution, 166
USDA (US Department of Agriculture), 56-60, 62-63, 70-71, 172
    See also: Department of Agriculture
    analysis, 65
    central planning agency for, 62
    economic activity in, 62
    economists, 61
    expenditures, 60
    land grant economists, 70
    land grant system, 60, 63, 66-67
    programs, 65
    research, 68, 75n
US Department of Commerce, 106
US Exploring Expedition of 1838-1842, 207
US income tax laws, 96
US Securities Acts, 82
use value, 279
usury statutes, 237n
utility maximizers, 245

V

value(s), 43
    normative analysis of, 13
    practice, 7
verbal pollution, 299
vertical
    integration, 278
    restraints, 278
vested interests, 82
vested interest groups, 94, 98
Veterans
    administration, 226
    assistance, 227
veto power, 32
visiting committee, 283
vocational bent, 114
vocational education, 135n, 224

W

Y

Z